Southern Fried Skeletons

Copyright © 2012 by Ellen R. Rigby

This book is a work of fiction. Names, characters, places and incidents are either products of the author's imagination or used fictitiously. Any resemblance to actual events, locales, or persons, living or dead, is entirely coincidental. All rights reserved. No part of this publication can be reproduced or transmitted in any form or by any means, electronic or mechanical, without permission in writing from the author or publisher.

First Edition
September 2012

Southern Fried Skeletons

Ellen R. Rigby

Acknowledgments

Many thanks to my professional Editor, Jon VanZile, at Editing for Authors for his encouragement and patience throughout this process. Jon, you're the best! Your advice and expertise were vital to making this vision come to fruition. A big thanks to everybody at 52 Novels for keeping us on track and making it happen, and to my cover artist, Jeroen ten Berge. Great job! My heartfelt appreciation also goes out to my friends who graciously became volunteer readers and whose feedback gave me the will to continue: Jane Marrazzo, Elaine Brown, Barbara Thompson, and Jeanne Connelly. Their advice, recommendations, and encouragement helped me remain steadfast through my ups and downs. With her psychology experience, I'm sure I'm Jeanne's worst nightmare. And last but not least, my gratitude goes to my frontline editor and dear sweet husband, who has endured along with me these many years and given his all to see that this book would happen for me. I love ya, babe!

Dedication

I would like to dedicate this book to Chris and Kelly, two brothers who lost their young promising lives to drug addiction a few short years apart, despite the significant efforts of their parents. Substance abuse and addiction in teens and young adults is an epidemic in America and has been since the 1970s. The toll taken on its victims, their families, and our society is incalculable, but nonetheless devastating. Unfortunately, it is worse now than ever, but there is now some hope and help that didn't exist when I was young. Rehab centers for these desperate youths are far and few, leaving many of them and their families to fend for themselves as best they can. The Chris and Kelly's Hope Foundation was started by their father, our friend, to financially assist organizations and programs whose purpose is to help adolescents and young adults who are struggling with substance abuse, addiction, and depression. The Foundation is committed to providing funds to help educate adolescents of the dangers of alcohol and substance abuse. Please visit their website for more information at www.chrisandkellyshope.org and consider making a donation. It will be money well spent, and I would be personally grateful.

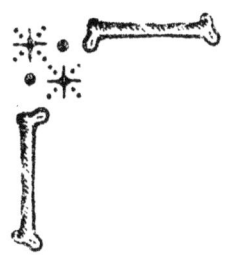

Prologue

The first time I tried LSD I ended up outside with my friends Beth and Willa wandering around the yard. I was fifteen and loving the hallucinogens. It was hard to walk because the ground was closer than it looked. The trees and sky looked amazing too. Even the dirt was awesome.

We rolled around on the grass and laughed so hard my stomach hurt. It was the best, and I suddenly *got it*. It all made sense. *Gotta get me more of this!*

We started around the front of the house when I felt the hair tingle on my head. I looked up and saw a flash of someone going behind a tree. Then I saw the freakiest blue eyes sneaking a peak out from behind the tree trunk and a shiver ran through my whole body. It was my sister's husband, Ted. The son of a bitch must have followed me to Beth's house. He was hiding and watching us and probably doing disgusting things to himself. He always knew where I was.

Damn it all to hell.

I freaked out and bolted into Beth's house, with Beth and Willa on my heels. Maybe it was the LSD, but I was hyperventilating when we got upstairs to her room. Talk about a bummer.

It was as if I had zoned deep into his eyes and had seen hell and torment in his soul, and I will never forget what that felt like. It was as if we were standing toe to toe, and I was being sucked into a dark vacuum. I knew what he wanted to do to me, but I also knew I couldn't say anything about it to anyone. Not Daddy. Not my sister Sara. And definitely not Mother. Mother was the toughest woman you ever met, but she'd already made it clear… we were not to talk about Ted and his little problem. Not unless we wanted my precious sister Sara to end up a single mother when her husband went to jail.

Couldn't say where that left me…well, maybe I *could* say where that left me and my other sister, Diane. Screwed. If Mother wouldn't do anything about Ted, it was like a green light for that damn pervert.

"You alright?" Beth asked. "You're not freaking out, are you? You look like you saw a ghost."

"It's nothing," I said. *Damn you, Mother!* I couldn't even tell my best friends that creepy Ted was following me and that I saw his freaky blue eyes in my windows at night, hoping he could catch me changing. Or that when he came over to our house, he'd hide at the bottom of our basement stairs, wanking it and hoping I'd see him.

I tried to shake it off and enjoy my first acid buzz. But I couldn't do this forever. Something was going to have to change before anything really bad happened. To me *or* Ted.

Chapter One

I was eight years old when the biggest, ugliest skeleton in the family closet first poked its head out from around the door and gave us all a jolt.

There were three of the five children in the family still living at home at the time: moi, the baby; my brother Buddy, who had just turned thirteen; and my sister Diane, who was fifteen. Buddy was at that sometimes terrifying age when raging hormones rule, and logic takes a back seat. One evening, he had yet another one of his mischievous ideas. Little did he, or any of us, know that what he was about to do would begin a series of events that would echo and ripple through the next fifty years of our lives, to no small ill effect on us all.

Buddy decided to climb a ladder at the back of our house under my sister's and my bedroom window. He knew that Diane had her pretty friend Suzanne over to spend the night, and he wanted to give them a little scare. Being a couple of years older than him, they knew, like most everybody at their school, he was a bit of a prankster. Snickering to himself about being the master of teenage terror, Buddy stretched to get one leg up from the ladder onto the spotlight on the side of the house. His intention was to lunge into the window and give the girls a little jolt. Well, okay, a *big* jolt!

Suddenly the ladder wasn't where it needed to be. It had been pulled out from under him. The girls caught a quick glimpse of a distorted face sliding down the window screen as he was falling and screaming, trying to get a grip on anything he could on his way down. It scared the girls so bad that Suzanne actually peed on herself. They were still screaming long after the crash was heard through the window.

I was in another part of the house, but as soon as I heard the screams, I came running into the bedroom. I looked out the window in time to see Daddy down in the yard, yelling at Buddy with a rage that sounded inhuman. Daddy was just beatin' the hell out of Buddy with his bare hands. My first thought was that he was either gonna kill Buddy or have himself a good old-fashioned heart attack. My second thought was that Suzanne was an incredible screamer.

"Wow, Suzanne!" I said as I looked out the window. "You ought to try out for some Alfred Hitchcock movies with a scream like that. I bet you gave everybody in the neighborhood a panic attack."

Meanwhile, Daddy was doing some screaming of his own… well, more like bellowing, I suppose. "Don't you *ever* let me catch you doing anything like this again, or you won't live to tell about it next time," Daddy threatened Buddy. "I saw you runnin' from me the other night when I almost caught you peeping in this same window. I found the ladder right down here."

"But Daddy," Buddy said, "that wasn't me. I have never done that before tonight. I swear! I was just trying to scare the girls for fun."

And knowing Buddy as I did, that was really all that was on his mind. Not any of the Peeping Tom pervert kind of crap. He was trying not to cry and be a big boy. But Daddy just took off his belt, and oh God!

"I don't care what you say you were or weren't doing. You don't *ever* look in somebody's bedroom window. Never. Never. Never!" Daddy emphasized each word with rhythm while he was tearin' Buddy's tail up with his belt. We girls were squirmin' like three worms on a South Carolina pavement in August, but only longer. Worms don't last long down here in the August heat.

I thought Daddy was going to beat Buddy until one of them died on the spot. We had never seen our father come unglued like that or dish out a beatin' like that either. Luckily for Buddy, Mother came out and starting beating Daddy to get him off Buddy. It was like a scene from a cheesy trailer park domestic violence police story or something. After Mother managed to break up the scene and herd Buddy and Daddy into the house, Diane just turned to Suzanne and me and said, "Well, that was interesting."

Then Suzanne said, "Now I have to go change my underwear. I do believe I have soiled myself." Diane and I thought she was joking, and we laughed and laughed even before we realized that she really did pee on herself. Now *that* was funny!

But then Diane and I got real quiet as Suzanne went into the bathroom to change. Diane looked at me and said, "What in the world was that all about? Daddy looked like he was possessed. I don't know what brought it on, but that was some scary stuff. That was even scarier than Buddy's face sliding down the screen." She almost chuckled. But then I noticed the worried look on her face. "Somethin' just ain't right. Buddy is a turd head, but he did not deserve that."

"Yeah, no kidding," I responded, worried and puzzled. "That was not at all like Daddy. Poor Buddy…and he's not a turd head. Well, maybe he is sometimes."

For the next couple of days, Buddy hid in his room. Nobody seemed to want to talk about Daddy going psycho on him, especially Buddy, and we felt so sorry for him. Facts were, his fingernails and fingertips were still hanging on the bricks on the back of the house, his face was missing a few chunks, and he looked so emotional. He didn't understand why his attempted prank had such an impact on Daddy. Even Daddy looked different around the eyes. I believe he did what he thought he had to do at the time but that he was ashamed and embarrassed for losing his self-control like he had.

I finally got up the nerve one day to ask Mother when we were alone in the kitchen what it was all about. But she would only say it was not my concern and it was just a big misunderstanding. She just kept frying chicken and making biscuits and such, acting as if I had never even posed the question. As for understanding, well, some of us children would learn way too much sooner than others. But it wasn't until many years later that all of us understood a lot of things. We had been taught to keep our mouths shut and not to talk about "such things." And definitely not to ask questions.

Suzanne never came over again after that. I do believe she had been so badly traumatized that she just couldn't take a chance on it happening again. And I do declayah, we were so proud of our family at that time. Not! I guess she thought our father was a child beater or somethin' dreadful like that. In actuality, we were at least as shocked as she was.

Buddy finally started showing his face again, but he looked different around the eyes as well. Buddy was a handsome boy, with the same dark black hair and brilliant blue eyes all my siblings shared. When I asked him what happened, he said, "I was just trying to scare the pee out of the girls."

"Well, mission accomplished, Bubba," I said and clapped him on the shoulder. He broke into a sly grin, and then I realized that he was going to be okay. It really did seem to make him feel a little better knowing he had accomplished his goal after all. The *king* of teenage terrah. Had caused the "hot chick" to pee pee in her panties. Oh yeah!

Still, I could tell Buddy was hurt, and he got serious again. "Daddy wouldn't let me explain," he said, and then it all came spilling out in a torrent. "He said he found the ladder against the house the other night under you and D's bedroom window, and he accused me of doing it. He said he saw somebody runnin' down toward the creek as soon as they spotted him coming. Since I wasn't in the house, he just assumed it was me. That was the first time I ever even thought of doing it, and that's because Suzanne was here and she's so hot, you know. But believe you me, I won't ever do that again. I thought he was goin' to kill me. It was so embarrassing in front of Suzanne. Man, he came flying around the house like a Brahma bull. He had to be cocked and ready, because he was all over me before I knew what was going on. And once he got started, he couldn't stop. He caught me in the middle of a snicker and scared the crap out of me. Man, I have never been so relieved to see Mother show up." And we both understood that, because Mother was usually the one who would rock your world when you were bad. "She actually had to pull Daddy off of me. I was terrified," Buddy said.

"That *is* bad when you're glad to see her show up," I said.

Then I thought for a minute, and said, "Did you mess on yourself?"

"MAGGIE!" he said with a surprised look.

"What? I hear ya'll say it all the time."

"True." Then he frowned. "I almost did mess on myself," he said. "I don't know who had a ladder up against the house before the other night, but it wasn't me. I swear it. But now I'm on the lookout, and Daddy can believe what he wants. And right now, he ain't believin' me."

"I believe you, Buddy," I said sincerely.

"Thanks, Sis." I could see he truly was grateful, even relieved, about me believing him.

We lived on a beautiful street in downtown Greenville, South Carolina. Our street was lined with huge oak trees that were over one hundred years old. It was a nice neighborhood with some lovely Southern homes. There were a lot of old widows who had that Suthun drawl. The kind you see stars trying to act out on TV shows and such. Hopefully none of them saw any of the redneck action outside our house that night. We weren't rich by any stretch, but we were comfortable enough to live in a safe area on a nice street. Or so we thought. We never locked doors or cars because there was just no concern for that back then. We rode our bikes and walked all over town without a worry, alone or in small groups. It wasn't a big deal back then. What we didn't realize was that a nice neighborhood had nothing to do with being safe.

We were a Catholic family with five children, spread twenty-three years apart. I had a niece and a nephew older than me in Florida. My oldest brother David had joined the air force when he was young and had two children before I was born. He was old enough to be my father. He eventually had four children, three girls and one boy. Much of my young childhood, he was stationed in Florida and later in Texas. Like all of my siblings, he was short and with age became stocky, blue eyed, and with black hair that was uncommonly curly for our family.

The next sibling after David was Sara, who was five years younger than him. Sara was a beautiful woman. Her cheekbones were more pronounced than the rest of us children, and her blues eyes were so bright they seemed to glow. She and her husband Ted lived in Greenville, only a few blocks from us. They were Elvis addicts and loved to dance. They had one daughter who was two years old, and Diane and I liked to stay with them, see the baby, and help Sara while her husband worked long hours. It was a good diversion for us, and Sara appreciated the company and the help. Diane was the most help since she was seven years older than me, and she got to go more often and stay longer. But I did my share of diaper duty as well. There were no disposable diapers then—the concept hadn't even occurred yet. You had to wash them out in the commode, then wash them in the sink, then hang them on "the line." In all honesty, I think I would now rather set myself on fire than have to do that again. Luckily, her first child, Carley, was constipated from birth, so her shit just rolled out easily into the commode. The next baby wasn't as easy. Oh my God!

On the verge of Sweet Sixteen, Diane was old enough to start dating before too long, and Sara would let her talk on the phone for hours while she was at her house. Sometimes Sara would even let Diane's boyfriend come over and visit without the poor guy having to deal with the wrath of Mother. They were always tying up Sara's phone. Everybody would get so pissed trying to call Sara to check on her and the baby and getting nothing but a busy signal. Mother actually got in her car one night, in her pajamas, and drove down to Sara's to see what the hell was going on. She made me go with her, also in my pajamas, and I thought she was gonna tear the door off the hinges when we got there. She was so worried about Sara and Diane initially, until she saw Diane on the phone. She walked straight up to her, jerked the phone out of Diane's hand, cracked her in the head with it, and slammed it down on the hook. She turned and walked out the door, we got back in the car, and we went home. That was very "Mother." We all learned at an early age that you didn't mess with Mother because you never knew when she was gonna sneak up and get ya.

Mother was mostly Cherokee Indian. She was born in 1916 in northern Greenville County and brought up poor and hard. She had to quit school after the third grade to help raise her three younger brothers and sister. Her father was a drifter, and her Mother had to work to keep them fed. She wasn't accepted in the white society, the black society, or the Indian, so she had to be mean to survive. And believe me, she was as mean as hell when she wanted to be (which was much of the time). You learned to never cross her path and to be very afraid if you did. It was an interesting mix of emotion and fear. She was mean as a pissed off rattlesnake till the day she died. Daddy always said she was the meanest woman to shit between two heels. At an overweight five feet, four inches, she still struck an imposing figure: jet black hair, the high cheekbones and full lips of her Cherokee lineage, and emerald green eyes that could brighten enough to warm a whole room or freeze your blood and cut you to slivers, depending on the situation. She had short, stubby fingers with a terrifyingly strong grip. And she had a radiantly beautiful smile that could belie the hard woman underneath. In their youth, Mother and Daddy were quite the handsome couple.

Her given name was Nora, but she was known by most everybody as Noni. Sometimes I think Noni was really an alter ego to Nora. Nora was the nurturing, protective mother hen that all mothers are. Noni was the rattlesnake you had to fear, respect, and keep a healthy distance from. The switch could flip in an instant…and sometimes flip back just as quickly. Sometimes it would stay flipped for hours on end, like when she had "took to drinking." Mother had a sixth sense, an awareness that was subtle and often shocking. She had feelings about people immediately upon eye contact, and she was right probably 99 percent of the time. She could be terrifying to those she did not trust or like, because she just told them right off what she thought about them. You never wondered where you stood with her, which is something I have also been accused of. She was known to have dreams of someone dying, and sure enough, it would happen. She would awaken from a deep sleep, covered in sweat and in a state of panic, and you would just hope she wasn't dreaming about you. Then we would wait for a phone call. It was very disturbing at times, but when you lived with it all your life, these little "glitches" become the norm. Or at least it was for us and for her.

Daddy worked third shift and had to sleep most of the day, so Mother ruled the roost with an iron fist. She was the one that would dish out the beatings if need be. Something that we learned quickly was to never let her get her death grip on you. If you did, you were doomed. She could filet you before you knew what was happening. She was also bad to grab anything within reach and bean you with it. It could be a dishtowel, a frying pan, a coat hanger, or whatever. So you learned to walk the line and not piss her off. And for God's sake, you didn't turn your back on her when she was after you. You didn't talk back, you said, "Yes ma'am," and you didn't argue with her. It was pretty simple, actually, but it could be life-altering until you learned the rules. The choice was yours.

She was sneaky and had rubber arms that could stretch out and reach you when you were sure you were out of the danger area. It was the damndest thing. Just when you thought you were safe, she would glide up on you without a sound like Bram Stoker's Dracula. Made you jumpy as hell. Even when you were innocent, you were looking over your shoulder like some Jack Nicholson stuff was about to happen. I'm surprised we didn't all end up on heavy drugs or something. Well actually, some of us did.

A true Southerner will admit having sweet tea in their baby bottle and sippy cup. It was—and is—a way of life. It was a true Southern staple that Mother made sure we had plenty of. And Mother could really cook. She was Southern to the bone, with her famous buttermilk biscuits, fried chicken, fried everything, sweet tea, and a cornbread dressing that was like no other. Yankees called it stuffing, but we always called it dressin'. Ain't the same. We usually could only talk her into making it on Thanksgiving and Christmas, so we savored it and hurt ourselves with it when we could get it. It was cornmeal based, but kinda soupy when it was fresh and then thickened some when it was cooked and cooled. Oh my God!

Daddy was born Elbert Keith in 1913 in Pickens, South Carolina, as thirteen pounds of auburn red hair and freckles (that's right, ladies...*thirteen pounds*). His father was also a drifter and lived a hard life. His tiny mother weighed only ninety-eight pounds fully pregnant with twins. She delivered the twin girls in 1918 and died two weeks later from hemorrhaging. So there was my Daddy with no parents and two two-week-old sisters, and him only five years old. He carried the babies in his arms on the only road there was to Easley, where an aunt took them in. Unfortunately, while the twins were treated well, he was treated poorly. They got the apples, and he got the peel. He went to work in the mill when he was six, and for a while was the only working person in the household.

Fortunately for him, he was eventually sent to live with his Uncle Jack and Aunt Bessie, who loved him and treated him like a son. Till the day he died, Daddy never would let any of our friends or family leave our home hungry, because he knew what that felt like for way too long. He was a good, honest man. He eventually finished high school and made a decent home for us. He never missed a day of work in over fifty years. He loved to drink him some beer occasionally on the weekends, but never daily. Unless he was on vacation. He could drain a full can of beer in about six seconds. And then do it again. Very impressive for someone who didn't drink on a regular basis. Or for anybody, really.

At five foot seven, he wasn't much taller than Mother, but he had big, broad shoulders, long arms, and huge hands and fingers (he wore a size thirteen ring). His hair was a subtle tip-off about his temper, but that was something he rarely showed (Buddy's little ladder incident notwithstanding). By the time I was in my mid-teens, he wore glasses and was somewhat bent from a long life of hard work, but he still enjoyed gardening and tinkering with the family cars. And he loved to play word games, often making up odd little twists on well-known rhymes, making jokes that used unusual, unexpected words and generally acting as a repository of quaint country sayings.

Chapter Two

"I'm going to Sara's for the weekend," Diane yelled as she headed out the front door. It had been a year since the Buddy incident, and Sara was pregnant—VERY pregnant. It had become Diane's Friday afternoon ritual to head straight over to Sara and Ted's. She was too anxious to get out of the house to wait for Mother and me to go with her. "Maggie and I will see you over there directly," Mother called back. Diane walked to Sara's with her overnight bag since it was only a few blocks away.

Mother and I headed for Sara's after we packed up some food. In the South, you never went to anybody's house without taking food. And you never left anybody's house without taking food home with you. Mother had apparently decided to stay a while and party that night, because she also packed some Wild Turkey and Winston cigarettes. Those were for Noni, who was soon to make an extended appearance. Mother wouldn't let me spend the night at Sara's because she would be left alone while Daddy worked third shift. I pouted about not being able to stay all night with Diane and Sara. She, of course, showed no mercy, and I sure as hell didn't argue with her, being trapped in the front seat of a 1958 VW bug with no way to maneuver out of her reach. No sir-ree. I ain't as dumb as I look.

As we walked in the back door of Sara's house, we heard some good old soul music blaring, and what we saw would be etched into our brains for eternity: Sara, looking twelve months pregnant and bent over with her hands on her knees, was dancing the Dirty Dog. Diane was rolling on the floor, hysterical. I probably should have gotten therapy for witnessing that. It was as comical as it was obscene, and I'm not sure which was more disturbing. *Is my sense of humor that sick? Apparently so…*

After a brief moment of shock, Mother regained enough control to stammer, "All righty then." She seemed to be trying to shake the vision from her head. "That's what got you in this predicament to begin with!"

"True enough," Sara admitted. "I'm trying to go into labor, if you don't mind. By the way, got any dynamite on you?"

"Not handy, sorry," Mother half yelled over the noise that still blared from the stereo as she headed for the kitchen.

Our family always loved music and dancing. It all felt so natural to just let go and boogie together. We might listen to Connie Francis, Elvis, Ray Charles, Jerry Lee Lewis, James Brown, Sam Cook, Junior Walker and the All Stars…it didn't really matter to us 'cause we loved it all. If we could dance to it, we would do just that. And if we couldn't dance, we would lip sync with our hairbrush microphones at our mouths while we choreographed our moves. I have to admit, those were some of the fondest memories of my childhood: I think I was always happiest and most carefree when I was dancing, especially with my family. In just a few years I would get to show off some of the dances I learned from my black girlfriends at school.

I was the only one of my parent's offspring that didn't have the black, Cherokee hair: I was a golden blond, with my family's typical high cheekbones and mouth and Mother's bright green eyes. I didn't know why I looked so different from my siblings, and at that age I didn't care, though in the years to come it would become a source of concern.

I sometimes thought I was meant to be black because I loved soul music and old gospel songs more than anything. I loved to dance with the black chicks in school 'cause they were the coolest. They had spirit and soul in their hearts that I felt all the way to my bones. I loved learning all the moves from them, and they liked me too because I didn't fall for that racist, segregation BS. I wasn't your typical white chick from middle class suburbia. I never saw black and white in a racial sense. I either liked you, or I didn't. It was pretty cut and dried to me. But in the deep South, that attitude didn't always sit well with some parents or peers. Especially in the racially charged mid 1960s.

Tough beans, I say. You're the ones missing out.

But I digress. The four of us girls hung out for hours, eating Mother's good cooking, listening to music, shagging with each other, and having a blast. It was really nice hanging with just the girls that night. But around midnight, we heard Sara's husband Ted coming in from what we thought was work.

Ted was a looker. He was over six feet tall, light blonde, with an olive complexion and ice blue eyes. Back then it was cool to look like Elvis (with blue eyes and blonde hair, styled like Elvis), so yes, he was cool. Those eyes could just cut right through you with a look that often felt disturbing. He would kind of slink around in the dark by himself, and now and then you would catch a quick glimpse of him around the corner. Ted's sneaky behavior was something nobody in the family seemed to talk about, but at my young age, I didn't think about it…except for those eyes. There was something about those eyes that made the hair on the back of my neck stand up. It was an intense stare, shifty and drifty, as if his mind was somewhere else. Like deep in the gutter.

When he came inside, we quickly realized Ted had been drinking. Mother's face went through the scary transformation to Noni. She jumped up and dragged Ted out the back door by his ear. "Oops, party's over," Diane said with a worried look. Sara just sat down and looked at me and Diane with more than worry. She was terrified, but she knew not to interfere when Noni was on the war path. We heard her quickly hitting her stride as she accused Ted of being a no-good drunk and telling him that if he didn't straighten up and do right by his family, she would make sure he never reproduced again. "Stop drinking, finish school, get your driver's license for God's sake, get a decent paying job or get the hell out of her life so she can find a good man like she deserves," Noni rolled on. "And in the meantime, you had better be here when she goes into labor, and you had damn well better not be drunk. Go man up, 'cause that baby's comin' tonight."

Well, that didn't settle too well with Ted. He had had just enough liquor to act stupid as hell. He grabbed Noni by the throat with both hands and said, while he looked straight into her eyes, "You ain't comin' into my house and tellin' me a damn thing. It's none of your goddamn business what I do."

"Oh my God! Please tell me that he did not say that to NONI!" Sara said, fear and concern accented by the tears in her eyes.

Then we heard Noni say to Ted, "You don't say…the hell it ain't," with great emphasis on "ain't." Then all we heard was a little feminine squeak coming out of Ted's guppie mouth—and then silence. "Do you want me to make a girl out of you?" Noni asked calmly. Ted seemed to have forgotten that Noni packed a gun when we girls were out alone. That is, until he felt it shoved up against his scrotum and heard it cocked. He was about a foot taller than Mother, so she had the best angle for the job. That was probably the only thing that would have gotten his attention at that juncture, and he immediately turned her neck loose. About that time, he looked up and saw all of us peeking out the back door, and he busted out crying.

"I lost my job today," was all he could say for a moment, his face paling. Noni's face briefly changed back to Mother's face, and she hugged him with one arm. He looked like a giant baby bawling his eyes out. When he finally calmed down enough to talk again, he said, in a most timid, meek voice, "And if you will kindly remove that gun from my scrotum area, please ma'am, so I can breathe?"

"Okay," Noni said, and she did just that. "That was a pissy job anyway. You can do much better than that. You just have to give it some effort. Here," she said as she handed him back his balls, "put these back on, and get out there and be a man. Elbert and I will help you get on your feet, but you have to straighten your sorry ass up. You're a father now. You have a family, babies, a wife. What do you want your kids thinking of you when they get older? Don't you want them to grow up proud, smart?"

Hanging his head again, Ted took his balls, turned to Sara, and said in a voice about two octaves higher than usual, "Will you please put these in your purse, dear?" He was no dummy, that's for sure. He knew he had to make a good impression right then and there or Noni would stay on him like white on rice. As far as the rest of us were concerned, his jewels were supposed to remain in that purse until they were needed for familial purposes. "Smart move," Noni said. Ted apologized to Sara and Mother, tucked his tail, took a shower, and went to bed to sleep it off.

Unfortunately, it turned out that Ted's balls spent way too little time in Sara's purse, but he had made the required gesture to appease Noni for the time being.

Noni announced that it was time for all of us, including Diane, to clear out and give Ted and Sara some time alone. Diane wasn't too happy about that, but tough grits. We'd had our fun before the turd was thrown in the punchbowl. On our way to the car, Diane turned to me with that look I had seen right after the Buddy-in-the-window incident and said, "When did we become trailer trash? Or have we always been and just didn't know it?"

That was one of my most memorable Noni lessons. I learned a lifetime of respect for her right then and there. We all did. Or maybe it was purely fear. Who knows?

Sure enough, the baby did come that night. Ted had to drive Sara to the hospital without a license and with a hangover from hell. And Ted was a different man from then on. Not necessarily a good man, but at least he took better care of his family. He did almost everything Mother and Sara told him to do, and he ended up with a decent paying government job with the help of our parents. Daddy took him to get his license and made him finish school, and Ted worked hard to support his family.

Chapter Three

A few days later, Sara and baby Ted came home from the hospital looking good and healthy. The first thing Mother asked her was, "How's your cootie feel?"

"Very funny. You ought to know," Sara said. "It's killing me at the moment. Help me get the sitz bath going, would ya?"

"Sure thing. They didn't have these when mine was torn all to hell," Mother grumbled as she was getting it assembled.

Over the next few weeks, Mother and I would go over to Sara's each morning to help out with the babies, and Diane would arrive in the afternoon and sometimes spend the night. I got to hold a baby for the first time in my life, and I fell in love with the thought of motherhood. Baby Ted was the sweetest little thing. He smelled like baby lotion, and I just didn't want to put him down. I was still young, so they wouldn't let me walk around with him, but that was fine with me. It was good that Sara could sleep for a while between feedings. I didn't like the breastfeeding thing. It felt embarrassing somehow. Too personal. We were always private at our house about nudity and such. It apparently hurt her to breastfeed 'cause she cussed a lot. It made me cringe, so I left the room, looking for something to do.

One afternoon, Diane arrived as scheduled, and Mother and I got ready to go home. I hated to leave the baby. What an incredible feeling to hold a newborn. I said to Mother and Sara, "I want to have ten kids one day."

Mother and Sara looked at me and Sara said, "What are you, retarded or something?"

"I think we'll leave on that note," Mother said. "I have to get Elbert's dinner and lunch ready and we have to start getting packed to go to Florida. God help us."

Our family went to Florida at least once a year to visit David and his family, and we all dreaded the trip, except Daddy. Diane, Buddy, me, and Mother and Daddy would cram ourselves into a 1958 Volkswagen bug, along with two cases of beer and all our luggage, and head off to Florida in the blazin' heat with no air conditioning. As we were ready to leave for our journey, Mother would line us up and hand out our puke bags, knowing we would need them—especially me. Because I was the smallest, I would have to ride in the very back in the hot sun with all our shit. And they wondered why I always got car sick. Hello?

Once the VW gas fumes started puttin' out good, and Mother got out the deviled egg sandwiches, I would start spewing. The combination of the heat and the smells made me pop every time. Then add the smell of puke to the bouquet, and everybody started to vomit. To this day, I hate deviled egg sandwiches. Just the smell makes me want to cram myself in the back of a 1958 VW bug in the hot sun for twelve hours without air conditioning.

To make matters worse, David and his wife Bonnie were raising a clutch of kleptomaniacs, and we were always the victims of their thievery.

As soon as Mother and I left, Diane started begging Sara, "Can I stay with you while they are in Florida? I would rather kill myself than go with them. Just the trip is the worst nightmare you could imagine. Then staying there is almost as bad, it just lasts longer. Those thieving kids of David's aren't gonna steal any more of my stuff. I'll run away before I'll go. I will have peeled the skin off my entire body by the time we get back."

"Just get your panties out of a wad, drama girl, and listen. Of course you can stay. I can use the help and the company. If you don't mind helping me around here, I would appreciate it at least as much as you would." Sara reassured Dianne that she would talk Mother into it. "You're fifteen now, so I don't blame you for not wanting to go. I can't stand that whole scene for more than one hour, tops."

Sure enough, Mother fell for it. Sara was convincing enough. At least we would have more room in the VW for the long, hot trip. Not that it would make much difference. I was getting too big to ride in the back, so Buddy and I would share the back seat. We tried to get a nap the day of departure, so we could leave at midnight. It wouldn't be as hot at least, and we could sleep. The trip would go by faster, and maybe Buddy would leave me alone for a while. When he got bored, he did horrible things to me, being a thirteen-year-old brother from hell.

The morning before we left, Mother and I went into the kitchen to whip up some breakfast. She had cooked some ham so all we had to do was throw some eggs in the pan and some toast in the oven. I was buttering bread, and Mother was crackin' eggs in the pan—with butter, of course. We were side by side when she let out this little squeal and said "DON'T LOOK!" Of course, that's the first thing you do when someone tells you not to look, and OH MY GOD…right there in the frying pan laid a little underdeveloped chicken, sizzling with the other eggs. Oh! Oh! Oh! The smell! Too much like burnt deviled egg sandwiches. We both just about died. She took the frying pan and flung the contents into the gravel drive, and I ran in the other direction.

After I had gained my composure, I went back into the kitchen, feeling a little green around the gills. Every time I started to say something, Mother stopped me. Finally she let me finish my sentence, which was, "I won't be having any eggs this morning."
"Whatever...just don't talk about it, okay?"
"Deal."
We were all packed and ready to go at midnight. "Okay, guys, here are your barf bags," Mother said as we got into the car for the trip. "Maggie, you get an extra one. I have been saving up for the trip." You didn't have the fancy Ziplocs and stuff then. You reused bread bags for everything. Dead baby chick...
"Tell me you didn't bring anything new or of value," Mother warned in the car. "You know they'll steal it no matter how slick you think you are. They do it every time. Bunch of damn thieves. How did we end up with thieves as grandchildren? It's a disgrace. The only one that isn't a thief is Mandy, and she's autistic."
"We have to have clothes, you know. I brought some records and some cards, but that's about it," I said. "I did bring my new sundress and my new tennis shoes. I had to. I'll wear it on the trip home so they can't get it. It's my favorite dress, and I'll have to hurt Sherri if she tries to take it."
"Boy, are you living in la la land! You know ya'll are almost like twins, so you know it'll fit her, and you know she'll steal it."
"Please don't say that," I said. "I don't want to be like her twin. She's mean and she talks funny. She spits all over me when she talks. I need a spit screen or something."
Buddy started laughing and started mocking her, and even Mother was trying not to laugh. Sherri had a bad lisp that we kids got a kick out of when she wasn't around. Buddy could do it just like her, and it kept us in sssstitchesss for much of the trip. We started getting sleepy, and just as I was about to nod out, Buddy grabbed my head and shoved it down between his legs

and let out a big fart. He held me there till Mother's rubber arm swung around and grabbed Buddy by the hair and shook him until he let me go. I started breathing deep and slow, trying to hold my supper, but that's all it took to get me fired up. Dead baby chick...oh God...

"She's gonna pop! Get the bag quick," Buddy yelled.

"She ought to spew on you, you moron. See what you did? She was doing fine until you crapped in her face."

"Ya'll shut up. I don't want to talk about it. That was just nasty, you bone head," I said, looking green around the gills. Dead freakin' baby chick...

Daddy rolled down the window, and I managed to hold it down with a breeze on my face. I managed to slip off to sleep. I woke up smelling something foul.

"Buddy stop farting," I said in disgust...dead baby chick...

"That's the deviled egg sandwiches," Mother said as she held one out to the back seat. "Youn't one?"

Nope! That's when I spewed for the first time during the trip, and I didn't stop until we got there. I prayed a lot. All I could think about was when Mother cracked that fresh egg that we got from Uncle Jack and Aunt Bessie's farm in the pan that morning and plop went the little half-formed birdie alien thing in the pan. Oh...the smell. Please just kill me now.

"God help me, please. Please God, make me stop. I'll be good for the rest of my life," I said weakly. Apparently he didn't believe me, because I just kept heaving.

"I'm gonna spew too if you don't stop. I can't stand the smell," Buddy said, looking a little sick himself.

"Just shut up, moron. This is your fault. Get away from me. Go ride on the roof or something. I hope you do spew deviled eggs, you butt head. I hope you have egg salad coming out your nose."

Well, that did it. Buddy thought about it too much, and sure enough, deviled eggs repeat. Oh my God! We all wanted to die. Between the smell of Daddy's beer, VW fumes, and deviled eggs, I knew I was going to die from hurling. Thank God we finally got there, because Daddy wouldn't stop the car for any reason. He would let us all perish and wallow in our own excrement before he would stop for a restroom. I remember Mother getting so mad about it one time that she grabbed the steering wheel from Daddy because she was about to mess on herself, and Daddy wouldn't stop. I remember her haulin' ass into the woods with toilet paper in one hand, in the dark. I have never seen her so mad, and our laughing at her didn't help matters at all. Oh Lordy Lordy, we were in a heap of trouble with Noni. I don't know what she did to Daddy after that, but he was as quiet as a little dead baby chick for days.

By the time we arrived at Shaw Air Force Base in Orlando, it was hotter than forty hells already, and it was only ten in the morning. David, my brother, greeted us, and as we were unpacking, Kathy, Mack, Mandy, and Sherri stirred from their beds to greet us.

"Where's Bonnie" Mother asked.

"She's not feeling well. Still in bed. Come on in and cool off. Let the kids bring your stuff in. And by the way, ya'll look like shit."

"You have no idea," Mother said wearily.

She automatically started thinking about them, the famous family thieves, taking inventory of our stuff. May as well let 'em. They seemed to have radars implanted. It was the damndest thing. It was a gift they inherited from their mother, the psycho-druggie kleptomaniac hypochondriac.

Speaking of whom, Bonnie heard us through her drugged-out haze and came stumbling out of the bedroom with her hospital hair all flat on one side and looking like platinum cotton candy that somebody ate one side of. She could barely walk as she swayed to and fro. I couldn't understand a word she said, and judging by the look Mother had on her face, she was at least as shocked as I was. Mother just shuffled me away so I wouldn't see or hear anything else.

The first thing I wanted to do was pee, then go to bed, so that's what I did. Sherri and I had to share a bed, so she was satisfied to go back to bed too. We slept half of the day away until suppertime, and then we woke up ravenous. David had cooked steaks, baked potatoes, and salad. He always was the best grill cook. We all ate like piggy kings and life was good—on the surface.

Bonnie had a lot of health issues and apparently had some good drugs. We found out later that she "procured" some prescription pads and was writing her own prescriptions. She wasn't dumb, but she was very manipulative. Poor David was so in love with her and had to work two jobs to keep things going. She was pretty much useless in that regard. The kids were wild as hell because, while David worked, she was drugged up in the house and locked the kids outside all day. They learned to survive by hook or crook, literally.

Bonnie loved Mother and called her Noni. She almost worshipped Mother, which was interesting because Mother wouldn't take any shit off her. Mother was one of two people who could handle her, the other being David. But David didn't know much of what went on because he worked all the time. Poor guy. He had to work some while we were visiting too, although not all week.

David and Daddy had made amends after a rough childhood. David was always in trouble when he was a teenager. He got with the wrong crowd and got in some big trouble with the law. My parents sent him off to military school, which probably saved his life in the long run, but David resented it for many years. He ran away and joined the U.S. Air Force. He lied about his age to get in, but he did well for himself and was able to retire when he was forty-two years old—but getting there was a bitch.

The next morning, David left for work early. We all slept in until Mother heard Mandy crying. She couldn't find her, and Mother started to get frantic. Mandy was about four years old, and being autistic, she got into all kinds of predicaments. Mother followed her ears and found Mandy in the closet, in the dark, in her crib. She had no clothes, no blanket, no pillow, and was in total darkness. Mother yanked her out of the crib and started to cry in anger. When Mother was mad enough to cry, you had better look out. By the time Mother got down the hall, Mandy was out of control and was hurting Mother. She was as strong as an ox and inconsolable. Mother took her into Bonnie's bedroom in a shaking rage.

"Tell me why this baby was in a dark closet."

"Well, I don't know. Come here, baby." Bonnie tried holding out her arms for Mandy, but Mother didn't hand her over.

"Would you tell me what in the hell have you been doing to this child?"

Bonnie was so screwed up that she couldn't even talk. Mother grabbed her by the arm and dragged her to the shower while hollering, "Kathy, get your ass up and come get this child immediately." She put Mandy down as soon as Kathy appeared, stripped Bonnie's clothes off and physically put her in the shower, turned on the cold water, and wouldn't let her out. The bloodcurdling screams woke everybody up. We all ran into the bedroom like our hair was on fire. Mother stopped us at the doorway and said, "This is none of your business. Go back to bed, NOW!"

I could tell the Noni transformation had occurred, and I ran like a scalded dog back to our bedroom. She didn't tell us for a long time what went on, but she did tell David and Daddy. Things got real tense for a few days, and Bonnie wasn't screwed up any more…at least not while we were there. Turned out, Mother had flushed all her drugs down the commode, and Bonnie was as mad as a wet hen about that, but she was also afraid of crossing Noni again, and what was done was done.

"What the hell is wrong with your navel? You have blood or a blood clot in your navel," Mother said to Bonnie as she was helping her get out of the shower.

"No, ma'am, that's where I had something removed."

"Like what?" Mother wanted to know.

Bonnie looking flustered for several reasons, looked up at Mother, and said, "That's where I had glued a ruby in the belly button and had to have it removed. I wanted to surprise David for our anniversary with an exotic outfit and a dance for him, and when I tried to get it out, it just would not come, so had to go to the emergency room to have it removed."

"Well, I bet he *was* surprised."

"Oh yeah, but it started hurting so bad that I had to get it out. That's when I realized that it wasn't coming out on its own. They had to—"

"I don't want to know any more, thank you," Mother interrupted. "I am sorry I asked. Now I can't get the vision out of my head already. Aren't you just full of surprises? Now, sober up. It's time to be a mother, wife, and hostess." Mother walked out of the room shaking her head.

Mandy was very difficult as a child, and apparently Bonnie just couldn't handle it. Bonnie couldn't keep up with Mandy's behavioral problems, especially when she was taking downers, and that was probably part of why she took downers. Which came first, the chicken or the egg? There's that chicken thing again. Anyway, one morning, we heard Mother yelling for help from the kitchen. Bonnie, of course, was still in bed.

"David, Elbert, somebody help me!" Of course, it was like a Chinese fire drill all over again. We could hear Mandy screaming and Mother yelling. As we entered the kitchen, we saw Mandy hanging from Mother's girdle. That child had actually pulled it down to Mother's knees. Now, I am talking about one of those torture devices with about one hundred little hooks and is so tight that I didn't know how she could breathe to begin with. Amazing! Mandy was biting and clawing and had a death grip on that girdle. It was hilarious to watch, but terrifying to think about what was going on in that child's mind. David pulled her off Mother, and Mandy turned on him. She had a fist full of his hair—and it was not attached to his head any more. He was bleeding from his nose and lip by the time it was over.

"What was she so damn mad about?" David asked.

Mother said, "I was fixing her breakfast, but apparently not fast enough. That's all I can say about that."

Any other child would have gotten a royal beating, but she knew Mandy needed serious help. It was all Mother could do to not cry in front of everybody. She wasn't the type to cry—she was too mean normally—but these two days had made her an emotional wreck, and we had another five days to go.

"Bonnie, do you have any nerve pills that I didn't flush down the commode? I know you have another stash somewhere, and I need one immediately."

"Actually I do. How about a valium?" Bonnie handed Mother one, and she downed it without water, but chased it down with Wild Turkey and water once she got back into the kitchen.

After a bit, I had never seen Mother so calm. I thought she might start drooling any second. It kinda scared me because it was so "not Mother."

"I am going to go take a nap now," Mother said as she glided to the bedroom about three inches off the floor like a slow motion ghost. "Elbert, watch the kids please and back off the beer till I am resurrected."

"Yes, ma'am."

Chapter Four

Meanwhile back in Greenville, Sara and Diane were taking care of two babies, with all the duties that come with it. Diane was getting a good dose of what motherhood involved, and she was not too sure she wanted to put herself through that when she got older. They were exhausted by nighttime and welcomed sleep. Sara was up every few hours to feed little Ted, and Diane would often get up with her.

Diane took a shower, talked on the phone for a while, and finally collapsed into a deep sleep. Suddenly, she felt a movement in her bed. She opened her eyes to see Ted's head under her covers with a flash light. She let out a scream that woke up the entire universe…Sara and the babies too.

"What are you doing in here?' she yelled at the top of her lungs.

"You shut the hell up," Ted hissed at Diane as he shone the flashlight up toward his face. He had the most frightening look in his face and eyes, especially with the freaky effects of the light. Then he jumped up and headed out the door, hiding his flashlight in his shirt.

Sara came flying into the room and asked, "What is going on?" as she looked at both of them.

"Oh, I noticed she was uncovered when I was on my way to the bathroom," Ted explained. "I tried to cover her up, and she woke up with a start. She was dreaming and I 'bout scared her to death. I'm sorry, Diane. I didn't mean to scare you, honey."

Diane lay as quiet as a mouse, shaking all over and clutching her covers. She knew not to say a word about it, and she was terrified now to go back to sleep, so she just quietly cried in the dark. The next morning, she got a glimpse of Ted as he was leaving for work. He had a serious, almost deadly look in those creepy-ass eyes as they bore down into hers, and she knew what that look meant. It meant just what he had said the night before: *Shut the hell up*—and she was scared enough to do just that.

That day, Sara and Diane went on with their chores, but Diane couldn't get over the incident. Sara appeared to be fine, and Diane couldn't bring herself to tell her what had really happened. All she could see were those evil, ice blue eyes in the dark, a sight that haunted her for her entire life.

"I am going to spend the night with Martha tonight," Diane told Sara.

Sara looked hurt and said, "Well, okay. I guess you had better tell Mother."

"I'll call her in a little bit," Diane said as she walked out of the room.

"If this is about last night," Sara said rather timidly, "Ted was only trying to help. He didn't want you to be cold. He's thoughtful that way. I guess being a Daddy has made him more aware about stuff. He felt bad about scaring you. I think it upset him more than it did you. He is such a big sweetheart."

Freaking pervert was more what I had in mind! Diane thought.

"Uh huh," was all Diane could force herself to say. "Martha and I haven't seen each other much, and she asked me to come over. If you need me, of course I'll come help. Her mother is fixing some Lebanese supper, and they invited me to eat. I'll stay with you till suppertime. Okay?"

"Just make sure it's okay with Mother. I don't want to be on her shit list, and neither do you."

"I will," Diane said, relieved and feeling guilty about leaving Sara. "Are you sure you're gonna be okay? I'll be back in the morning to help you."

"Yeah, I'll be fine. Ted can help if I need it. Go, have fun while Big Chief is out of town."

That's what Daddy called Mother, and it really pissed her off…which is why he did it, of course.

Now it was time to make the dreaded call to Mother. Just as she touched the phone, it rang, and Diane just about jumped out of her skin.

"Hello?" Diane said, trying to hold back the anxiety.

It was Mother. "I had a dream about you last night," she said with a stern but worried voice. "Are you okay?"

Not really.

"Yes, but please tell me I didn't die in the dream. I was just about to call you."

"I know you were, and no, you didn't die, but you were crying and scared."

She could barely hear Mother over all the background noise at David's house. It sounded like a hundred people were there.

Diane thought, *God, I am so glad I am not there.*

"What's the matter?" Mother asked.

A perv had his freaking head under my covers.

"Um, nothing," Diane said. "I just wanted to tell you that I am spending the night with Martha tonight and maybe every night until ya'll get back."

"And why would that be? What's wrong? I know something happened."

My brother-in-law is a freakin' perv.
"I'm fine. I just don't want to stay here at night."
"What happened, Diane?"
"I don't want to talk about it right now. I am fine."
NOT.
"Just tell me it is okay, please?" she said to Mother. "I am begging you. I don't feel…comfortable here."
Terrified is more like it.
"Okay, but we will talk about this when we get home, if I survive this shit down here. Just check in with me so I'll know you're all right. Okay?"
"I will. I'll be fine."
Just get me the hell away from the devil man.
"I'll help Sara during the day and spend the night with Martha. Talk to you tomorrow. Bye, Mother."
"Please be careful and stay out of trouble."

Chapter Five

Back on the Florida battlefront, all stayed pretty calm until Thursday morning. Mother was fixing breakfast as usual. The biscuits and gravy and grits were done, and the bacon and eggs were almost ready. Mother served Mandy's plate before anybody else, or else the child would turn psycho at the sight of anyone eating without her. Buddy was served next, and he decided to put an egg in his grits while they were as hot as molten lava. He liked to whip an egg into his grits to add flavor. The grits cooked it almost immediately. He had started to eat when Mandy noticed that his grits were more yellow than hers.

Now, Mandy really loved butter, and she thought Buddy had more butter than she did. So she went off on him, trying to grab his plate so she could get to those beautiful, golden-colored-from-butter grits.

Buddy, of course, being as stubborn as any Keith can be, held his plate close and tight while she tried to take it away from him. He was determined to keep it and continued trying to eat. But Mandy decided to fling her plate like a Frisbee straight at him. Luckily, it hit the top of his head rather than his face, and still he held on to his breakfast. Mandy started screaming and trying to remove Buddy's hair from his scalp and his plate from his grasp, when Mother—Noni by now—returned to the kitchen.

"What the hell? Holy mother of God, what is going on now? I leave for one minute and all hell breaks loose!" Noni's voice got louder with each sentence. Mandy was out of control and hollerin', and Buddy was trying to explain what had happened with blood oozing down his ear and grits, bacon, and eggs all over him and the kitchen.

"Just give it to her!" Noni almost yelled at Buddy. "Do you have a death wish or something? Jesus Christ, Buddy, you know not to mess with her. What a goddamn mess." She started to clean up and get a handle on Mandy at the same time, but talk about *Mission Impossible*. "It looks like she got you pretty good. You're bleeding, and you have a nice gash in your scalp. And she *still* got your breakfast, you dummy! When will you learn to leave her alone? Go let David look at your wound and see if you need stitches. And your britches are crackin'! Pull your britches out of your crack and go show David your battle wound. Now go!"

Before Buddy could get out of his chair, everybody showed up. Talk about late for the fire drill…

"What in God's name has happened now?" David asked, looking like it had already been a long day.

"Well, let me see, Mandy just came unglued because she thought Buddy had more butter in his grits than she did. Buddy's britches are crackin', and he has a hole in his head the size of a quarter." David tried to calm Mother, but she already had her momentum. She was getting louder with every word, and it was too late. "There is food all over the kitchen! Somebody needs to get Mandy another plate and quick! I have a hemorrhoid hanging down to my damn knees, and I may have to kill somebody! Does that about cover it?"

Noni's hair was frizzin', and her nostrils were flarin' like a rodeo bull's. Real bad sign, that.

Buddy shook his head and slinked out of the kitchen. He knew that when Noni had a "rhoid," you had better get to steppin' and stay the hell out of her way.

"And somebody get me some goddamn Prep H before I have to pinch somebody's head off!"

In a split second, there were three sets of keys jangling—belonging to Elbert, David, and Bonnie—and people running around, trying to escape with their lives. Finally getting organized after they had escaped the kitchen, they split up. David took Buddy to help him get his britches out of his crack and stitches put in his head. Bonnie went to the PX to get the H meds. And Daddy stayed the hell out of Noni's way. After Bonnie returned with the H meds, and David and Buddy returned with three stitches in Buddy's scalp, everybody in the house sort of collapsed for a while. Some of us went back to bed.

A few hours later, we'd all had our chance to relax, Noni was getting some relief from the Prep H, and our guards were dropped. That's when things got interesting again. Somebody realized that Mandy was missing. She could usually be found dancing in the same spot, sometimes for about sixteen hours a day. That is, when she wasn't eating. She loved music second only to eating, and would stand and rock back and forth, tapping on a cigar box with a pencil on a string, smiling and happy as a clam. She was very docile most of the time, especially when music was being played.

But *do not* try to take her pencil-on-a-string-attached-to-a-cigar-box. She would turn animal on you in a flash. Her older brother Mack was mean sometimes, and he loved to worry the hell out of her and take it from her. She would chase him around, screaming at the top of her lungs until he gave it back. He was really cruel that way. Of all the thievin', conivin' members of the closet full of skeletons that was my brother's family, Mack was the baddest news. He stayed in trouble, in and out of jail all of his life, and probably met the worst end of them all. Hard to tell sometimes...but again, I digress.

We looked all around the house and yard for Mandy. We found her cigar box with its attached pencil out in the yard, which made us go from worried to nearly frantic. We called and called. No Mandy. We scattered into the neighbors' yards, looking and asking around, but no one had seen her. The neighbors knew her and were aware of her disabilities. And her capabilities. We had gotten just about everybody the neighborhood into a panic when somebody happened to look up and see Mandy. On the freaking roof! Bonnie screamed, David and Noni cussed, and Mandy just grinned. We were baffled at first how she got up there, but then we noticed a little tree beside the house. It just happened to be about the only tree on the entire base. She had climbed the tree, which was no simple task I can tell you, having a great deal of personal experience climbing trees myself. Sizing the tree up, I knew I could get on the roof by climbing it, but I would have never thought Mandy could. But there she was, walking around casually as if nothing was wrong.

"Now that we've found her, how are we going to get her down?" Daddy asked.

"I have a ladder in the garage. I'll go up there and get her down somehow," David said.

He climbed the ladder to the roof, but Mandy would not come to him. He was afraid she would jump or fall, although she was very agile and *strong* for her age. It was about a hundred degrees outside and probably nine hundred degrees on the roof from the looks of David, so we got some cold water for him and

Mandy…because it took about two hours to get her down. She was afraid to get on the ladder backward and go down.

"Offer her some food," I finally suggested, wondering why the thought hadn't occurred to me a long time ago.

"Good idea. Get those chocolate chip cookies out. That'll get her down," Bonnie said.

Sure enough, it worked. They usually didn't let her have many cookies because it made her hyper. So she fell for it. She whipped around like she was on a mission and climbed down the ladder with ease. Like she had done it a hundred times. They eventually had to cut down that little tree because she quickly learned how to get cookies. She clearly was not dumb. But she got really pissed when the tree was gone because her cookie supply went with it.

Things kind of settled down, and we had a pretty good time for the rest of the week. Mother got her rhoid under control before the trip back home. Thank God! That would have made a trip from hell even worse. We took inventory, knowing that the thieves would be doing their best to steal anything they could before we left, and packed up our stuff. Then we slept for a while since we would be leaving around midnight again. We got up, our parents had some coffee, and they lined us up for our barf bags. Bonnie was crying for Mother not to leave. *Yeah, uh huh…* We got into our little spaces in the VW and waved our good-byes.

As we were pulling out, I looked out one last time and hollered, "Are those my tennis shoes Sherri is wearing?!"

Sure as shit stinks, there she was, smiling and waving goodbye, wearing my only pair of tennis shoes. "For cryin' out loud! I need those, Daddy!"

"Well, I'll be damned," Noni said, starting in on another roll. "If that just doesn't take the cake! No telling what else they lifted. We had everything packed in the car. How the hell did she do that? Forget it, Elbert, just keep going. We'll get you another pair, Maggie. Let's just get the hell out of here. I am ready to get home. I don't know how David can stand it, poor fella. I'd probably be an alcoholic if I had to live here. No wonder he works all the time."

"Well, at least the heifer couldn't take my sundress off my back," I muttered. Mother was so pissed at Sherri and Bonnie and the whole situation at David's that she was finally speechless. Daddy, as usual, kept on driving with his mouth shut. He knew anything he said would just get Noni stirred up even more, and what he wanted most was some quiet.

We were so tired that Buddy and I slept all the way home without barfing. That was amazing for me. But when we got home and started unpacking, there was more bad news: Buddy realized his records were gone. Mack had outsmarted him once again, despite that fact that Buddy had hidden them deep in the bowels of all our stuff in the car. The thieves apparently rummaged through the car while we were getting in our pre-trip nap. *Whatever…the damn morons…*

That night after supper, I overheard Mother and Daddy talking. "They're gonna have to do something with Mandy. She is downright dangerous to herself and others," Mother said to Daddy.

"I know, and they need to do it soon," Daddy said. "I talked to David about it, and he's in the process of finding a good school for autistic children, hopefully nearby. He was exhausted and couldn't stand the thought of us leaving."

"Well, that's too bad because there is no way in hell I could take it much longer," Mother said. "I feel for him, but I'm too old to deal with that mess. My nerves are shot, and we were only there for week! I don't know what else we can do for him but pray."

Chapter Six

We all felt better the next day, but Mother and Daddy were still worn out. They weren't young anymore, and it had been one helluva week, emotionally and physically draining. And here came Ted early that afternoon, trying to be the sweetest Southern gentleman you could imagine. He said he'd come to help us unpack and stuff. "Did Diane tell you I scared the hell out of her the other night?" he asked Noni. She had transformed into Noni the instant Ted walked in the door. Noni just nodded affirmatively and gave Ted her death look. "Yeah," he went on nervously, "must have been having an awful nightmare when I tried to wake her from it. She screamed and backed up so fast she hit the wall. Started cryin' and wouldn't let anybody touch her. I've been worried about her, poor thing. She hasn't talked to me since."

"Yeah, she told me," Noni finally spat out. *You son of a bitch! I know Diane didn't tell me everything. Yet!*

Mother turned tail and walked out of the living room, leaving him standing there. She already knew there was a fox in the hen house. She really hadn't needed anything more than her own daughter's voice on the phone to tell her that much. Ted's little performance just now only confirmed it. But she would wait and talk to Diane before she did anything…or didn't do anything, as the case sadly turned out to be.

Mother and Diane talked in private that evening. I was no dummy, and I knew something was up. I knew my sister well, and she was on edge like I had never seen her before. So naturally, when Noni shut the two of them in her bedroom and gave me that "Go find something to do" look, I pretended to obey, but doubled back to listen at the door. I could barely hear what they were saying. There was no yelling or crying, and the only impression I got was fear and doubt. Finally Diane came out real quiet like, leaving Noni looking at her and me with a cold stare that showed pain, worry, and anger. Not a good combination for her. I knew nothing about what had happened at Sara's while we were gone, but clearly something was up. They didn't tell me because they didn't want me to be scared of Ted. Sara and the babies were doing well. She was lonely because Diane stayed away. I wanted to spend the night, which I had done a couple of times before, but that was not allowed anymore. Things had taken a weird turn, and I didn't know why. I was mad because all of a sudden I had no outlet. Mother and I would go to visit and help during the day, but no more jammie parties at Sara's. What was up with that?

Ted got into the habit of making nightly visits to our house to check on us. He just wanted to make sure we were okay since Daddy worked the third shift, you know. Yeah, sure. He would slink around in the dark living and dining rooms, maybe sit in the bedroom with Mother and me for a few minutes as we watched TV. Then he would go down to the basement and stay a while.

He would always leave the basement door open, and it took me a long time to find out why. But when I went into the bathroom, I could barely see him down there at the bottom of the steps. I don't know what he did when Mother passed by the doorway, and I didn't know for a long time what the heck he was doing to begin with. Turns out, he was busily letting off some pressure. But I was only ten years old. I just knew that he was so sweet at times and weird and secretive at other times. He paid a lot of attention to me. He loved for me to dance for him, and I loved showing off. I had also become a hula-hoop champ, and I showed everybody why. Looking back now, I can only imagine what it did to Mr. Sicko's imagination to watch that. I was clueless then.

But not for long. One day I got a little dirt on my bathing suit bottom, right in the front, from playing in the sprinkler in the yard. Ted was visiting, or rather he was watching me play. He offered to help "get that dirt off of there," but I declined. Even at only ten years old, I knew that was off limits. And then it clicked. I suddenly felt a sensation of revulsion and fear. I turned off the water and went inside to change out of my bathing suit, and Ted left. The feeling passed in a few hours, my young, inquisitive mind finding other things to occupy it. But it had started, though I was barely aware.

One aspect of our lives that didn't fit the traditional Southern stereotype was our religion. We were raised as Catholics, and almost exclusively by Mother. On Sunday mornings, we went to Mass at 6 a.m. Every freaking Sunday. Mother, Diane, Buddy, and I got all dressed up and Sunday-morning clean. How on earth my Mother—three-quarters Cherokee and one-quarter Southern redneck—ended up being Catholic I never have been able to divine. But for most of my childhood, not attending Sunday morning Mass was not an option for her or any of her children. Daddy was somehow exempt, and he always exercised his right to stay away.

South Carolina in August is hotter than hell. For much of my childhood, we sat by a fan during the day, slept by a window fan at night, and praised the attic fan in the evenings once it was cool enough to turn it on. When I was about ten or eleven, we finally got one little window air conditioner for the whole house. It was in Mother's bedroom. During the day, we played in the sprinkler to cool off. Back then, we lived every summertime moment just to go outside and ride our bikes, play softball, or walk to the corner drugstore for a fountain drink. I was quite athletic, especially for a girl. And I was inquisitive, always trying to figure stuff out, how things worked. Anything from dolls and watches to roller skates and sewing machines, I wanted to know how they worked. Unfortunately, that often meant disassembling things, and they could not always be reassembled properly.

But I gained a knack for ingenuity at some things. I remember making my own skate board out of an old pair of skates. The kind of skates that just tightened with a little tool until they fit your shoe. I had long ago learned how to take the skates apart. So I nailed them onto a board, and *Voila! ME. HAVE. SKATE. BOARD. NOW!* My parents were all like, "DAMN!" Especially my father, who was the mechanical type and could appreciate my efforts. Those were the days.

My siblings were not the only ones to receive nurturing under Mother and Daddy's roof. Several of the neighborhood kids, mostly those around Buddy's age, spent a lot of time and ate a lot of food at our house. Mean as my Mother could be, she had a very soft place in her heart for children, especially those less fortunate than us. She and Daddy both had hard upbringings, and she just couldn't stand seeing a child go through what they had gone through. One kid I remember most was Robbie, who usually showed up on his bike. He was one of Buddy's friends, and he was such a good guy that Mother took him right in. His parents were always gone, and he stayed hungry a lot and was often locked out of his house. It was not uncommon to wake up to find Robbie asleep on our front porch in the morning after his paper route. Sometimes it was hotter than hell outside, and sometimes icy and snowy. Mother or Daddy would find him, and bring him in, feed him, and let him sleep in the house. He was a great guy I might have married one day if he hadn't felt so much like a brother. We grew up together, and he was five years older than me. And Buddy probably would have broken his arms if he had ever come on to me.

Another friend of Buddy's was Nathan. One day he knocked on the door, with his little brother Chris beside him. Nathan looked up at Mother, his eyes spilling over with tears and said, "Mrs. Keith, my little brother is hungry. Do you have any food?"

Mother almost cried in front of him. "I sure do, honey chile. You know there's always a place for ya'll at our table and in our hearts. Have you eaten, Nathan? There's plenty of food for everybody. You're a good big brother, you know that? You two get in there and wash your hands and I'll have you something good in no time. I was just fixin' to make some biscuits and gravy. Sound good?"

"Yes, ma'am, but if you'll just feed Chris, we would be most grateful. I'll be glad to do yard work or anything you need if you'll just feed my little brother. I'll be okay." Little Chris couldn't have been more than six or seven years old. He was skinny as a rail and dark around the eyes.

"Don't be foolish, honey chile. There's plenty of food here." Nathan and little Chris came into the kitchen, and there sat Robbie, stuffing his face.

"Hey Robbie," Nathan exclaimed. "Funny meeting you here. I had to find something for Chris to eat. He was looking poorly and wanting to sleep too much, and I was worried. I knew Noni would feed him."

All of our close childhood friends called Mother "Noni" at her insistence.

"We haven't seen our parents in a few days, and there is no food anywhere in the house," Nathan said.

"I know what you mean," Robbie replied. "I don't know what I would do without the Keiths, do you?"

Nathan agreed and knew exactly how he felt, except he had a little brother to worry about as well. It was beginning to look like a foster home in our kitchen, but it made us happy that they had us and felt comfortable coming here. And they were so thankful and never stopped offering to pay or work off the hospitality. These were all good guys as it turned out, and they grew up to be good men. They just had shitty parents.

We all had lots of friends. Mother and Daddy seemed happy when they had us all around the house, joking and playing music and dancing. I guess as long as we were where they could see us, there were no worries. If you came to our house for any reason, you had to eat. That was just the way it was. Even if you said you had just eaten, Mother would force-feed you something. If you refused, that was the ultimate insult and not to be forgotten. And Mother was like an elephant with grudges. She took some of them to her grave, I am sure of that.

I was about eleven years old when Diane started dating. I only remember her dating one guy, Michael. They were then, and always have been, "the one" for each other. But in order for her sweetie to come a courtin', he would have to endure the wrath of Noni. She was awful on our dates, but Michael didn't give up. He soon learned that proper respect paid to Noni was the key to seeing Diane on a regular basis. Sometimes when he came to pick Diane up, I'd be waiting, knowing she would be doing some last-minute primping before going out. I'd run outside as soon as he pulled up, hop in the front seat, and he would take me for rides in his really hot car. I thought that was so very cool. We were buddies from the beginning, me and Michael. Noni tortured that poor guy for years, but he didn't give up on Diane, he just kept on comin', and she kept going out with him.

Chapter Seven

We found out shortly before Thanksgiving one year that David and his family were coming for two weeks at Christmas. Oh my God, somebody kill me please! Then again, everybody was a few years older, so I hoped maybe things would be a little more in control…oh, who was I kidding?

We had seen them for the past four or five years on our annual trips-from-hell to Florida. So now, the Christmas from hell was coming up. A week before they were to arrive, we started hauling our valuables over to other family members' houses and to Michael's. We kids didn't have much stuff, but my parents had some valuable things, including silver, jewelry, antique china, fine clothing, etc. It all had to be removed before the family thieves came. Buddy and Diane still lived at home, but Diane wasn't there much, especially now that David and his brood were coming. Diane would stay at Michael's or at one of her girlfriends' houses almost the entire time, though she did come by the house for a short visit once a day.

We never knew just how much David was aware of the juvenile delinquent gang that was his three oldest children. My parents didn't want to hurt David's feelings by asking him a lot of questions. Personally, when it comes to thievery, I thought, *Screw that!* Stealing is stealing. And stealing from family is even worse than just stealing. But Mother Dearest would not allow us to talk about it to him, just like she wouldn't let us talk to Sara about dear Ted. Always trying to hide the skeleton. I often thought, as we were making trips to everybody's houses with our worldly possessions, *Now isn't this just dahlin'? Thieves in the family, but will we tell their father? Hell no...*

Little did we know that this was going to be a most *special* visit.

They arrived as scheduled on the twentieth of December. *What a shitty time to go invade someone's life, don't you think?* The whole fam damily! God help us. If only I was old enough to drink...David and Bonnie looked pretty good, and the kids did too. Kathy was tall, blonde, lean, and rather pretty—until she opened her mouth. Mack was built like a Mack truck, short and stocky like David, with dark, shifty eyes under heavy eyebrows, and a perpetual smirk of mischievous confidence on his face. He was used to not just getting into, but also creating, trouble. And getting away with it too often. Sherri was slowly shaping up like me. Mandy was the youngest, and she appeared to be more in control. They had her in a special school, and it was helping with her control issues.

God, I hope it lasts while they're here!

We did our hellos and got them all moved into the house. Later that evening, the weather was nice, and we cooked out on the grill. I know, it was the holiday season and you're supposed to grill in the summer, but this is the South. Barbecue is fit for eating any time of year...maybe not Christmas Day or Thanksgiving Day, but just about any other time. Daddy told us all kinds of stories, mostly about his youth when he lived with his Uncle Jack and Aunt Bessie. They were the parents his could never have been. They took my father and in when no one else in the family would treat him right. Daddy hated being separated from his little twin sisters, but he knew they were treated well by the relatives they lived with. So Jack and Bessie loved him and raised him as if he was their own. They were just plain old, good, salt-of-the-earth types who worked hard and lived honest, Christian lives. They never complained about their lot in life, hard as it was. Uncle Jack worked a full-time job, and they had a challenging daughter and a big garden with chickens and acreage. Daddy nearly worshipped the ground they walked on…and with good reason. Following his uncle's example, Daddy worked the farm and had a full-time job before he was ten years old.

Anyway, Daddy was spinning yarns while some of us sat in awe, others, like Noni, listened with trepidation. Here we all were, eating barbeque ribs, chicken, and pork with all the fixin's, when Daddy started into what, after this day, became one of his favorite stories. Why he had never dropped this one on us before, I don't know, but what a debut…

"Well," he said, with the slyest of little grins, "Uncle Jack needed to replace the old front door in the living room. So he went and got him some seasoned wood and started sanding and cutting. He'd been working on it for a few weeks off and on as he had time. Uncle Jack could do anything when he put his mind to it. He just didn't have a lot of spare time. He had a workshop out back where he did all his woodwork and carpentry. He was in there sawing on that door one afternoon, and Aunt Bessie and I were in the house washing vegetables we'd just picked. Suddenly, we heard Uncle Jack hollerin' real frantic like, with a sound like we'd never heard come outta his mouth. We ran out the back door and saw Uncle Jack walking toward us, blood everywhere.

"I cut my finger off, Bessie!" Uncle Jack said, looking about the same color as his white T-shirt. "Go get it off the floor, Elbert, and get a towel or two to wrap my hand up. We'll have to go to the hospital, maybe they can sew it back on."

"Well, I ran into the shop, but then ran I right back out real quick and said, 'I don't think so Uncle Jack. The dog's eatin' it. He won't give it to me.'"

Well, Daddy's entire, formerly enthralled but now thoroughly disgusted audience went "EEEWWWW…"

Noni said, "Dammit to hell, Elbert! What did you have to do that for? You went and made everybody sick at the dinner table."

But Daddy, perhaps emboldened by several beers, continued his story despite the negative response of the women. "Uncle Jack's eyes rolled back in his head and he toppled over like an old oak tree. We had to get him some help soon 'cause he was bleeding like a stuck hog. Aunt Bessie and I tried to pick him up, but it was like trying to pick up a 230-pound piece of wet liver. Not gonna happen. But we figured out pretty quick that you could drag a body a lot easier by the legs. So we dragged him all the way across the back of the house and down the driveway so we could get close to the car. We finally got him in the car, which just about killed us both. Actually, it made Aunt Bessie poot when she strained too hard," Daddy said matter-of-factly.

"Elbert, shut up!" Noni was ready to murder him.

"Anyway, Joe started waking up right about the time we got to the hospital, and all he would say was, 'My damn head is killing me.' We looked, and oops! The back of his head had dried blood, grass, and dirt on top of several purple lumps, as well as chunks missing from his scalp. He was so hung up on his head problem that for a while there, he forgot he was missing a finger. We never told him why his head was so beat up, we just let him think he'd hit his head when he passed out."

Daddy almost looked like he was daydreaming and said, "I knew I should have fed Duke the dog earlier that morning, but I was working the garden before it got too hot. Ever since that day, nobody wanted to watch Duke eat anything, and things just weren't the same after that. All I could see when I looked at him is that bloody finger going round and round in his mouth."

"Jesus, Elbert, will you please just shut the hell up?" Noni said with that nasty glare of hers. She turned away and went into the kitchen to smolder. For some reason, the barbeque wasn't looking so good anymore. Daddy and the guys thought it was funny as hell, but the women all looked a little queasy. Once we all got over the shock and awe, it became kinda humorous for the rest of the week and a source of fun.

Please forgive us, Uncle Jack.

But Noni stayed royally pissed at him for messing up a good welcome dinner, and she wouldn't talk to him for a couple of days.

We were all trying to get in the Christmas mood. But it was kinda hard with too many people in the house, and having to share your bed, bathroom, and everything else got old pretty quick. Mother took Bonnie shopping the next day, partly just to get out of the house. Sherri and I were hanging out a couple of hours later when we heard Mother and Bonnie return. Or rather Noni and Bonnie, 'cause they were raising hell at each other, and that was rare. Bonnie NEVER tried to argue with Noni—she had too much respect for and fear of her to do so. Sherri and I went running into the living room to see what was up, just to get turned around by both parents and told that everything was fine (a sure sign that yet another skeleton was trying to make a daylight appearance while Noni was furiously trying to shove it back into the closet). We could tell that Bonnie had been crying, and Noni looked like she had been run over by a truck.

Okay, fine, liar liar, we'll just turn around and go back into the bedroom.

Later that day, we noticed secret meetings among the parents, whispering, shifting eyes, etc. Whatever...but there was no telling what had happened.

Things settled down to a quiet evening. Sherri and I were sitting in the living room watching the aluminum Christmas tree with the rotating multicolored spotlight, drifting in and out of sleep. Bonnie came out of the bedroom and headed for the front door. I looked up in my sleepy stupor and saw her going outside. She noticed that I saw her and said, "I am going out to the van to get something. I'll be back in a few minutes."

Whatever...

She left the front door open slightly, and I proceeded to nod in and out of a semiconscious TV coma. After a bit, Bonnie came back in and leaned over Sherri and kissed her on the head and said, "Bye, baby, I love you." I thought that was odd but rather sweet, because that is something that my family didn't say normally.

Then I looked at my pink, fuzzy bedroom shoes and saw a large amount of blood on them. There was a trail leading from them to the front door. I looked up and saw that Bonnie was bleeding profusely all over the couch, the floor, and Sherri. I started screaming for Mother and David as I looked for the source of the blood. I wish I had not gotten such a close-up view of the wounds, because I still see it in my head now. Bonnie had gone out to the van and slashed both wrists with a razor blade, and like a true Southern Belle, come back in to tell everybody goodbye. What a fucking mess. Noni came charging into the living room and started dishing out orders immediately: "Bonnie, lie down right now! Maggie, bring me some towels. Buddy, call an ambulance. Sherri, go get your father up! Dear God, Bonnie, why…what…Jesus…"

Bonnie, crying and looking a little pale, said, "I know I did a bad thing today, Noni, and you were so mad at me. I let you down. I can't stand it when you're mad at me."

"Now you know we already talked all that out today," Noni growled. "You didn't have to go do something like this. You could have died out there, and you upset the girls too. Look at the goddamn mess in here. What the hell were you thinking, Bonnie?'

"I was ashamed Noni, and I didn't want to live. I love you so much, and I know that I upset you today and I am so sorry."

"Well, you've got one screwed up way of saying it, my dear. You listen here, and I'm gonna tell you…You are going to get your ass on that stretcher, and go get some help. And I mean some serious help, not just for your wrists." A few moments passed before we could hear the siren approaching. "The ambulance is here now," Noni barked. "David, are you ready to go? They're here!"

"Yeah, Mother." David looked like he had the weight of the world on his shoulders, and quite frankly, he did. We still didn't know what Bonnie had done that day to make Noni so mad. We figured we would probably find out after they left, but until then it was kept…yeah, you know, in the closet.

The ambulance took Bonnie away with David in the back, leaving Mother, Buddy, and me with all the kids and a hell of a mess to clean up. God help us!

Chapter Eight

Bonnie was taken to the emergency room, and once her wounds were stitched up and she was given a unit of blood, she was transferred to the nearby mental hospital. They said initially they would keep her for at least a couple of weeks. They wouldn't let anybody see her for a few days except David. He would come back all wrung out after just an hour visiting with Bonnie. She was seriously drugged, and with her pharmaceutical history, it took a LOT to knock her out.

She was apparently enjoying the buzz, but she was really pissed off that she couldn't have her fingernail file or any other sharp objects. Even after just having tried to kill herself, Bonnie was vain enough to want to look her best. She wanted her "hayah dressah" to come in and do her hair and nails, and she was willing to do anything to get it. She may have been crazy as hell, but she always looked pretty and immaculate, so the "hospital lock-up look" was not doing it for her. And she was getting near violent about it.

She also insisted that she use a bedpan for her bowel movements. No one could understand why she would want to do that, since she was ambulatory. They refused to bring her a bedpan, so she rigged up a way to make her next BM on the food tray that her breakfast came on. She felt nature call, took the tray into the bathroom, and made her deposit. She had managed to procure some gloves from somewhere or somebody along the way, so she put those bad boys on and started picking thru her stool specimen while she sat on the bathroom floor. Just as she was getting the hang of it, the bathroom door opened, and there stood David, Nurse Ratched, and an orderly the size of a refrigerator, all looking down at her with the same bewildered stare. She looked up at them and said through her drug-clouded haze, "Ha-a-a-ay."

David didn't faint, but he did blow breakfast at the sight of his prissy wife playing in her own doo-doo. He did not know what to say—he just ran and threw up in the nearest trashcan. Bonnie tried to explain what she was doing and why, but no one was buying her justification for such extreme behavior. Except Bonnie. They proceeded to pick her up and haul her prissy, stool-picking ass down to a padded room in lock-up, hospital hair and all. David convinced them to let him talk to her for a few minutes first to try to figure out what in the hell she was doing.

They put them in a secure area to let them talk. "Okay, what's it all about this time, Bonnie?" David demanded. He wasn't naïve enough to think Bonnie wasn't up to *something*.

"I swallowed a diamond ring yesterday, David," Bonnie said through sobs. She always could get into his heart by crying.

"Who's ring?"

"I stole a ring yesterday when Noni took me shopping. That's why she and I got into that big fight. She told me that I had to take the ring back, and I knew that if I did, they would probably arrest me. So I swallowed it right there in the car on the way home. If Noni hadn't been driving, I think she would have shoved me out of the car or knocked me out."

"Jesus, God in heaven help me," David muttered. "Well, she should have. I have a good mind to just let them take you and keep you forever. That was the stupidest thing I think you have done yet. Now what am I supposed to tell this hospital? They want to put you away in a padded room and throw away the key, do you realize that? You are fucking killing me!"

"Just tell them I swallowed my diamond to keep somebody from getting it. And…go make sure they don't flush my sample. The ring is probably in there."

"You are truly insane. Sometimes I wish I had never met you."

She gave him that killer smile and batted those big blue eyes that had always melted him. Except this time. He left the room to start damage control. When he got back to her room where the specimen had been on display, he found that, sure enough, they had disposed of it. And that was actually a relief. While it didn't produce the evidence, the story at least kept Bonnie out of the padded room in lock-up.

David finally came back to our house, where we were all hanging by our claws, and he looked so defeated. It was now morning, and he had been at the hospital all night. Mother stopped him in his tracks, put a hand on each of his shoulders and took one long look at him, and he fell to pieces. All the kids left the room out of respect for him, although I wanted to hear the scoop. I was wondering what had happened with Mother and Bonnie and the big fight the day before. Since I knew the house better than anyone else, I managed to position myself so I could hear their conversation in the bedroom. David was having a hard time controlling his emotions, and he was still in shock from the hospital incident. He eventually was able to tell Mother what had happened, although he couldn't look her in the eyes. Noni just sat there and took it all in with those short little Indian arms crossed, that typically intense look in her eyes. I think David kinda forgot how intense she could be, having not lived with her for so long.

She proceeded to tell him what had occurred the day before: "Bonnie and I went into several stores yesterday. I knew to watch her, but I swear she has gotten too good, because I never saw her take anything. I knew she probably had, but I couldn't tell for sure, and she was so relaxed. She went into a jewelry store, and I freaked out immediately and followed her in. I threatened her before we went in and she promised, 'Don't worry, Noni, I'll be good.' And I told her, 'You'd better be, because I ain't going to jail for you. If something happens, you're on your own.'

"Bonnie asked to see some bracelets and rings," Mother continued. "She tried on several ring. I never left her sight, and she never left mine. She thanked the clerk, and we got back into the car to head for home. We got about halfway home, and she started pulling shit out: she had a ring in her mouth, a bracelet in her beehive hairdo, a scarf in her bra, and a new purse under her coat. I slammed on the brakes and told her that was *bad* shit, that she was going to take that ring back if I had to carry her. She immediately put it back in her mouth and swallowed it just as easy as you please. I get the feeling she had done that before, but I still couldn't believe it. I was speechless. I knew that if we went back into the stores, we would be arrested, and I was afraid to do that. Then she started crying, and we had a big fight. I told her that I was never going to take her anywhere again, that I was ashamed of her. I told her that our family didn't do things like that, and if she was going remain a part of this family and be welcomed here, she was going to have to straighten her ass up. She kept saying how sorry she was, but I was hard on her. I am not going to put myself in that position again. *Ever.* And then she has to go trying to kill herself and make me feel like the bad guy, and I am sorry, but it ain't gonna work on me. You're my son, and I love you with all my life. I know you have your damn hands full, and I do feel sorry for you, but we cannot have that shit going on here. Understand?"

"Yes, ma'am. I'm so sorry, Mother. She pulls that guilt shit on me and the kids all the time. What scares the hell out of me is that the kids are just like her. They stay in trouble all the time too. Mack has been brought home by the police more than once, as well as Kathy. I work two to three jobs to pay for all the stuff she wants and buys and all her medical bills...They bring home stuff I know they can't afford. You just wouldn't believe what I deal with. I don't know what to do any more, and I am too damn tired to think. I have to lie down right now while I can. I'm so sorry, Mother, for everything."

Mother gave him a hug and a peck on the cheek. "Go get some rest, Son, you need it," she said sadly. She knew there was nothing else she could do.

We were never a physical family, and we rarely said, "I love you" to each other. We never doubted that we were loved, and I never knew the difference until I started going to other households and saw there was a difference. We were not the norm. And as I got older, I began to realize just how true that really was.

The next day, David went to the hospital to see Bonnie. They let him in with supervision. They opened the door, and there she was in all her beauty, sitting up and smiling big for him, with a shiny new ring on her finger. The nurse said, "Well, Bonnie found her ring this morning after all. I'll leave you two alone."

"Yeah, I see that. That's great, honey," David said as he looked over at Bonnie. She winked at him and batted those big blue eyes. She and David had managed to convince the hospital staff that she wasn't playing in her stool just for the hell of it. She had a good reason. Yeah, uh huh...They sat in almost complete silence for the visit, not talking about the ring. David just kept looking at her, then the ring, and shaking his head as if to say, "I am so screwed. My life is shit. I don't want to know. I don't want to talk about it."

Bonnie said they were considering letting her go when her wrists looked better. And yep, with her looks and charm and intelligence, and probably a whole lot of bullshit on her part, they agreed to discharge her in a few days if she continued to behave. Bonnie didn't care that David was mad; she knew it wouldn't last forever. She was happy. She knew David loved her, and she used that to enable her to get away with anything this side of murder. She had her husband, good drugs, her new ring, and soon, her freedom.

Meanwhile, back at the ranch...what a mess. The cleanup was intense, and you could still see and smell the blood days after it happened. It was going to take a professional to get it out, and they had yet to arrive. The natives were restless. David's kids were used to running loose on the air base, but Noni wouldn't allow them to hardly leave the house and yard. They were possibly going to have to stay longer than planned because of Bonnie's little "predicament," so we were all a bit anxious about how long that would be. Diane came to visit every day, I guess to see that we all hadn't killed each other. One day she had a look on her face that was like a deer in the headlights, like somebody who had had too many plastic surgeries. You know, like she was in a constant state of surprise. The phone rang, and she jumped suddenly, and it made us all jump as well. She answered it as if she was expecting an ax murderer to be on the other end of the line. She handed the phone off to Mother with a look of relief. What was that all about?

Buddy and Mack usually took off in the mornings on bikes, but they always came back to eat. And they had to be in by dark. "Your asses had better be here when the street lights come on, or I'm coming after you," Mother would always say. And believe me, they didn't want that. They were always home before dark.

Sherri, Kathy, and I had virtually nothing to do but walk to the pharmacy and get a fountain drink and window shop. I never had any money, so I had no reason to go into the shops at the Plaza. They catered to the richer clientele, and they stayed on your heels if you went in there. Boring! And humiliating…they would follow you around like you were going to steal something. Imagine that…

So finally, one day the two of them convinced me they just wanted to look around in a couple of the shops. I gave in and we went into Patterson's. Everything in there was outrageously priced. I had never owned anything to the likes of that inventory. The sales clerks, of course, were all over us. "Let's get out of here," I said. "There's nothing in here for us." I just wanted to get them out of there before something went wrong.

"No, wait a minute," Kathy replied. "I want to try on this sweater and slacks." I sat down in one of the chairs provided for the bored husbands and worried. Sherri continued to pretend to "shop." It was taking too long, and I was getting antsy. I knew what they were capable of, but I had never been in the middle of it. Sherri kept going back and checking on Kathy, but I just sat my ass still and started to sweat. Kathy was the transporter of the items, and Sherri was the distractor/provider. They had a system that worked. I saw it all happening with my own eyes. *Finally*, they were ready to leave, and we bolted out the door. I immediately noticed that while we had on winter clothes, Kathy's appeared fuller than before. I think that was when I had my first panic attack.

I turned to them and said, "I. Don't. Want. To. Know. Anything. AND I am never going anywhere with you again. I live here. These people know me and my family. Mother is on a first-name basis with the owner of that store! So you know what? I'm telling. As soon as we get home."

"They don't care anyway," Kathy said. "Mother does it all the time. How do you think we learned, you dummy?"

"I'm not telling your mother, you dummy. I'm telling Noni!"

They both started to chase me all the way home. The "Noni" word got their attention. Little did they know that I was the fastest runner in my elementary school, and I had already made my mark at middle school as the fastest sprinter. Including the boy's division. After running less than a block, I looked back and they were so far behind I knew they would never catch me. Instead, they started begging me not to go to Noni. I just let them holler and beg until they were out of breath and had to stop to rest. I had to do it.

If anyone noticed us, they would know me, and I would be in trouble for something I didn't do. So I told Noni as soon as I got home and caught my breath. As soon as I had finished spilling my guts, she got "the look" in her eyes and slowly and quietly walked into the living room and waited for Kathy and Sherri to get home.

They came sneaking in like she wouldn't know they were there. They didn't know her nearly well enough. Those rubber arms appeared out of nowhere, grabbing Sherri by the hair and then Kathy. She dragged them into the dreaded bedroom, locked them in, and whipped their asses raw. After about ten minutes of what sounded like a hellacious three-way cat fight, there was hair and clothes and snot all over that room. Of course she whipped them after she stripped them down and found the stolen clothes. Then Noni got the clothes together, put the girls in the car, including me, and we went to Patterson's. Mother went straight to the manager and apologized profusely. The clerk recognized me and knew I was innocent by the way I had just sat there hyperventilating when the three of us girls were in the store earlier. She had known something was up, but we had gotten out of there so fast that she didn't have a chance to catch us.

"Are you going to file charges?" Mother asked Mrs. Patterson. "You should, you know. That's the only way they're going to learn."

Mrs. Patterson thought for a bit and said, "No, but we can call the police and give them a scare if you want."

"Honestly, I don't think anything scares them, Myrtle," Mother sighed. "I'll just be glad when they pack up and go back to Florida."

"I know what you mean, Nora," Mrs. Patterson replied. "Thank you for coming in and returning everything. Just keep them out of here, and we'll be even. Now, your daughter is fine. I know she isn't the guilty one. She was terrified and she did the right thing by telling you."

"Whatever you want to do, Myrtle, I will support you. And thank you for understanding. I am so sorry for the trouble. I hope that's everything."

On the way home, Mother gave us the guilt lecture from hell, during which she threatened to whip those asses again. But she agreed to not tell David because he had enough on his plate already. I think she was afraid he might have a heart attack or something, and then they would never leave.

We got home, and I immediately had to get away from them. I went down to the basement, and there were Buddy and Mack sitting and eating candy by the fistfuls, a mountain of it on the bed. "Where did that come from," I asked as I drooled at the sight.

"Mack bought it and said I could have all I wanted," Buddy said.

"Well, shut up and give me some," I said, looking at Mack, "or I'll tell on you too! Mack doesn't have any money, Buddy. None of them do, so keep that in mind in the future."

"Here, you little bitch," Mack said as he shoved some candy into my chest.

Wrong thing to say and do! I saw Buddy's eyes light up, so I grabbed what I wanted real quick and got out of the way. Like lightning, Buddy hauled off and hit Mack so hard with his fist that he flew off the bed. "That's for stealing!" Buddy yelled. He went around the bed and hit Mack again while he was down. "And that's for calling my little sister a bitch!" Then he kicked him in the ribs. "And that's for lying!"

"Buddy, don't kill him!" I yelled. "Jesus! Even though he deserves it…"

I think he would have kept going if I hadn't stopped him. He appeared to be just getting warmed up. Buddy loved a good fight. But then suddenly, everything changed. They both started getting all pale and sweaty, and before you know it, they both jumped up and were throwing up. Chocolate. Smarties. Fireballs. And God knows what else. Technicolor, I'm talkin'. Buddy made it to the basement door, thank God. Mack spewed all the way out the door. No telling what all they had eaten before I showed up and ruined the party. I confiscated the remainder of the booty, knowing they couldn't say a thing. I did share it later with Buddy, though, because he took up for me and he was innocent. He was rarely innocent, but he didn't *ever* steal from anybody. He just liked to fight. Period. "Ya'll are cleanin' that mess up," I said. "So bye!"

By the time I got upstairs, David was back from visiting lock-up. "They're gonna let Bonnie go home tomorrow. They've arranged therapy for her in Florida so we can get home," he told Mother.

"Well, thank God for that," Mother replied. "Ya'll need to get the hell out of here before we all end up in prison or kill each other, or both." Mother had an uncharacteristic defeated look. I never saw anybody else who could wear her down like they could. But they were relentless, she was no longer young, and she was whipped.

David, clearly afraid to ask, finally did, "What the hell is going on now?"

"Nothing, Son, we're okay," Mother lied. "I can handle them, but not for much longer without killing them with my bare hands."

David looked equally defeated. "I know," he said. "I'll get our stuff together and be ready to go tomorrow night after midnight."

"I'm sorry, Son. I am too old for this shit, and your father can't know most of it because he can't handle it. I can't carry this burden, and you have enough to deal with right now just getting Bonnie home. We had our own issues that we are dealing with here before ya'll came."

"What, Mother?"

Yeah, what? I knew something wasn't right—I could hear the skeleton bones rattling sometimes, but I couldn't put my finger on what it was.

"It's okay."

Rattle.

"Something that we can't really talk about."

Rattle, rattle.

"We're okay, so don't worry. It's someone else. A friend."

Shake, shake, rattle!

"Now go rest up so you'll be ready for tomorrow night."

Chapter Nine

It was no friend Mother had been talking to David about. I could tell she was worried about Diane and what had been going on when she was staying at Sara and Ted's. She had told Diane to keep her mouth shut about Ted, especially to Sara and me. And Diane did just that. Mother thought she was protecting me from the harsh truth at a young age. And she thought she was protecting Sara from a lifetime of humiliation and destitution. If her husband went to prison for sex-related crimes, she wouldn't be able to support her family.

As if to mirror her myopic outlook on that particular situation, it seemed that Mother's sixth sense had dried up over the last couple of weeks. And that troubled her as much as the immediate situation. It was as if she'd never had it. Usually she knew what was happening within the family, in some cases before it happened. I think the stress of the Bonnie affair, along with the effort of trying to keep David's kids out of jail (and keeping the truth of it all from David himself) had her just slap exhausted.

But now it was time again: time to hide all our remaining valuables before the thieves left and took everything that wasn't nailed down. Clothes, records, jewelry, whatever…we had to hide it all before tomorrow night. I realized once again that I really didn't own much of anything. I had some nice clothes, more than any other child in our family for some reason. Still, not a lot. Buddy and I did the best we could to stash our favorite stuff while David's kids were busy elsewhere.

The following afternoon, we waited until they were sound asleep, then we checked their luggage and anything else we can get into. Sure enough, I found some of my albums in Mack's suitcase and some of my clothes in Sherri's suitcase, along with my favorite bracelet. *BINGO! You scumbag! I can't believe...yes, I can. Just get the booty and go hide it quick!*

Meanwhile Buddy was doing the same thing. We couldn't get into their van, unfortunately. God knows what was in there that we weren't ready to part with. Diane wasn't home to look for her stuff, but we were on the lookout and found some of her stuff in Kathy's suitcase. *Unbelievable!* She had stolen Diane's London Fog coat, the one she saved for months to buy with her baby-sitting money. But I got it back! *Ya-a-ay me...*

I went to bed after putting our recovered goods under my mattress, and I lay down on top of it as if I had been there all night long. I was able to get a few hours of sleep in before the big bon voyage that we had been all praying for.

Everybody got up, Mother made breakfast and a boatload of coffee for the traveling party. We all said our good-byes, although not fast enough. I was feeling pretty proud of myself for having rescued our possessions from the thieves. As I saw them waving good-bye from the van, there sat Kathy waving like a maniac... with Diane's London Fog coat on. What the hell?!

I felt a sense of panic and ran to my bedroom. I pulled up the mattress, and I'll be dipped in doo if they had not taken everything back that I had rescued earlier. How in the hell did they do that with me sleeping on top of it? You just couldn't win with them. All my records, clothes, necklace, and Diane's stuff—and she was going to have a dog shit fit! Oh my God! They were professionals. They knew exactly what we were going to do, and what they were then going to do. We thought we had outsmarted them, but NOT! They were in a league of their own.

After they left, Buddy and I started whining about our stuff, but Mother and Daddy said, "Just shut the hell up and go to bed. We're too tired to think about anything. We'll talk later. There's nothing we can do right now anyway."

So that's what we did. We slept and slept. Until Diane came busting through the bedroom door and woke me up, looking for her London Fog. *Oh, crapola!* I could see she was starting to get into a panic over her coat, and she was looking for someone to blame. Like me.

"Go away!" I found myself saying, my hackles up from being so rudely awakened from a much-needed sleep. Taking a page out of Noni's book I said, "I'm too tired to deal with it! Kathy took your coat, *after* I had already rescued it once. I can't explain how, they just did it. We just don't think like they do. I'm sorry, Diane. I had it hidden under the mattress and I slept on it, but they got it anyway. You should have taken it with you. You knew it was at risk, so don't blame me. I have been through hell for the last two weeks. I have had Miss Lisp spitting in my face for two weeks. I have almost been to jail, I have had to clean up clotted and dried blood, I don't even remember when Christmas was, I—"

I was failing to notice, caught up in my rant as I was, that Diane's face was slowly getting redder and more distraught by the second.

"You have no idea!" she shrieked with tears streaming down her face and flew out the door.

I'm not sure what that meant, but if it was worse than what I have been through, then it must be really bad.

Diane looked as drained as we did, like she hadn't slept in two weeks, and she looked different in the eyes. Something was up, but nobody was talking as usual. Once again, I was getting a not-so-good feeling. I wanted to run after her, but I was so tired that I couldn't move. I know she was upset about her coat. It had been her pride and joy...

David called later on that day to say that they got home safely. They were pretty washed out too. Hopefully, we had all learned a lesson and wouldn't have to go through it again. I knew my parents almost didn't survive it. Daddy was lucky because he had to work during the worst part, while the rest of us had to deal with it. We kept most of it from him, because there was no reason to tell him all the little gory details while he was trying to work and sleep during the day. But Mother was also afraid that he would have skinned some butts if he'd known what was going on. She didn't want a repeat of what happened to Buddy that night under our bedroom window.

Diane moved her stuff back home immediately after David's circus left. We were all feeling edgy and tired, but glad to be back to normal. About a week afterward, Buddy was feeling spunky one day and decided to pick on Diane. He snuck up behind her and grabbed her from behind as she was walking through the dining room. Bad move.

Diane always seemed so meek and mild, but lemme tell ya, she could think fast on her feet. She grabbed the closest thing she could lay her hands on, which happened to be one of those colossal cans of Final Net hair spray. She swung around Bruce Lee style and brought that bad boy down on Buddy's head with all her might. Very impressive sound effect too, I might add. There was just the right amount of Ring! to the concussive blow, making it even more realistic. The light in Buddy's eyes flickered out, and he melted to the floor at Diane's feet just in time for Daddy to come out if his bedroom and say, "Damn, Diane, did you kill him?"

"I hope so," she said, looking real proud of herself. "Teach him to sneak up behind me, the pin head."

"Gotten a bit jumpy, huh, Diane? Take it down a notch before you kill somebody else," Daddy said. Buddy was stirring and holding his head. "You okay, Buddy? Let's get some ice on that thing before it swells any bigger. You already have the big head."

Fortunately Buddy lived, but he did thereafter reconsider when the thought of sneaking up on somebody occurred, especially Diane. Lesson learned. She had apparently been practicing her defensive skills. Or she'd had wa-a-ay too much sweet tea. We were all used to sweet tea, seeing as how we had it in our baby bottles from birth and then our sippy cups as toddlers. So it probably wasn't that. Whatever the case, Diane was bundle of raw nerves.

I helped ice Buddy's head while he whined. "It's kinda pretty, like a purple Easter egg," I said, "and from the front, you actually look taller 'cause of the way your hair stands up on the egg."

Buddy was not impressed with my humor. His black, curly hair covered it up nicely, so he just kinda had that "pin head look." And he really was a little taller. He liked hearing the part about looking taller, but the next morning when both of his eyes had turned black, he was not happy. He looked at himself in the mirror that morning before he got in the shower for school and screamed, "Diane, I'm gonna strangle you, you little be-atch!" We all knew Buddy was joking, but Diane's mood hadn't changed much.

"Well, you are a PIG FROM HELL! So there! You deserved it, pea brain!" Diane shouted back.

A few days later, we were in the living room when the phone rang. Diane jumped and froze in place. Normally, she would steamroll you to get to the phone, but his time she kinda snuck up on it like it was going to deliver an electrical shock or something.

"Hello?" D said with that deer in the headlights look on her face. She immediately slammed down the phone and ran to her bedroom.

"What has gotten into her lately?" I asked out loud.

Suddenly Daddy's head poked out of Mother's bedroom door.

"Go get your mother. NOW! Then go to your room, and tell Diane to get in here," he barked at me. I ran like a scalded haint, 'cause Daddy normally didn't bark at me, and it scared me. It actually hurt my feelings: I was a daddy's girl. Mother and Daddy and Diane went to their room and talked with the door closed. I didn't know what was said, although I tried to listen. But if I got caught, it would not be good for me, so I couldn't try too hard.

As usual, nobody's talkin'!

But the next day we had deadbolt locks on the inside of our bedroom doors. *YES! Me likee!*

But why would Mother and Daddy want to do that?

Chapter Ten

Time goes on…some shit gets stranger, and some stays the same. Sara had always been a looker, and Diane had become a beautiful, very shapely young lady. And though I didn't yet realize it, I was gradually becoming a woman myself. Buddy was a handsome thing with dark curly hair and gorgeous bright blue eyes. He was a real heartbreaker. David was short and handsome, but he was showing strain from his daily hell in Florida.

It was the late 1960s, and America was deep in the crucible of those times, the very fabric of our society seemingly being torn apart. But my parents did the best they could to shield us from it all, especially me, the baby. Vietnam, race riots, the antiwar movement, drugs, sex, assassinations—it was all out there, but it didn't really affect me. Yet.

The first jolt of reality came for me when Michael got drafted and sent to Nam not long after graduating from high school. I remember being so worried about him. Diane was always pining for him, though she rarely showed the fear I knew she carried in her heart. Protected as we had been, we knew the boys we grew up with were getting plucked up and shipped off. And we knew so many of them who didn't return. Thank God, Michael came home alive after thirteen months, with a purple heart. Though he did get back in one piece, he was a different man, as were all the boys who became men over there and saw combat. He was nervous as a whore in church, had nightmares, fear of crowds... you name it. But he managed to keep himself under control, with Diane's help and family support. Our prayers had been answered.

By that time, I was the big thirteen, going on fourteen, and I thought I was hot stuff. I also sprouted boobies overnight: 36Bs that appear suddenly will get some male attention for sure. And those bad boys hurt like a muh-ther! It was like having two big sore testicles mounted on your chest. "Taking shape" was putting it mildly. I was getting into the sorority thing at school. I had good looks, personality, I was smart enough in class, and I had a lot of friends. Guess I got lucky that way.

My figure would soon turn out to be more of a curse than a blessing, though I didn't know that then. I was the baby, and I had Daddy wrapped around my little finger. Mother, on the other hand, couldn't be wrapped by anyone or anything. Ted was getting more nervous around me and paying us more nightly visits. Diane and Buddy were seldom there anymore, so usually it was only me and Mother at home. After a while I made it a point, whenever Ted came over, to stay in either Mother's bedroom with her or in my own room with the door closed. I didn't realize it at the time, but I was getting caught up in the game. And the skeleton was making it all happen.

Somehow I got selected to run for class president in the eighth grade. I didn't even know I was popular, but apparently things had taken a turn for me. In the seventh grade, I was a nerd with nerd clothes. But by the eighth grade, I had a popular boyfriend I had landed at the end of seventh grade. He dumped me just as summer break started, and I was just dumb enough to take him back at the beginning of eighth grade. Now the two of us were running against each other for class president. Oh boy!

I worked on a speech for a couple of weeks, with the help of a friend's dad. My parents were happy, but clueless about what it all meant. As a matter of fact, I was clueless as hell myself. I was able to get a new outfit out of Daddy for the speech, but I had to pull the whole thing off alone. My parents were not in attendance, as usual. They were interested and supportive, yes. Involved, no. Whatever...

Anyway, the big day came at last. I gave my speech, the crowd roared, and I was so surprised at the reaction that I didn't know what to think. Except that none of my family was there for me, and that hurt.

A couple weeks later, the votes were in, and yes, I was now class president of the eighth grade. My boyfriend was vice president. He wasn't too pleased about it, but we still were boyfriend and girlfriend. Until summer break, of course, when he dumped me. Again. I guess it was so he could run wild all summer. Sometimes I just didn't learn. We wouldn't be going to the same school next year, so I guessed this was it for us. But for the time being, I was in my sorority, he was in his fraternity, and we did have some good times. I learned about making out, or at least getting to first base. I learned about running with the town's elite families, which was fun. There were big parties at mansions, good bands, alcohol-spiked punch, pool parties, a country club crowd...you name it. I thought I was pretty cool stuff, but I had no idea how I got there or just what I was supposed to do with it. I was just enjoying the ride. At the end of the school year I was voted "Best All Around" by my peers.

Home was still home. We weren't rich like many of my new friends, but we still had a lot of old friends who came and went. Mother continued to take in the strays and kept them fed and in school. She had a heart for the kids who were hungry, and she treated them just like she did us. But she didn't take any shit. You went to school every day, you said "Yes, ma'am" and "No, ma'am," you got a job as soon as you could, you didn't use foul language in front of the ladies, and you minded your manners at all times.

All the kids liked to come to our house because Mother would let us drink and smoke as long as we didn't go anywhere. She figured that we were going to do it anyway, so we might as well do it where she could monitor us. She always said that if any of them told their parents, she would deny it, and they would never be welcomed again. So, naturally, nobody *ever* said a word, and nobody ever got behind the wheel drunk leaving our house. It worked for everybody. Rarely did we even get drunk. We just horsed around, played loud music and danced, and if we wanted a beer, we would get a beer, and that was okay too. It made a difference in the way we thought. We were all relaxed about it and didn't get the craving to binge like most teenagers do when they finally escape from their parents. It was nice. Of course, it was legal to drink and drive then, as long as you were eighteen, which we weren't, but we didn't argue with Noni. We had a good thing going, and we would be stupid to mess that up.

The summer before the ninth grade was busy for me. The sororities had to rush the new girls in, which was fun. Initiations were brutal, and some of what we did isn't even legal any more. Now it's considered hazing. When September rolled around, I was a freshman in high school. And to my surprise and shock, I was voted to run for freshman beauty queen. Oh my God! My life was out of control. It was basically a popularity contest, and I loved everybody. I still had friends of all colors and social backgrounds, so I guess that helped. But we had to get ready for the pageant. I was so not believing this, and I felt like clawing my own eyes out for weeks. Mother took me shopping, and I got this kick-ass outfit: a short dress, a red brushed-suede skirt, a tight navy blue sweater top with matching red suede jacket, high-heel navy boots...yeah, baby!

There were ten of us voted in for the pageant, where we were all "presented" to the class. Of course, no one from my family was in attendance, so I have no pictures to chronicle the event. As usual. Whatever...I placed in the top three! We three faves had our photo shoots done, and we picked out our favorite pictures. They were sent to Ryan O'Neal—*Ryan O'Neal!*—so he could choose the placement. All three of us were close friends, and it was a little awkward for a while, but we tried to forget about it during the rest of the year.

We had plenty of distractions. Lots of sorority parties, fraternity parties, ball games, and was I ever dating the cutest, sweetest guy in the universe, Marty. We were just wild about each other. He had sandy blondish hair and green eyes, both almost the same color as mine. He just made things in me come alive. Things I had not felt before. He was from a rich family, although his daddy had dropped dead at an early age. But he left Marty's momma with lots of money, a big fancy house, a farm with many hundreds of acres, and two kids, one boy and one girl. I couldn't have cared less about the money. I didn't know about any of it for a long time anyway 'cause he never talked about it. We were together as much as my mother would allow, which wasn't enough for us, but we saw each other at school and all the parties, and he could come over to our house on the weekends and "hang." Mother watched us like a hawk and would occasionally catch us smooching, which didn't go over too well. But we were willing to risk it, 'cause we were in love. Love, Love, Love!

My social life continued to bloom. I was voted Most Valuable Member of my sorority and ninth grade's Most Likely to

Succeed. I was past class president and running for freshman beauty queen. *Hot stuff!* Or so I thought. Life was good in so many ways. I had done all these things on my own. Nobody ever asked why my parents were never present, so I never talked about it. It was just me, myself, and I. My parents were so old when I was born, I guess they just didn't have the energy to try to keep up any more. Everybody who saw them thought they were my grandparents, for God's sake. Daddy still worked third shift, and Mother just wouldn't participate. I don't even have any freakin' pictures of that part of my youth. They didn't think of that either. Whatever…

I rode the bus to school for years. But when I became a freshman, I started riding with my best buddy up the street, Beth. She did the sorority thing for a while, mainly because her sister and cousins did, but also because I did. I would walk home from her house every day, unless it was really cold or raining and then she'd take me the rest of the way. I didn't mind the walking, it wasn't very far and it gave me some alone time.

Buddy got his draft letter early in my ninth grade year. And he had a low lottery number. We all panicked and I cried about it. But lucky for him, he was turned down as 4F. I didn't know why, I only knew we were all greatly relieved. The Vietnam War was still killing lots of American boys, and it was good to know that no one else from our family would have to go. Not long after that, Buddy caught his longtime girlfriend fooling around with his best friend. He was crushed, and I think I felt almost as bad as he did about it. I realized then that I cared a lot for my older brother, even after years of his pranks.

"I'm home," I would always announce as I came in the door from school. One Friday when I got home, I found Mother with a really sick look on her face. I was afraid to ask her what was wrong, but I did anyway.

"Your brother is getting married," she said with tears in her eyes.

"Oh. My. God!" I gasped. "When did this happen, and who is this person he's marrying?"

"I don't know, he just met her a couple of weeks ago. And I feel sick to my stomach about it. He's supposed to bring her over to meet us this weekend. He seems so happy, and he says she is beautiful."

"Yeah," I said dejectedly. "I thought Margaret was beautiful until he caught her fooling around with his best friend, Donnie. Well, at least he's moving on now. I was worried about him for a long time after the Margaret thing. We'll see what happens. This too will pass."

"I don't think so," Mother said, clearly downcast. "They've already set the wedding date. Big affair and everything."

"Holy shit!" I exclaimed. Then I caught myself. "I mean, wow! Sorry, Mother, that just came out."

"It's okay. That's how I feel too."

Saturday came, and I was so busy all day selling donuts for my sorority that I forgot all about Buddy bringing his fiancé over. I got home and was about to take a nap when Mother reminded me. I had just enough time to clean up and put on something decent for the show. Buddy arrived home with his new squeeze and called out for us. Mother and Daddy and I went into the living room to meet her, and for the first five or ten seconds, all we could do was look at her with surprise. And shock. Nobody could speak, including her, until Buddy broke the ice.

"Linda, this is my Mother and Father, and my little sister Maggie," he said, clearly a bit unnerved at our initial response. Or lack thereof. Linda was not only FAR from pretty, she was haughty and about two feet tall. Actually, she was about four-foot-ten and really was, to be polite, not very attractive. We could have gotten over that part, but she had such an attitude. She wouldn't talk to Mother or Daddy at all, and she only seemed interested in my popularity contests of late. I tired quickly of the topic and excused myself to go to bed.

When I got to my bedroom, I just felt like crying. Brother Buddy was getting hitched. Sure enough, he went through with it a few months later. And I really did cry at the wedding, throughout the entire ceremony, and most of the high-class reception afterward. I had finally admitted to myself that I loved my brother very much and I wanted him to stay at home and live with us. Linda's family had a lot of money, and they sure spent plenty of it marrying off their daughter. As if all that money could make up for her unfortunate looks and shitty disposition. I was depressed for weeks after the wedding, but I eventually accepted it. He was the one who would have to live with her the rest of his life, not me. I had too much else going on in my life to dwell on it for long.

One day after school, I was moping around in my bedroom when the phone rang. Lately, it had started every day about this time, but Mother usually answered it. It always seemed to be a wrong number, because no one said anything when she answered. They just hung up.

But this time I answered it. "Hello?"

"I want to be your dear," a man said in a whispery, creepy voice.

"What did you say?"

"I want to be your dear."

"You must have the wrong number," I said as I hung up. *That was really weird. What exactly did that mean?*

Creeped me out for sure. Shaking it off, I started to change into some more comfortable clothes. I opened my underwear drawer to take inventory, and I saw a piece of paper that looked like a magazine page folded in quarters. *What is this?* I opened it up to find the most disgusting porno pictures. With animals! It was a deer having oral sex with this really sleazy girl. *I get it now!* That explained the phone call. *I want to be your deer, not dear. I think I'm gonna be sick. That's just nasty as hell.*

I couldn't show this to Mother; it was too disgusting. How and who in the hell would do this? Being a virgin, and knowing absolutely nothing about sex except smooching (and what little we learned in our sex education class), I found it very disturbing. As I thought about it, I had a pretty good idea who was behind it. And that didn't help me feel any better about it at all.

Suddenly my little world was upside down. My brother had gotten married, and I had these disgusting sexual images in my head that I couldn't seem to get rid of. Isn't it amazing how your life can change in an instant? I kinda went into this depression, or regression or something. I didn't even want to be with my sweetheart, which got his attention right away. I just shrugged it off when he asked what was wrong. I decided that I couldn't go on feeling like this forever, so I made myself get back into the swing of things. But it took me a few weeks.

My sorority had a big spring dance coming up, so it was time to make some money. We had to raise our own money for everything because dues barely scratched the surface. We sold doughnuts by the truckloads, and we had car washes and bake sales. That's really all there was to do to raise money back then. And we sure did it. By spring, we had enough for the band and the dance hall. It would be the "end of the year" blowout before summer, a tradition. Meanwhile, I really didn't like school for some reason. I used to love school, but there were only a few teachers I liked, and if I didn't like my teacher, I had to force myself to make good grades. But I did because the alternative would be to lose my freedom. So between school, chores at home, piano lessons, sorority fundraisers, and a boyfriend, my schedule was pretty tight. But I was happy that way. My parents were just going to have to get used to "the baby" being grown up—or almost. I had responsibilities outside the home environment.

Evening was about the only time I had to do homework and practice piano. I had to practice after Daddy got up to go to work or in the morning before school. So I would do my homework in the kitchen where I could spread out and make a little noise if I wanted to without waking Daddy. I kept feeling like someone was watching me, but I didn't see anything. One night, a knock at the door made me jump. It was sleazy Ted. I was told I had to let him in when he came calling. I opened the door without looking at him other than through the peephole.

"Hey!" he said with vigor, as if he was so glad to see me.

"Whatever," was all I could get out of my mouth.

"I still want to be your deer," he managed to get out before I could get out of earshot, thinking he was being funny.

"Well, that ain't gonna happen," was my immediate response. "EVER!"

I went back to my studies, but I had a helluva time concentrating. I saw some movement out of the corner of my eye, but I was afraid to look. When I did, I saw Ted standing in the dark with what looked like an arm in his hand, shaking it. When I got a better look, I realized he had his enormous dick in his hand, and he was workin' it in a frenzy. I immediately screamed, "MOTHER!" I never saw Ted move as fast as that. He packed it up and was out that door in a matter of seconds. I felt like my heart was going to burst from fear and confusion. I had to tell Mother what I saw, and it made me cry. Why would he, or anybody, do that? I didn't really understand what would make somebody do something like that outside of their own privacy. I knew about masturbation, but it wasn't supposed to be in front of somebody else.

Mother was very quiet about it. She said to me, "You can't tell anybody about this. I mean *nobody*. If this got back to your sister, she would kill him and go to prison. Then what would happen to the kids? Huh?"

"I don't want her to go to prison. I want *him* to go to prison."

"No, you don't want that. Then what would Sara do? She can't support those babies and herself. She would have to move in here. Would you like that? I can't take care of babies at my age while she works. It just can't happen. We are going to just have to look the other way. When he comes from now on, you need to either go lock yourself in your room or come in here with me."

"Okay, but—"

"Don't okay, but me, just do as I say and keep your mouth shut. Just stay away from him."

Well, that's about the dumbest thing I have ever heard.

But you didn't argue with Noni. I still couldn't show her the animal porn. It was just too disgusting to believe, and I didn't want to put that image into anybody else's head. So I had to learn to deal with a sexual pervert in the family and all the images that I had acquired that very day. Just how many more would there be? *Now* I knew why Mother and Daddy put deadbolts on the bedroom doors. *So they knew before I did. Uh huh…*

Chapter Eleven

School got more demanding of any spare time in the evenings. I would eat supper, practice piano, do homework, and then if there were any time left, I would get on the phone with my buddies. Sometimes I kept all my homework spread out on the kitchen table, but as long as I stayed in there, the perv would hang around. So I had to lock myself up in order to get him to go home. When I was in my bedroom, I could hear him go into the basement. I could only guess what he was doing. He had caught me by surprise many times before, so I tried to avert my eyes at all times.

One night, I was in my bedroom, and I heard him in the basement. I decided it would be a good time to sneak and go use the bathroom while he was down there. Of course, he left the door open so I could see him doing "his thing." *Not again!?* Anyway, I was sitting on the commode, and I noticed a light as I looked down between my feet. We had an old shag carpet in there, so I pulled it back and I'll be damned if there wasn't a hole as big as a quarter in the floor. I could see him in the basement looking up at me with his dick in his hand. Those eyes! *Those freaky damn eyes!*

I froze and felt like I couldn't breathe, but at least I had enough control to cover the hole with my foot so I could get my clothes back on and run into Mother's room. Of course, he knew I was onto him, and he left suddenly without a good-bye. I told Mother, and I was so furious at him and her at that point that I screamed at her through tears and hysteria. She stood her ground and took it. Then she slapped the hell out of me, right in the face. She marched into the bathroom and examined the hole, and I could tell she was more upset than she let on. I could see it in her eyes. She told Daddy when he got up to go to work, and I could hear him cussin' all over the house.

I was getting more freaked out by the minute. I felt so violated. I locked myself in the safety of my bedroom and tried to finish my homework, then I went to bed. My bed might just as well have been on fire that night. I couldn't get comfortable. I kept hearing things outside the windows. And I couldn't clear my head of all the nasty shit that I would never have dreamed up in a thousand years.

To make matters worse, I started having a lot of trouble concentrating on school. *Well, no shit!* My boyfriend and other friends asked me the next day if I was okay. Even the teacher caught me daydreaming and put me on the spot. Actually, it was more like an X-rated horror flick rather than a daydream. I kept seeing those pictures of the deer thing, the hole in the bathroom floor, that giant dick, and those damn, freaky ice blue eyes.

I had to get that out of my head. Somehow, I had to get it out. I couldn't live with it in there forever.

"Maggie! Maggie! Are you okay?"

I jumped at the sound of my name in class. My teacher had asked me something, and I didn't even hear her. "Yes, ma'am. I'm sorry, but I'm not feeling very well. I'll be okay."

"Why don't you go to the school nurse and let her take a look at you?" Mrs. Huff suggested.

"Really, Mrs. Huff, I'm fine now. I just didn't sleep well last night," I lied.

"If you're sure you're okay."

"I am, thank you for asking, Mrs. Huff."

God, I thought, that was embarrassing as hell. I feel like my life has gone from top of the world to the bottom of the shit pile in a matter of a few days.

I felt so dirty, so violated, even guilty. Mrs. Huff was looking at me again as if she had asked me something else, but I really had no idea whether she did or not.

Somebody please just shoot me or something.

"I think you need to go to the nurse, Maggie. It's okay, just go and give her this note. Do you want me to go with you?"

"No, ma'am, I'll be okay," I said as I finally gave in. *What the hell am I supposed to say to the nurse? I'll just tell her the same thing. That should be okay.*

I felt so guilty as I walked those quiet halls alone, hearing the clicking of my shoes on those old hardwood floors as they echoed all around. I felt like I was in a dream, it had become so surreal. *Am I okay or not? I just don't know.*

"Hey, Maggie," the nurse said as I gave her the note. Everybody knew me because, for some damn reason, I was probably the most popular person in the school.

"Hey, Ms. Smith," I managed to get out of my mouth somehow. "Really, I'm okay. I just didn't sleep well last night, and Mrs. Huff caught me drifting off. It just isn't my style, you know. I don't mean to cause you any trouble."

"You are certainly no trouble," she said as she was getting out her stuff to check me over. She listened to my heart and lungs, took my temperature, and that's about all she could do.

"Everything seems okay, Maggie, except that look on your face. Is there something you need to tell me, or tell somebody? Is something going on at home that you need help with?"

Yes!

"No, ma'am." I made up some bullshit about my sister and her kids having to stay with us and how I had to share my room and bed, and blah, blah, blah…

"Well, I can certainly understand how that could mess up your sleep. You can lay down here for a little bit if you want to. It might help you make it through the rest of the day. I can tell you are distraught."

"Honestly, I find that offer too hard to resist," I said. "Thank you so much." I laid down in one of the little cubicles and felt so safe and tired that I could have slept all day. She woke me up after an hour of dreamless bliss to return to classes. I felt much better for the remainder of the day, but my mind was churning as I walked the empty halls again.

What a wonderful nurse she was, but I thought she was a little suspicious of me. I wouldn't be able to let that happen again. I thanked her profusely and tried to look her in the eyes, but I just couldn't. I didn't seem to be able to hide from my peers either. It seemed I was in the spotlight all the time, and I was feeling self-conscious when I never had before. I had always had the feeling of complete confidence. But now I felt so violated and so abandoned by my own family. All I could do was look out for myself as best I could and try to concentrate on school and the positive side of my life.

I have a lot going for me, right? It's going to be okay. Right? For one thing, I'm going to have to quit talking to myself.

That seemed to be a visible sign of distress, and it had to be eliminated to keep the world from knowing I was having "issues."

It was hard enough to be judged for my looks. But along with that came the pressure of the constant attention to everything I did, wore, said, talked to, and dated, plus my sorority status. I could go on and on—but none of it had bothered me before. It all came natural, because I didn't care what anybody thought. Now I was just plain freaked out and paranoid about everything.

Okay, already, I thought. *Get a grip. I am so looking forward to the weekend. I need some serious sleep. I'll lock myself in my little room and sleep all this weekend if I want to.*

Next weekend was the sorority carwash, so it would be a full weekend. If I pulled a disappearing act this weekend too, my sweetie might think I didn't love him anymore, and that certainly was not the case.

The week slid by without any more incidents at home or school, thank God. I was feeling some better and interacting again, even though I was dressing in the dark, on the floor. *I feel like a freakin' nutcase.* I had to make myself act normal and happy, but I was glad I did. It made me happy to be sociable. Mother and Daddy were going to try to make me go to Uncle Jack and Aunt Bessie's on Sunday, because that's what we did almost every Sunday afternoon for as long as I remember. But I didn't think I could do it anymore. Talk about depressing as shit. I was tired and too busy to dedicate every Sunday any more. I knew they needed help gathering eggs and tending the garden, but I had other responsibilities now. I just had to convince Mother and Daddy.

That Saturday, I pretty much stayed in bed from Friday evening until Saturday evening. I finally got up to eat, and whaddya know…there stood Ted in the living room, lurking around in the dark. I guess he had been missing my strip shows lately, since I was lying on the floor in the dark to get dressed now. *Son of a bitch!* I waited in Mother's bedroom with the door closed until he left, then I started slinking around the house like he did without thinking about what I must have looked like. I was diving under windows, wearing too many clothes around the house, and walking around in the dark.

"What is he doing here sniffing around? I asked Mother.

"Shut up, chile. He came to get the dirty clothes for Sara to wash for me."

"I'd rather do them by hand than give him another excuse to come in here. And Mother, I can't go to Uncle Jack and Aunt Bessie's tomorrow."

"The hell you say."

"I'm serious as a heart attack, Mother," I tried to explain without losing my temper again. "I have things I need to do for school. I need to get ready for the car wash, make posters for it, organize it, and I need to meet with Laura, Anne, Becky, and Sandie to get ready. Please, Mother! I have more responsibilities now, and all I have are the weekends to do everything. I had to sleep today, so tomorrow is booked solid. Okay? Please?"

"Oh, all right," Mother relented. "I know you have a lot going on at school now. Uncle Jack and Aunt Bessie will miss you, though. And as for tomorrow, I really don't want you here by yourself at all. And your father will have something to say about it."

"I can deal with that," I said with relief. "For today, I have to run get some poster material and markers. Can I drive the VW to the Plaza real quick before they close? I'll get us a hot dog from Pete's while I'm out."

"Okay, just don't let the grass grow under your feet. Go and get back before Elbert gets home. And don't get caught!"

"I won't be here for long tomorrow. I told you what all I have to do. Beth is coming to get me, and we're going to Laura's to make posters, and—"

"Okay, okay, Jesus! You just make sure you aren't here by yourself. You need to leave when we do. You know what I'm saying."

"Yes, ma'am. I don't want to be here alone any more than you want me to, believe me. I appreciate it, Mother."

"Your father is gonna have a conniption fit. He does not want you here alone, and he doesn't want you to grow up."

"Well, that's too bad because I'm up to my butt in commitments now. Is it okay if Marty comes over for a little while tonight?"

"Sure, just stay where I can see you. You two are getting a bit too cozy, and your daddy can't handle it. Trust me on that one."

"Okay, thanks! I'll let Marty know and go get the posters real quick." I called Marty, and he was relieved to know that I still wanted to see him despite the fact that I had been very distant and jumpy lately. I took off to the Plaza, got us a few hot dogs, and was back in two shakes. It's amazing how a little inspiration can get the lead out. I jumped into the shower and started getting ready for Marty.

I was looking out the window, waiting for him to arrive, when I suddenly hollered out to Mother, "He's here! Whoa, what is he driving? It's a big new shiny gold thing. Pretty!" I ran out to see him and the wheels he was getting out of. "Oh my god, this thing is beautiful. And huge! Is it yours?"

"No way," Marty said. "It's Mother's new car. It's a Buick LeSabre. Let's go for a ride."

"Lemme go tell Mother!" I ran into her bedroom and said, "We're going for a spin in the new car for a little while. Okay?"

"Okay. But don't stay out too long, ya hear?"

"Yeah, yeah. Come on, Marty, let's roll. I can't believe your mother let you drive it so soon. This is so cool. It's beautiful. God, I feel like I'm in an airplane. But then I'm used to the VW, so what do I know? It feels like we're floating. I could get used to this."

Marty looked in my direction, afraid to take his eyes off the road, and asked, "Are you okay? You haven't been yourself lately, and I thought you didn't want to see me anymore or something. I didn't know whether to leave you alone or just keep on calling. I was about to freak out, but I feel better now."

"Thanks, but I'm okay," I lied again, doing my best to look relaxed. "It's just family shit that I don't really want to talk about. I'm not interested in anybody but you right now. I haven't been doing much of anything, just trying to get some rest and get my head straight. Maybe one day we can talk about it." I looked out the window as we were pulling away and whaddya know, there was Ted walking up the street. "I swear he is every damn where I go," I said as we drove by him.

"I just passed him on the way in too," Marty said with scowl on his face. "He's weird."

"You have no idea," was all I could say without opening a huge can of worms. "Let's go cruise Main Street and show off your car."

"That's what I was hoping you wanted to do. Slide over here closer to me. I have missed you something fierce," he said as he looked at me with those killer green eyes.

As I slid over to him, I said, "I've missed you too. I feel better when I'm with you." I snuggled up to his shoulder as we were heading toward Main. "I feel like I should be wearing a tiara and doing the Miss America wave, like on a parade float or something." We got a big laugh out of that as I mimicked the wave and smile of the beauty queens of America. Strange that I had just gone through that on a much smaller scale. It was not something I would have chosen to do myself. But since I was the "chosen one," I would do it for my classmates, who were responsible for putting me in that position. And I had to admit, I was kinda getting used to the attention. It was getting me places I had never been, helping me meet people I would probably not have been associated with otherwise. Some I liked better than others for sure. Marty didn't appear to care about any of that, although I think he was proud of me.

After we had cruised for a while I said, "I guess we had better go back home before Mother goes on the war path. You really don't want that, and neither do I."

We got back to our house, turned on the TV in the living room, and I'll be dipped in shit if Ted didn't walk in. He had a kind of crazy look in his eyes. He was nervous, agitated. The way he just appeared had me backing up until I bumped into the coffee table. *Jesus, I'm gonna need therapy or drugs before long.* I rushed over and sat beside Marty, feeling a bit shaken at my own reaction.

"I don't like the way he looks at you," Marty said real low, almost with a growl.

"Aww, you're just crazy about me, that's all," I fabricated, putting on a fake but convincing smile. "He's fine, just a little weird. Just ignore him. That's what I do." Now I was doing the cover-up thing with Marty too. *Skeletons are such fun.*

He put his arm around me, rubbing my arm. "Then why are you shaking?"

"He surprised me, that's all. Let's go in the kitchen and watch TV in there. Let me go get my cigarettes, and I'll be right in there."

As I went down the hall to my bedroom, I saw Ted slinking in the dark toward the basement. *Good!* I locked the basement door so he couldn't get back in. At least I left the light on for him, the damn freak. Just the thought of him made me shiver all over. I had to think why I even came back here, and then I remembered my cigarettes. I opened my underwear drawer where I kept them, but when I grabbed them they felt funny. I turned on the light and saw that the perv had been in there and left me a little present. It was another porno picture, wrapped around my cigarettes. Not just Playboy stuff, either, I'm talking really XXX and nasty as hell. I dropped it like it was on fire, and then I got mad. I picked it up and marched into Mother's room and tossed it on her bed. "Enjoy, Mother dearest. It's a present from your dear son-in-law. Maybe you'll like it more than I do, 'cause I don't like it worth a damn."

"Come here right now!" Mother demanded.

"No. I've had enough of his shit. You need to fix this problem, or I'll fix it myself."

Mother looked at me with those green eyes that felt like they were burning holes through me and said in her calm voice, "You cannot and will not get involved."

"You don't think this is involved?" I said, pointing at the picture. "What are you thinking? You don't give a damn about anybody but yourself and your darling Sara, and you sure don't give a damn about me."

Mother did another Bram Stoker's Dracula, and before I knew it, she was all over me and had slapped the ever lovin' crap out of me again. Damn near knocked me off my feet. All I could do was stand there with my hands over my face. I could feel every heartbeat throbbing in my face, and I started to tear up. I heard Ted go out the basement door. Apparently, he had heard what was going on upstairs and decided it was time for him to leave.

"I'm sorry," Mother said, trying to control her temper. "I can't have you talking to me like that. I'll take care of it."

When I returned to find Marty, he had apparently heard something because he looked kinda nervous. "Are you okay?" he asked softly, which made me break down again. I went over to the sink to get a cold, wet paper towel and saw movement at the back door window. That blue-eyed devil was staring at me through the curtains, which he had apparently opened earlier for his viewing pleasure. *I can't believe this is happening to me. And I'm supposed to act like nothing is going on? Yeah, sure.* I closed the curtains with his eyes about a foot from mine without making a sound. That was, for some reason, one of the hardest thing I have ever had to do. "Yeah, I'm okay. Mother and I just went a round, and I don't want to talk about it. I really just want to go to bed."

Marty gave me the puppy dog look and said, "Okay, I guess that means it's time for me to go."

"I'm so sorry," I apologized. "I just had the wind taken out of my sails, and I have a long, busy day planned tomorrow. I have sorority duties. We're doing a fundraiser next weekend, and we have to do posters and plan for the car wash. Make sure you bring that car, too."

"Yeah, I get it. I know you don't want to talk about what just happened, but I want to help you if you'll let me. I love you, Maggie."

Well, didn't that just open up the flood gates again. "I love you too, Marty. I can't wait to be with you, *away from here*. Hang in there for me, please," I begged him. "We're going through some weird shit right now over here, so just hang in there. Okay?"

"I'm cool. I'm just worried about you. Your face looks painful. She shouldn't have hit you like that."

"Well, let's just say that I asked for it and leave it at that. We are having major stress right now, but it's okay…I'll be okay."

"I get the feeling it has something to do with creepy Ted," he said as he looked so deep into my eyes that I could feel it in my heart. All I said was, "Yes, it does. Leave it at that for now, please."

"All right then, give me some sugah and I'll leave. Can I call you later?"

"I think I am going to sleep. If I don't, I'll call you. Okay?"

We had a few sweet kisses, nothing too juicy. Too damn many witnesses to be sure, and I was too freaked out to enjoy intimacy in any capacity. Marty and I had only been to first and second base, but tonight I couldn't even leave the batter's box.

After Marty left, I had a major crying spell in my bedroom. In the floor. In the dark. That was the only place I felt safe without being in Mother's room, and I was too pissed off at her to go in there. It was getting late, so I figured Ted would be back at home by now. Sara would flatten him at the door if he walked in too late. *I think he gets up when she and the babies are asleep and walks around the neighborhood and somehow ends up HERE.* I had learned to dress in the dark and slip into bed. *He can't see in here when it's dark, right?* Lying by the window gave me the heebie jeebies. Even though we had hidden the ladder, he could still jump up and grab the ledge of the window that was next to the driveway. That's the window that worried me.

I was totally washed out and finally did a face plant. I woke up to the sound of Mother and Daddy arguing over me going not going to Uncle Jack and Aunt Bessie's. *Well, tough shit, I ain't goin'. So Daddy can just get the hell over it. I'll run away before I'll go there every weekend.* I worked like a slave over there, and I knew they needed help. It wasn't that I didn't care for them. I just had a different life now. I had new responsibilities. I had always disliked going over there in spite of my admiration for Uncle Jack and Aunt Bessie. But it was depressing as hell. Every weekend, I felt like I was waiting to have all my nails pulled out or something, in anticipation of going over there. *God, could life get any worse?*

I was so tired I just turned over and went back to sleep. I knew that in the morning Daddy and I would have a confrontation to work out over going to Jack and Bessie's. And I knew it would be pretty intense too. But I just didn't care at the moment. *Sleep...*

The next morning, way too early for my liking, Daddy and I went a few rounds, and I just flatly refused to go with them. "I have too much to do now, Daddy, and too many people counting on me."

I ain't going! Get over it. You'll have to kill me to get me in the car.

He had the look in his eyes that said he was slowly losing his baby girl. The last of five, all grown up. I almost felt sorry for him, but I didn't give in. "I'm sorry Daddy. I can't be everywhere at the same time. I know you worry about me, but I won't be at home while you're gone. Beth and several of us are going to Laura's to make posters and get ready for the car wash fundraiser. I'll be gone about the same time that ya'll leave. It'll be okay. And I really have no choice in the matter. Tell Uncle Jack and Aunt Bessie I love them and I'll see them later. I'm going back to bed, so wake me about an hour before you leave so I can get a shower and get out of here. Okay?"

Daddy still looked hurt, like he'd just lost his best friend. Or his baby daughter. "Okay, honey. I don't want to leave you here, but I understand you're growing up so fast now, and you have other things to do than be with your ole Daddy."

"Aww, Daddy, don't make me feel bad about it. It is what it is. Please understand."

Daddy walked out the bedroom door, looking pretty pitiful, finally resigned to the fact that I was growing up. I tried not to feel guilty and just covered up my head until I had to get up. Mother came in an hour later and told me to get up and get out of there because they were leaving.

"Okay, I'm up. I'll hop in the shower and I'm outta here too. I'll call you later and let you know how things are going. We have a lot to get done."

"Okay, bye," Mother said. Then she briefly got "the look" in her eyes and added, "No boys. I mean it!"

"Mother, we don't have enough time already. Quit worrying." I started gathering up my clothes for a shower, and I realized I needed some cigarettes. I just happened to know where the keys were to the station wagon, so as soon as I heard them drive off, I jumped in and shot down to the gas station, bought some cigarettes, shot back home, and fired one up. *Oh yeah…good stuff.* Tarlton 100s were my faves. *Okay, I gotta hurry.* Front door, side door, and basement door were locked. I got my clothes and stuff so I could dress without leaving the bathroom. I stripped down, looked at my face up close in the mirror for a zit check. Everything looked good…but then I thought I saw something move behind me in the mirror.

I didn't have time to react when the shower curtain flew back and the blue-eyed devil had his arms around me from behind. I was totally naked, and he had one hand over my mouth and one between my legs. He was so huge and strong, there was no way to get away from him. I could feel his erection against my back. He felt my breasts and used his fingers to take my virginity, probing with them as far as he could reach. I felt like I had started to bleed, and he became detached from reality. I could see it in his eyes in the mirror, and they reminded me of a starving animal protecting raw meat. I realized this was my chance to break free if I was going to, while he was so distracted. And I saw the perfect weapon just within reach. I pivoted away as he removed his hand from my crotch (why he did I have no idea), and I literally grabbed the opportunity and armed myself with…yes, the Final Net hairspray can.

He was not prepared for me to fight back, just as I had not been prepared for him to be in the goddamn bathtub with the curtain closed. I whirled around (having developed lightning fast reflexes as Buddy's little sister) and cracked him upside the head with the biggest can of freakin' hairspray ever manufactured. It had that satisfying ring to it, as I gave the swing all I had. The asshole sprayed blood all over the place from where his forehead and eyebrow were split open. *I hope I broke his fucking eye socket and skull.* I ran into my bedroom, slid the deadbolt to lock, and yelled, "Explain that one to your wife, you sick son of a bitch, and get the hell out of here before I call the cops. And don't bleed all over the house. Clean that shit up and get out, and leave me the *hell* alone!"

I slid down the dead-bolted door, naked, humiliated, and terrified, and wept while I smoked a cigarette with one hand and clutched the Final Net with the other. I heard him leave, and I could tell he was pissed. He was cussin' me all the way out the house. Suddenly, I stopped crying. That's when I decided that I wasn't going to be scared any more. I was too royally pissed off to be scared. I started to channel my fright into anger and defensive strategy.

Thank God I had a phone in my room. I called Beth to come and stay with me while I got in the shower. Of course she said okay. I didn't tell her anything. She knew a little about the Ted problem, but she had no idea how bad it had gotten. I found that I was bleeding some since I was still a virgin, although I didn't feel like one now. *Those goddamn beefsteak hands, long fingers. I'd really like to hear what he tells his family about his head being split open. He wants to play dirty, by God I'm ready.*

I couldn't talk about it to anybody, but I would be prepared from now on. He'd have to deal with the consequences.

Chapter Twelve

While this had been by far the worst experience of my life to this point, I found that pulling myself together after this particular Ted episode was easier than I would have expected. I suppose it was because I now knew that one, I was no longer powerless, and two, this shit wasn't going to go away until I moved away. Or I killed him. Hopefully, someone else will do that for me. Bad as all this is, he's not worth committing THE mortal sin. Going to hiney heaven (or, as is the case for women, clitoris heaven) for the rest of my life had no appeal to me. I had too much I wanted to do and see in my life.

Okay, so I think I just cleared a big hurdle. I can and I will defend myself, and I will hold my head high, for I have done nothing wrong!

Beth came right over after I called her, and she could tell with one look at me that I was upset and had been crying. She and I were best of buddies, and we knew each other so well there was little we could hide from each other. I told her that Ted and I had just had a little "round," and I didn't really want to talk about it. I just wanted to talk about the stuff we were going to do that day. She gave me a long, worried look, but she knew when to let something go, and if I wanted to talk, I would talk. I put all the safety locks and chains on the doors, and I finally got in the shower and tried to wash away the filth I felt all over. At least on the outside.

I felt better after the shower, though I still didn't feel clean enough where it mattered most. *Get it out of your head, girl!* By sheer force of will, I put on a positive, upbeat attitude and came bouncing out of my bedroom and proclaimed, "Let's go make some whip-ass posters!" *And not act like I was just practically raped.* "Oh, Beth, will you stop at the pharmacy and let me buy some hair spray?"

She gave me a puzzled look but went straight to the Plaza without asking. We stopped, and I ran right in and back out. In my bag was the big bad Final Net. I wanted a can near me at all times.

"What are you going to do with that? You don't use hair spray, do you?" Beth asked.

"I do now!" I answered with a sly grin on my face. *But not like you think.*

We got to Laura's, and everybody was happy and all into the project, feelin' alright! I felt like I was going to be okay as long as I stayed focused on what I needed to do right then. But if I thought too much, I found myself getting freaked out. I kept my mind on our projects, because the group was relying on me to do much of the artsy work. Laura's parents were just awesome. They had lots of good food, and they let us play our favorite music as loud as we wanted. We always had to dance a few jigs to get warmed up. We had to do the Tighten Up and Funky Broadway for starters. Then we put on Junior Walker & the All-Stars and let it go. When "Shotgun" started, we had to jump up and dance like maniacs, and then when it got to "What Does It Take to Win Your Love for Me?" we all grabbed a pillow and slow-danced.

The posters were soon done, and Laura's parents knew what we needed to wash the cars with, and they were all over it. Her father even agreed to supervise the car wash so we didn't do something stupid to somebody's car. We liked that idea really well because we had no idea what we were doing. But we were all into it and ready. We had spread the word through the school that we were doing a car wash, and we were all wearing short-shorts and bathing suit tops. Holy God in Heaven, was that ever effective! The best-looking girls in middle school dressed like that...oh yeah! I just prayed that my father didn't drive by and make a scene or have a heart attack.

The flip side of all that advertising was that we had to endure the whole week leading up to the car wash with all the sleazy comments about our upcoming attire. But hell, it wasn't that different from what we were wearing to school anyway: the shortest skirts you could imagine, with garter belts and hose. And by the way, I still don't know how in the hell we did that. I wouldn't consider trying it now, even with panty hose, much less with a garter belt.

Saturday came, and we were pumped. We had on our bikini tops, our tiny little shorts, our buckets, rags, brushes, detergent, and glass cleaner...you name it, we had it. I stepped out onto the porch when Beth came to get me, and Holy Mother of God, it was freezing outside! *What the hell?*

"There ain't no way I'm going out there like this," I said. I ran back into the house and got my sorority T-shirt, a little jacket, and some jeans, and we took off for Augusta Road. When we got to the little gas station where we were having the car wash, the girls were huddled up against the sunny side of the building. But we had a job to do, and we had promised everybody that we would perform. So we would perform, by God. We just hadn't expected it to be so damn cold. *But that could work to our advantage...*

Time to put the skin strategy to work. "Come on, girls," I shouted. "Let's get those fannies moving to the music. Get your signs out. Get those little hard nipples out here. Let's make some money!"

"We will if you will," they shouted back.

"You got a deal!" Off came my T-shirt and pants, and I was down to my skimpies. *Holy moly, it's cold!* "Very nipply out here, huh? April weather? Okay, whatever, let's get this done!"

So there we went, signs, shorts, navels, nipples, and all. Several of us went down to the road with our signs to draw the customers, and the others got ready to do the wash. Within twenty minutes, we had a line of cars two blocks down Augusta road. I swear I saw Ted drive by a dozen times. He had a bandage on his forehead, and the injury was now a week old. *Yes!* As he drove by one time, I stepped toward the curb and locked eyes with him. *Come on, you bastard. Come and get some of this, I dare ya. Lemme get that other eye!* I was ready, armed, and cocked for his sick ass. I had become dangerous, and with that one look I gave him, he knew it.

Before long, we didn't need to flag down cars any more. We just needed more water hoses. With our soul music blaring, and us singing and dancing, we damn near caused a riot. As sorority sisters, we had had a lot of practice dancing together, mainly soul dancing in a line. So we put on a show while we washed cars. I have never been so tired or so sunburned by the time we were done. That Southern sun started heatin' up the pavement by 10:30 a.m., and we were cookin' by noon. Meanwhile, the eastside girls of our sorority were doing almost as well using the same skin strategy. I guess we were better looking and better dancers, you reckon?

When we had our meeting the next day, we were impressed to find that we had made some easy money: Over $500 that one day, at $5 a car plus tips. And we got a lot of tips. The eastside girls came in at just under $500. We had already sold doughnuts every weekend for what seemed like months. So now we had enough money for a band, refreshments, rental of the Poinsett Hotel ballroom, floral arrangements, etc. We were too young to drink alcohol, so that wasn't an issue. The chaperones were free, and we knew which ones to invite. So we were set for the big spring fling. Hot damn!

The car wash was the talk of the school—and the entire Augusta Road section of town as well—for weeks. The sorority Spring Dance was the first Saturday in May, after which time everybody was headed for Myrtle Beach for Spring Break. I was invited to go with Anne and her mother to the beach, but I doubted I would be able to afford it. That would be cutting it close with the expense I was about to lay on my father: I had to find a formal gown that Daddy would pay for. And that I liked. The problem was, Daddy was practically having a cow over paying a lot for something that would only be worn one time.

But the Spring Dance was going to be huge for me: the announcements of the new sorority officers and my placement in the freshman beauty contest would be that night. The beauty contest winners would already be known by then, but since I was the only one from my sorority nominated for the contest, I was going to be put in the spotlight for a few moments of recognition. *Gotta look good. Real good!* Since my parents were not involved in my social or academic activities, Daddy had no idea of the importance of things like a beautiful, classy gown on a teenage beauty queen.

Fortunately for me, Mother did, so with her help I finally got Daddy to agree to buy a gown. He put the limit at $100. I looked all over hell and half of Georgia for a gown in that price range, which was a challenge because I had limited transportation. My parents were old and uninterested, and I had the most important night of my life right around the corner, with no dress! I was starting to panic, even though the dance was still weeks away. Finding the right dress was only the beginning of apparel preparations, as any self-respecting Southern girl would know.

My sorority sisters and I had been running around like headless chickens. The officers were the ones who had to pull it all together, and even though I wasn't one, I had been voted Most Valuable Member, and it was sort of expected that I help them with the planning. And there was a *lot* of that to be done. We had to arrange the band, the stage, the flowers, the refreshments, the photographers, etc. School was buzzing with excitement over the Spring Dance, but time seemed to creep along so slowly.

The next week, we were getting ready for exams, and classes were getting more serious. I came home exhausted each day, but one afternoon I just happened to remember Ted's little injury. I hadn't heard anything about what he had told the family, and I hadn't seen him since the drive-by at the car wash. *What the hell, she might just tell me.*

"Mother, what happened to Ted's face?"

Noni gave me a strange look and said, "He says he ran into the cabinet door in the dark the other night." Then she returned her stare to the TV. "Would you happen to know anything about that?"

"Why no, ma'am," I responded, but when her eyes darted back in my direction I couldn't meet them. It didn't matter, she could read me either way, and said, "That's what I thought." I was not going to admit to anything, otherwise I'd never get to stay home alone again until I was at least twenty-one years old.

"Wonder how he managed to do that," I said thoughtfully. Noni looked back at the TV. "Maybe Sara hit him again with the frying pan. I wouldn't blame her if she did. She almost killed him last time. And she should have."

"She says no, he came in like that Sunday night, and he had to get stitches the next morning."

I spewed my Coke when she said that. *Holy cow, it was as effective as it felt! And I loved that ring. Let's hear it for Final Net!*

Mother looked at me with a sly grin, nodded, and I slowly turned away. No more said. But I did keep my full new can of Final Net at the ready. I also had a hatpin that was about four inches long. Noni had armed me with it years ago. I actually used it once on this creep at school who wouldn't leave me alone. I got him in the hall, half-hidden among a bunch of other students. I bet you could have heard him scream like a little girl two miles from the school. Now, Ol' Ted might still peep, but he wouldn't get near me again without getting a big surprise. I guaranteed, at every opportunity, a wound of some kind. I'd had enough, and I had decided he was not going to ruin the rest of my life. I would not allow him that.

Diane came in later that afternoon with a long garment bag and hanger, grinning like a Cheshire cat. "Look what I bought," she said brightly. We peeled back the garment bag to find the most beautiful chiffon gown. It was formal length, with brown and gold sequins around an empire waist and between the breasts, with a medium low V-cut and see-through sleeves, all ivory. I could have just died.

"Where did you get that and where are you going to wear it?" I asked, already in the pleading mode. "I need this so bad!"

"I got it at Patterson's, and I don't know where I'm going to wear it, and no, you can't wear it." Patterson's, the scene of the *Kathy and Sherri Shoplifting Show* just a few months before, was an exclusive, very expensive shop. Which explains why I hadn't found this gown. I knew I couldn't afford Patterson's, so I didn't even think to go in there. Besides, I never wanted to be seen in there again after, you know…

"I need it so bad," I begged. "I can't find one anywhere, and you know how Daddy is about the price. You know what a big night this is going to be for me, and I have nothing to wear." She started to walk out of my room. "Please, I am begging you. You don't even have any plans to wear it. I'll get Daddy to pay you, just please let me wear it. I'll take care of it, I promise."

"No," was all she said as she stuck that nose in the air, spun around, and left me standing there, trying not to cry. Mother must have talked to her, because she came to me later and said that if it fit, I could wear it. "But if you stain it or tear it, I'll do something horrible to you in your sleep that will be life-altering."

Diane seemed meek and mild, but behind closed doors she was one mean little shit. I thanked her profusely and promised to take good care of her gown.

All I had to do now was buy some matching shoes. Back then, you bought white satin shoes and had them dyed to match your gown. Diane and I wore the same size clothes for the most part, but my feet were bigger than hers. With three weeks to go before the big dance, she had saved my life because there was still time to get the shoes done so they would match. And I was sure she would make me pay until I was deceased. Mother took me to get the shoes, then we left them to be dyed ivory to match the gown.

And *now* I could concentrate on exams.

Chapter Thirteen

One night about a week later, Mother woke up at 3 a.m. in a cold sweat, shaking. She had been crying in her sleep. She got out of bed and went straight to the living room, and there she was: the Madam Alexander doll, her eyes blinking continuously. Again. She had a bright red Spanish dress accented with black lace, plus black lace on her head and partially over her face and eyes. She would occasionally start blinking, and when she did, she would usually blink for days. It took us a while at first to figure out what was going on. Nothing seemed to stop the blinking, even if you picked her up and turned her at different angles. She wouldn't stop until she was ready.

So when Mother's dreams turned bad *and* Madam Alexander started her blinking, we knew something bad was about to happen. At this point, Mother did not know exactly who was involved or when it would happen, but she probably would know who in the next night or two—if she was able to sleep. *Oh God, here we go again.*

As if she were in labor, she started pacing around the house, and she did so for the rest of the night. When morning came, she called around and see if the family was okay. We waited in anticipation and dread, knowing we would soon be mourning.

But school had me so busy that I didn't dwell on all that once I was away from the house. The big Spring Dance was coming up fast. Final exams were also underway. Actually, taking the exams was the easy part for me…no big deal. It was the anticipation leading up to them that wore me down.

For years, I would often hang out with some of the black chicks I got to know at school. Even though I was brought up in a racist home in a racist city in a racist state, I never bought any of that crap. I didn't see color as having anything to do with who a person really was. My initial connection with the black girls was music and dancing, of course. There were cultural differences between us, but as I got to know them better, I realized most of them were really no different from me on the inside. And we really enjoyed hanging out and dancing with each other.

Lately, I was spending more than the usual amount of time with the black girls between and after classes. As you might guess, the sorority sisters and the black sisters didn't mix too well, but I really didn't care what anybody else thought. I was trying to learn some new moves from my black friends, whom I had always called "the sisters." One afternoon, they taught me the Slide, and we were working on several others. We were laughing and having fun dancing in a line together. My sorority president spotted us and started waving at me, trying to distract me. She was trying get me to stop dancing and come talk to her. I let her flap her arm for a good while before I stopped dancing and went over to her, suspecting what she was going to say. And she said it. "You shouldn't be associating with them," she hissed, with an emphasis on "them" as she tipped her head toward my dance buddies. "It looks bad for you and gives the sorority a bad image. You will have to stop that."

I looked her straight in the eye and said, "These are my friends and have been for years, since elementary school, and not you or anybody else can tell me who my friends are."

I turned away without giving her the chance to respond, went back to my real friends, and started dancing again. The sisters hugged me and said, "Thanks for doing that." They hadn't heard exactly what Miss Prez said, but they heard what I said and figured the rest out for themselves.

"You don't have to thank me," I spat, starting to get mad. "She's just a twitty twat and an embarrassment to the human race. I feel I owe *you* an apology for her narrow-mindedness and ignorance. That just totally pissed me off. I am so sorry. You'll have to forgive me for having any association with her. I had no idea until now what a bigot she really is."

The sisters all chimed in, "That's okay. We know you're not a racist. We know you ain't that way…you're pretty cool for a white chick! You all right." They made me feel more accepted than I was starting to feel in my own sorority.

"Thank you, girls. We go way back, you chicks and me, and you mean the world to me. I'm finding out there are only a few of those twitty twats that I really like. The rest of them can just kiss my entire ass!"

After lunch, we went back to class for the last of our exams. *God just get this over with, so we can get ready for the big party.* After the last exam was over, we were still sitting in the classroom. A girl from the junior class came in, talked to my teacher for a second, and they both looked at me. She motioned for me to come into the hall, and my teacher nodded the okay at me. Oh crap. The junior introduced herself as the editor of the high school yearbook, which was when I noticed the volume tucked under her arm. She opened the book to a marked page and turned it toward me.

I almost fainted. There I was, "Freshman Beauty Queen." Ryan O'Neal had picked me! *Oh my God!* There it was in black and white. I didn't know whether to laugh or cry or just holler. Actually, I felt a little embarrassed. The editor told me to keep it strictly to myself until the yearbooks were handed out, although she admitted there would probably be leaks.

I wonder what Miss Twitty Twat will think about it when she sees the winner, the girl who dances with black chicks.

It didn't really matter to me anyway, her year as president was almost over. It was time for the freshmen to move up and take offices for next year.

God, I hope I am not elected. It was too difficult for me with my parents being so uninvolved and having to get rides with everybody in order to attend meetings. I didn't want or need any more responsibilities.

At last, exams were over! It was a hot bus ride home for the beauty queen that afternoon. I still couldn't believe I had won. I knew my parents would freak out about it. When I got home, Mother had made some fried chicken with gravy and biscuits for dinner, and she was bustling around trying to act busy. But I knew right away it was only her nerves and that she was tired. She looked like hell.

"I see the doll is still at it," I said to her, having checked on my way through the living room. "Have you slept at all?"

"Very little," she said quietly. Then she blurted out, with tears starting to flow, "I just found out that Sarge has lung cancer. It's bad, and they don't expect him to live long."

Sarge was a very close, very dear family friend. "Oh no, Mother! I am so sorry," I said with tears in my eyes too. "I know how much he means to us all. That's awful. So that's what all this Madame Alexander stuff is about, I guess?"

"Yes, of that I am sure," she said. "We'll just have to wait. I'm going to go see him tomorrow while he is still up and around some. Do you want me to wait until you can go with me after school?"

"No, thanks. I don't know what to say, and I might cry or something. I don't think that would help anybody."

"Okay, then. Maybe Sara will go with me."

"I do have some good news, although it's supposed to be a secret for a few more weeks. I WON!"

"Won? What did you win this time?"

"Well, since you didn't bother to even come and see me at the pageant, I guess you did forget all about it." I caught myself, feeling guilty for what I had just said. "I'm sorry, Mother. I know you have a lot on your mind. That was a low blow. I'm sorry…I even forgot about it for a while. I won freshman beauty queen."

"You're shittin' me!" Mother exclaimed, looking excited and a little ashamed.

"No, I am quite serious. I just got the news today and saw the yearbook. Pretty cool for trailer trash, huh?"

"You are NOT trailer trash, and don't let me catch you saying that again. That is wonderful news. Congratulations, baby girl. I am so proud and not at all surprised. Your Daddy is going to be so happy he'll just explode!"

"Well, I hope not! It caught me off guard, that's for sure," I said. "I really didn't think I had a chance. You'll see it soon, when the yearbooks come out. The big picture they used is the one you and I picked out together. They sent that one, along with the other contestants' pictures, to Ryan O'Neal for him to make the final picks. I really didn't like the picture that much, but it worked. But please just keep it amongst the family for now."

"Okay. I am so tickled! I needed something good to think about. I'm calling everybody now. I can't wait to tell them."

"Whatever...to tell you the truth, this is embarrassing to me."

"Oh, you stop it. What's wrong with you? That is an honor and a privilege to be voted as a beauty queen. You're the third one in the family so far! Your Aunt Sybil and your cousin Judy were beauty queens."

"I know. I know already. Just tell them to leave me alone about it, okay? I am trying to get used to the thought of it before it's announced at the dance. And right now I am basically terrified."

"You're gonna have to look real good," Mother went on, clearly glad to have something more upbeat to talk and think about. "Let me see that dress on you. When do you get the shoes back from being dyed?" All of a sudden, Mother was all into the image thing. Better late than never, I supposed. Mother started working on that phone, and I retired to my bedroom to catch my breath for a few minutes. I had actually drifted off to sleep on my bed, when the phone in my room rang. I must have slept longer than I meant too...

"Hello?" Nothing. But I was too sleepy to think quickly enough. "Hello? Who is this? Say something, or just hang up."

"I want to eat your pu—"

AWAKE!

I hung up so fast it sounded like I broke the receiver. I didn't need to hear that end of that sentence.

"What was that all about?" Somehow Noni had heard that brief encounter. Hell, even I forget sometimes that Noni could hear EVERYTHING. ALWAYS.

Hot potato.

"Wrong number," I told her. Then the phone rang in her bedroom. She answered it, talked a minute, and hung up. She came down the hall and said, "Ted is on his way with the clothes. Come in here with me until he leaves."

"Okay. Jesus. I don't know how much longer I can handle this crap," I mumbled to myself. Mother dear heard me, but she had no remark.

I went into her room and lay down on her daybed to wait for the sleazebag to leave. He came into the bedroom to say hey, as if I wanted to see him. I just had to comment, "Your eye's looking better, Ted. That was either one hell of a cabinet or you were going way to fast to be in the dark. Are you sure Sara didn't crack you with a rolling pin or something?"

"Very funny" was all he could say since Mother was there. As he sat down, he had a shit-eatin' grin on his face, but a mad look in his eyes. I bet he was thinking about payback. I looked down and saw that, even as he sat on the edge of Mother's bed, he had an enormous erection running almost all the way down one leg to his knee under his pants. *Oh, for God's sake. I wonder if she sees this stuff.* I casually picked up the Final Net that I kept near me at all times, and slowly walked toward him. But he got up real quick and said "Well, I'd better go. I need to use your restroom if you don't mind, Noni."

You need to go some damn where else with that shit. He is unbe-fuckin-lieveable.

"Course not. Thanks for bringing the clothes. You want some fried chicken? It'll be done soon."

"No, ma'am. I need to get home, but thank you. I'll just stop in here for a minute and I'm gone. Hey, is the doll still blinking?"

"Yes she is, and it's wearing me out. I know what it's about, though. It's Sarge, you know. All we can do is wait and pray that he doesn't suffer long." Mother's nerves had her talking more than usual. "My brother Ed went through the same thing, but it took months. We were all exhausted, and that damn doll never stopped blinking the whole time. Finally I woke up crying one night. The phone had just rung, but nobody was there when I answered it. And I knew that he had died. I called over to his house, and when Barbara checked on him, he was dead. She didn't even know until I called. As soon as I hung up the phone I went into the living room, and the doll had stopped blinking. *Finally*. I just collapsed and cried my heart out."

"Yeah," Ted mumbled, "I really hate that Sarge is going through that. Is there anything I can do for you before I go?"

"No, but thanks anyway. We'll get through it," Mother said, suddenly noticing my posture and my eyes. She gave me a quick look that said she knew I had turned the corner with Ted… and with her. Ted headed for the bathroom, and I went into the kitchen with Mother until he was gone. And it took him a while, too. *Sicko.*

Daddy got up, and we had dinner together. I told him my good news, and he was so proud that he had tears in his eyes. He wanted to know everything…when, where, how…but I really didn't know everything yet. He strutted like a peacock after dinner. He was so cute and such a sweet man when it came to his baby girl. He really was a good father, and I loved him so much.

He got in the shower for work, so I went into my room to get my jammies on. I got out my jammies, turned out the light, made my little pile of clothes on the floor and got dressed in the dark. On the floor. I had gotten real good at that. I put on a robe that would cover everything down to my ankles. As I was going through my underwear drawer to get tomorrow's stuff ready for school, there they were…more pictures. *Oh my God.* Nasty, nasty stuff. Gross stuff. Stuff that I never would have dreamed of and sure as hell wish I had not seen. OK…what to do…I opened my pocketbook, and I swear, there were more of them in there. *God in Heaven! Should I be scared or pissed or both?* I knew not to get into it with Mother again, especially since she was worried about Sarge and hadn't been sleeping well. But I did have an idea…

After Daddy left for work that night, I took the nasty pictures and put them in Mother's pocketbook. See how she likes the nasty element of surprise. I didn't want Daddy to find them, so that was a safe place to hide them. The pocketbook was off limits for all of us.

Surprise, surprise, Mother Dearest, and good night!

Chapter Fourteen

"Morning, Sunshine! Time to get up'n at 'em, my little beauty queen," Mother sang loudly. At 5:00 a.m. 5:00 freakin' a.m.!? Go. To. Hell. Definitely not to be said aloud to Mother Dearest, unless you wanted her to turn into Noni and get your face rearranged.

But the smell of bacon, eggs, and Mother's buttermilk biscuits started drifting in, and like any normal Southerner, I found myself being pulled toward the kitchen. Mornings were never my best time of day. *Especially after a night of porno dreams, big dicks, nasty pictures, and the killer Final Net.*

Heaving a sigh, I put on my robe and stumbled into the bathroom, then into the kitchen. Mother was already jabbering away about "the beauty contest, and when do we get the yearbook, and the gown, and the shoes," and on and on. I wanted to say all kinds of mean things, but as I watched her happily cooking breakfast I just didn't have the heart to ruin her good mood. One of her rare moments of simple joy of late. Still…

Where were you when my terrified ass was walking across the stage with freaking floodlights from hell shining on me in front of hundreds of teenagers and teachers? You know, like, you could've taken a picture or something?

Bitterly, I remembered the day of the pageant, walking from the show back to class, feeling like an orphan. *A pretty and popular one, but an orphan nonetheless.* My friends were all around, and I knew they couldn't help but notice my forlorn demeanor, which was so out of character for me. Some of them knew why too; they had noticed that I had no family there to see me compete. But they didn't say anything about it. Ever. And that's what I called good friends.

Mother apparently had not yet found her nasty nurses and fun-with-farm-animals photos. She was too happy about me at the moment. She had been so upset about Sarge, and it really was nice to see her happy for a change, even though it would be short-lived. With perhaps a trace of guilt creeping in, I considered finding the porno and taking it out of her purse. I was getting cold feet. I couldn't help myself—I jumped up and went into her bedroom real quick to see if I could steal them back. Oblivious in her happiness to my abrupt behavior, she was on my heels, still jabbering. Giving up, I returned to the kitchen to finish my breakfast.

I thought, *Oh well…the shit is getting ready to hit the old fan, and I probably can't do a thing about it now. I guess I'd better just stand back, let it fly, and see where it lands!*

The food was awesome as always: milk gravy and biscuits, eggs, bacon, country ham, and grits. *Man, I'll miss this one day.* Mother did all the talking, while I just ate. My mind was swirling with so many things, but I didn't have the time or the energy to say them aloud. Mother could usually read me anyway, but she was so distracted that she didn't notice the turmoil in my head. I thanked her for breakfast and ran to get ready for school.

I gathered my stuff and went into the bathroom. I was doing a zit check in the mirror, and suddenly I thought I saw the shower curtain move behind me. In the blink of an eye it was, *Oh shit! Oh…nothing…?* Part of me wanted to scream and attack like a wild woman. Part of me wanted to curl up in a tight ball and cry. Part of me wanted to believe it was just in my mind.

It's just a flashback, I hoped. *It's too early in the morning for this crap to be real.*

Still, I grabbed my weapon of choice just in case and whipped back the shower curtain…and nothing was there. But I couldn't stop the visions that flooded into my head. And then I was crying. I felt like I was losing my marbles, when this should have been the best time of my life. Until now, my life had been pretty boring, although carefree and happy. I was always a happy child, not afraid of anything, and now I felt like a paranoid schizophrenic who was afraid of the shower curtain. And the telephone. And windows.

And who now cries all the time.

But the shower I finally took when I could step into the bathtub helped me recover, and I once again psyched myself up to face the day at school. The word was out about the winners of all the various class officers and beauty queens. It was supposed to be a secret until the yearbooks came out, *but that wasn't gonna happen!* My friends who were competing against me apparently had heard as well, because they weren't talking to me or even looking at me. They were in the "other" sorority anyway, so it was no big deal. I still liked to dance with my black girlfriends, I liked everybody, and everybody apparently liked me. Life was good, for the most part. I was determined to make sure of that.

I am not letting that pervert bring me down and miss out on life.

I received lots of congratulations when I got to school, and at first I felt embarrassed to be judged just by my looks. It seemed to me so shallow, just like judging people by the color of their skin, or where they lived, or how rich or poor their Daddy was. The whole popularity experience had brought some things into focus for me. Things were looking much clearer...

But as the reality of who I was, and what I was, sank in, I gradually got used to it. And as there was nothing I could do to change it right then, I tried to shift my focus from myself to the people who were responsible for the label that now defined me in so many ways: my friends. *We the people.* The people who thought enough of me to give me the honor of being their president, now their past-president, and beauty queen. And although I still felt self-conscious, I started to feel proud and ever so thankful to have been blessed with so many friends.

So life goes on, ever changing. The changes can be slow, but the shift in our perception of what they mean is often sudden and dramatic. I had just learned a good lesson: *Just go with the flow and be sure not to change the things that make you who you are and that got you where you are.*

After what seemed like a very long but exciting day, I hitched a ride home with Beth. "Thanks for the ride, chick," I said as I closed the car door. I let myself into the front door of our house, feeling pretty washed out.

"It's me, Ma," I called out. Nothing. "Mother? Mother?!"

Aha!

Her bedroom door was closed, and I could hear her talking in a low, serious voice. She was having a down-and-dirty with somebody. I went into the kitchen, got a sweet tea fix, and started to play the piano softly. I couldn't help but notice the doll's eyes were still blinking, but I tried to ignore it. Shortly after I got comfy at the piano, Ted came out of Mother's chamber with his tail tucked deep between his legs. As he walked through the room, he looked over at me with real hatred in his eyes, his face red.

"What's the matter, Ted?" I sank my claws in quietly. "Get your balls waxed?"

He didn't answer and immediately exited the house. Mother walked through the living room and barely glanced my way, but she couldn't look into my eyes. I'm glad, 'cause I couldn't look into hers either. I thought about the porn I had planted in her purse, and I was sure that she had just ripped Ted a new one about it. The unspoken truth hung heavy in the air, but rather than initiate yet another fruitless round of the question-and-evasion game we had been playing lately, she kept quiet. She knew exactly how that trash got into her purse, but she wasn't going to bother accusing me of doing it. *Was I really learning how to play her?*

The phone rang, and I answered without hesitation, knowing it couldn't be Ted so soon. "Hello?"

"Hey, this is Sybil from Suttons. Is this Maggie? Your shoes are back, honey, and they're beautiful! I know this is a big dance for you, and I think you'll be pleased with them."

"Yes, ma'am, thank you! I'm so excited to see them and wear them to the dance. I'll talk to Mother and see when we can come pick them up."

"That'll be fine. We have lots of shoes going out for that dance. Just don't wait till the last minute to make sure that they are okay. We're already pushing it mighty close, so come as soon as you can. It's your night to shine, girl!"

"Yes, ma'am, we will. And thank you so much for getting them done so quickly. See you soon. Bye-bye."

I hung up the phone. There was a lot going on, and I really just wanted to do a face plant. Just then Diane walked in and said, "Look what I bought!"

"Holy shit, watch where you're pointing that thing!" I exclaimed as I jumped back two feet. She was holding out a very shiny, very new, and very dangerous looking *gun*! Talk about a reality check!

"Ain't it purdy?" she said as she watched how the light reflected off of it. She had a psycho look in her eyes that I found troubling. "It's a semi-automatic, blah blah blah…" That's all I heard from her mouth because I was so shocked. "I'm keeping it in my purse," she finished.

Mother walked in and said, "Oh, Diane, that's a lot like mine! Except yours is so new and shiny."

"What is wrong with you two?" I yelped. "Why do you want to carry a gun? Put that thing away. I am terrified of those things. Ya'll are too weird!"

"Weird? No. Serious? Yes," Diane said. And judging by the way she caressed that thing, she was *dead* serious. As I pondered this, I realized she had it out for Ted. But she never did say so, not for many, many years to come. But that day, and for a whole lot more, she and I never talked about our little problem with Ted. We were sworn to secrecy by Mother Dearest, but I was sure that Diane had had it at least as bad as I had. *It made sense…* She wouldn't go down to their house anymore. She answered the phone like it was going to blow up in her face.

Like I do now, in other words. Have I been dumb or what?

Things were, for the second time today, more in focus. Things that had not occurred to me while at school. But these were not up for discussion. *Yes, life goes on…*

"So why would you need a gun when you have Final Net?" I asked Diane. "It's very effective, you know."

Mother cut those green eyes at me as if to say *That's what I thought!*

I tried to look away, but she locked in on me, and I couldn't move. She had a way of paralyzing you with her eyes while she probed your brain, a very effective way to get the truth out of you. She'd known all along what had happened to Ted's face! Trying to change the subject, I asked Diane, "By the way, can you run me up to Suttons to get my shoes? Please?"

Diane answered quickly, probably to save me from the brain probe, "If we go now. Michael is coming to get me and teach me how to shoot before it gets dark, so hurry. Annndd as for the Final Net, I don't want to get that close to anybody, and this baby is much more effective."

"Aren't you afraid of hurting somebody?" I asked.

"No, I look forward to it," she said with a calm that was chilling. I just let that go. I never knew D had this dark side to her, but then I had recently discovered a new side of my own as well.

I followed Mother to her room, in search of money. "Mother, I need some money to get my shoes out of hock." She handed over some cash, which is how it was most often done in those days. Only an occasional check was used. Diane and I took off without another word, but as my eyes glanced over to her, she definitely had a smirk on her face. She was enjoying every bit of a newfound air of confidence. I hoped she was in control of her little temper and her nerves and hopefully backed off on the sweet tea. We often communicated without words, and we had a whole butt-load of conversatin' going on right then. We understood each other well, but I had to say out loud, "Thank you for letting me wear the dress to the dance. I don't know what I would have done otherwise."

"I know," was all she said. I had to wonder if she bought it for me anyway. She had no dance to go to, and once again, we understood. *Sistahs! Ya' can't live with 'em, ya' can't live without 'em.*

The shoes and the dress were perfect. I looked like a movie star when I looked in the mirror. I thought I would really feel like a star at the Poinsett Hotel, walking down that elegant, winding stairway in my beautiful dress. The hotel was downtown

Greenville's first and finest. There was lots of elegant, hand-carved trim, marble, gold leaf, and enormous crystal chandeliers sparkling everywhere. I was getting so excited that I was having trouble sleeping again, but this time it was good stuff causing my insomnia. I was feeling pretty carefree, but underneath I was a little nervous. For one thing, Marty's mother kept fussing about his hair being too long. It was actually, but he was so cute with it that way. She wanted it to be short for the dance and the pictures, and they were goin' 'round and 'round about the issue. I personally didn't care one way or the other. More and more kids were wearing their hair long, and like I said, he was cute that way.

I called Anne, Beth, Laura, Becky, and Nancy and asked, "Are you wearing your hair up or down?" The overall consensus was "DOWN." Ok, down it would be. That was good because I didn't know who was going to do my hair if it had to be up. If it was my Aunt Sybil, it would end up being a beehive thingie with about a gallon of liquid cement.

And that isn't gonna happen.

Yearbooks would be out the next day, and that made me nervous. Most everybody knew who won what already, but I had only told my family and Marty. We were excited, nervous, and proud. *I don't think I am gonna sleep well tonight,* I thought, *but I feel exhausted. I am going to bed early.*

When I got home, I thought I'd go ahead and get my jammies on and climb into bed. So I got out my jammies, turned out the light, got on the floor to put them on, and the phone rang. *Crap...*

"Hello?" I said while in the floor in the dark.

"I'm gonna get you, you fuckin' bitch. When you least expect it."

I tossed the phone like it was on fire and left it off the hook. I pulled my knees up to my chest and just rocked in the dark for what felt like hours. I started to cry, but after a few minutes I decided that I'd had enough of that shit. And I didn't want my eyes to be swollen tomorrow during the yearbook day signings and stuff. I went to the bathroom, got one of Mother's hemorrhoid suppositories and put it under my eyes. Worked like a champ! I pulled my pajamas on, treated my swollen eyes, and went to Mother's room. I felt I would sleep better in there, but I hated to wake her up.

"You okay?" Mother asked as she stirred.

"Yes. I just wanted to sleep in here. Bad dreams. Okay?"

"I'm sorry, I understand. Come on in. I'm having some trouble sleeping myself," she said.

I slept like the dead that night. I had weird dreams all night, but at least I slept hard. I guess I felt safe and could relax enough to really zone out.

The next morning, Mother looked like hell, and I didn't look much better. I made compresses for my eyes and followed with the Prep H. They worked pretty well. Mother and I didn't talk about yesterday's events. It was understood, although she didn't know about my late-night phone call from dear Ted. She must have really lowered the boom on him, because now he was out to get me. I would need to be with somebody all the time for a while—and be armed at all times.

Mother had gotten up and fixed a big breakfast as usual, and we ate together in near silence until I reminded her that we would get our yearbooks that day and that the next night would be the sorority Spring Dance. That seemed to perk her up a bit, but she still looked pretty down. The doll was still blinking up a storm. Tentatively, I asked Mother, "How's Sarge doing?"

"He's worse of course," was her miserable reply. "He's in the hospital, and they don't expect him to live much longer, maybe a few days or so."

"I'm so sorry," I said as water filled my eyes again. "I'm sorry I asked. Now my eyes are swelling again. I give up."

"I know. We all love him. We have been close for so many years." Looking at Mother suddenly made me wonder just how close. *Judging from the pain in her eyes, she held something deep down in there for him.* She saw that I had read her for a change, and she turned away with tears spilling onto her face and a look that broke my heart. *Oh shit.* I really didn't want to know what that was all about, so I finished breakfast and headed for the shower. I dressed up a little more than usual, so as not to disappoint my friends who thought so much of me. I was grateful for them, but I really did not feel that I deserved the honors they had so graciously handed me. *If they only knew what I had to deal with at home, and how dirty I felt.*

Mother always liked to see how we girls looked before we left the house. I walked into her bedroom just as I was leaving to say bye and wish me luck. The first words out of her mouth were, "Yer titties look s'purdy. Stick 'em out real nice, back straight." She slapped my back and whirled me around. "Turn around and let me see yer butt."

"Jeez!" *Just do as she says.*

"Yer butt looks purdy in that skirt. Good luck today. I can't wait to see that yearbook! My baby is a beauty queen."

"Okay, thanks, Mother." *Whatever.* "My ride is here. Bye."

God help me, that woman is a trip, I thought. At least she had something to take her mind off Sarge, even if just for a little while.

Chapter Fifteen

When I got to school that morning, everybody was buzzing, congratulating, singing, and dancing in the aisles and in the halls. It was hard to keep my mind on classes when there was so much to say, so many yearbooks to write in, so many good-byes. My classmates were getting excited about the sorority dance the next night. The teachers were very patient, letting us sign yearbooks for a while during each class. We got our exam grades and our final report cards too. What a day it was! I thought again how lucky I was to have so many good friends. Sometimes it was easy to take things for granted, but if I just looked around I realized how much there was to be thankful for. It helped get my mind off other things to read the comments in my yearbook from all my buds. I knew this would be something that I would show my kids and grandkids one day. That would be awesome.

It was a fun day, but exhausting. It was hard to believe the school year was over. I started to gather my books to go home, but then I realized that my yearbook was nowhere to be found. I was running around like a maniac to see who had it, probably writing me a silly note. NOT…*some-damn-body stole my freakin' yearbook that I waited all year for, and my parents paid for, and my friends all signed. What the fuck?!?*

I couldn't even think about going home without it. Totally deflated, I gave up and had to go home without it. People can be so cruel sometimes. Just when you think people are good, somebody comes along and knocks the shit out of ya.

Well, Daddy was brokenhearted. Mother was just plain pissed off. They called the school, and Daddy went up there that day and bought a new one, even though he had to work third shift that night and had done so the night before. My parents were happy after all, but it cut me pretty deep that someone would just take my yearbook right from under my nose. Probably the competition, who knows? I'd have to get some friends to sign again. *Dammit to hell!*

I just wanted to get ready for the dance and have some fun. Sleeping would be hard. I went into the bedroom to do my usual routine of undressing and dressing on the floor in the dark. *I'm a prisoner in my own home. From fame and glitter to this, in a matter of a few hours. What was wrong with this picture?* I got ready for bed, all creeped out as usual. Something about sneaking around on the floor in the dark makes you real paranoid. I decided to sleep on Mother's daybed in her room.

"Ma? I slept better in here last night, do you mind if I do it again tonight?"

"Of course not," she said. "I sleep better with you in here with me. Climb up here. This king bed is plenty big enough for us, and then some."

"I can do without the 'and then some,' thanks," I said. I deadbolted the bedroom door and crawled onto that giant bed in the dark. Mother said softly, "Ted got his leg chewed up by some big-ass dog last night. It was pretty serious. God knows what he was doing."

"I bet I could tell you what he was doing. Serves him right!"

Silence followed. *Payback is hell, ain't it?* I'm sure he was peeping somewhere and got a BIG surprise. He always blamed his injuries on his job with the postal service or some freak accident. But we knew better. In most cases, he was being a pervert. "I wish that dog had chewed his dick off," I muttered quietly.

I tried to stifle a laugh as best I could as I turned into my pillow. I could hear Mother doing the same thing, and before you knew it, we were both hysterical with laughter. You cope however you can sometimes.

I guess it was better than Ted getting shot by my sister and her new gun.

But the more I thought about it, the more freaked out I got about Diane having a gun. She had gotten so nervous lately that I could actually see her using it. I understood now why she was acting so squirrelly, and I was following in her footsteps in the nerves department. There was more silence, and the next thing I heard was Mother saying, "I am sorry, you know." We always could communicate better without words than we could with them. I knew exactly what she meant. That was the best she could do at the time. It was about the whole screwed-up mess and her part in it.

"I know," I said.

And the next thing I knew, I was waking up at 10 a.m. in a panic.

Gotta do my nails, eyes, hair, skin care, makeup, oh my God!

Marty called and said he was ready, although he still didn't get his hair cut. His momma was pissed—and mine probably would be too when she saw the dance portraits. *But who cares?* I spent the day pampering and beautifying. I talked to all my sorority buddies, and of course all of them were doing the same things I was. At least I had some professional help from my cosmetologist

Aunt Sybil and my dear sisters. This was the most important night of my life so far, and I didn't want to look like a ho in a chiffon evening gown.

Marty showed up, with his mother driving. He brought in a beautiful orchid corsage for my dress, and we struggled awkwardly while attaching it, trying not to do any damage. His mother obviously had seen my dress and coordinated appropriately. She was very classy and had been to many social soirees in her lifetime. As for Marty, he cleaned up pretty good in his midnight black tuxedo. Mother frowned at his hair, but I shot her an eye dagger, and she didn't say anything. No pictures were taken before we left, as usual. I don't think we even owned a camera. Daddy even got up early to see us off, and he had tears in his eyes. I had to get away before I started crying too. He loved his baby girl. Even Marty's mother was proud and all keyed up about him behaving and looking the part. She was bragging about my yearbook pics. This was going to be a long night, and everybody was making me really nervous about it.

The arrivals started to trickle into the elegant Poinsett Hotel, and the girls all congregated upstairs in the elaborate ladies lounge area, refreshing our makeup and pampering each other. Then we got to float down that beautifully elegant staircase. Every girl in Greenville who went to a prom or a sorority dance looked forward to that special moment. Our dates all hung out at the bottom of the stairs and watched us descend in our formal gowns. I just prayed I didn't get my stacked heels hung on my dress and tumble down forty-seven steps with my dress over my head.

Finally we got done with our grand entrance! The Fantastics started to play, and the hooplah began. They played several songs and then started the announcements, which I had forgotten all about. I desperately thought, *I just want to get this over with and have some fun.* Of course, they made me wait until the last, as we all had to walk from the back to the front of the ballroom. *Lights, cameras, nerves, hot as flaming hell!* I could feel my makeup sliding down my face.

Our sorority president was announcing the awards, and she finally came to me. "Last but certainly not least, we are so proud to have her as our sorority sister, past class president, voted best all around, voted our sorority's most valuable member, and FRESHMAN BEAUTY QUEEN 1972, Maggie Keith! Let's give her a hand and all of our sisters a big thank-you and congrats for all their hard work!"

Ya-a-ay, woohoo, please just shoot me.

God, I had to pee, and I didn't want to have to go all the way up that glamorous staircase again. My feet were already hurting, and we had barely even started. *Lord have mercy on me.* We finally got to dance to some old Myrtle Beach favorites, fast and slow. Somebody spiked the punch bowl, thank God, and that helped a little with the overall pain factor. The band stopped playing at 11:00 p.m., and we all sadly limped home or to a pool party at one of the mansions in the historic area. I felt like somebody had beaten my feet and toes with a goddamn claw hammer. Whoever in hell invented high heels should be castrated slowly while wearing a push-up bra, a garter belt, and stiletto heels.

I could only go to the breakfast party following immediately after the dance for a short while. I was surprised Mother agreed on a 1:00 a.m. curfew. That was a first! Marty's mother transported us to the breakfast, where we changed into more comfortable clothes. God, it felt so good to take off those cruel shoes. It felt like I peeled off flesh with my hosiery, it hurt so good. Nobody really went dressed to swim, but the party was around the pool.

The house was at least as magnificent as the Poinsett Hotel, just not quite as big. I couldn't imagine living like that every day. There was another gorgeous sweeping staircase that looked like solid mahogany, with an oriental runner down the middle of the staircase. Above was a crystal chandelier that looked like it was the size of our entire house. *Unbelievable!* I felt like Cinda-fuckin-rella. I was so hungry I felt like I could eat a horse, so I went to check out the vittles. I walked down those beautiful stairs after changing into a cute little sundress and sandals, feeling pretty good about how things had gone at the dance and so glad it was over. As I looked down at my pretty little sandals, I noticed that my throbbing toes resembled ten perfect little strawberries.

I found my way to the pool area, and oh my God what a beautiful sight! I was so awed by the surroundings that I didn't see everybody poised for my arrival. The boys scared the crap out of me with a lot of whistling, wooing, and all that testosterone stuff, and I almost fell into the pool. If I hadn't already had a steady beau, I could've had any one of them, or so it appeared. Marty looked all puffed up about it, so I had to give him some extra attention—when I could find him. His short little ass kept disappearing, and I noticed that he looked and acted kinda strange.

I finally got a good look at him and asked, "What's wrong with your eyes?" They looked like he'd been swimming at the Y or something.

"Nothin', just tired I guess," he said as he headed for the spiked punch. I noticed that he kept his distance as much as he could from me, but he looked pissed when any guy talked to me or congratulated me. They were saying things like, "You need to get rid of him and date me." Even though he was one of the rich frat boys, they didn't care. But I loved that short little dude, and I told him so often. He'd always respond with, "I love you more." And I felt like he did, but I didn't think he was enjoying the spotlight any more than I was.

Marty came back over to me after checking out the punch bowl, and I said, "I'm tired too. This last month, and especially this week working up to this night, has been a drain. I'm sorry I haven't had much time to hang with you. But now we can be together more with summer here and all. Right?"

"Yeah, sure," he responded. "Can I come over tomorrow?"

"I don't see why not. I think Daddy's finally given up on me going to Uncle Jack and Aunt Bessie's, but I'll have to come up with an alibi. They don't want me staying at home alone."

"Why not, you're a big girl now! You and I could have some alone time finally."

"That'll be nice. I'll give you a call tomorrow when I get it all figured out. Just hang back till I call, okay?"

Things had been heating up between us sexually before all this busy work started, and I knew I was gonna get pressured to go all the way. I could feel it coming. We had been dating for a while, and I loved his cute little ass off, but I was terrified of doing the nasty, all-the-way thing. This image kept coming to mind from back when I was younger, I guess about six or seven years old. I had walked in on my Daddy while he was bent over putting on his underwear. I saw Junior and the Twins, up close and personal. *Oh my God!* That was one of the few times in my entire life that Daddy yelled at me. I was traumatized enough from that view, and getting yelled at scared me so much that I cried. I thought something was wrong with Daddy, that maybe his tonsils or something were hanging out of him. It took Mother quite a while to calm me down. *Anyway...*

Marty and I snuck off into a dark corner of the meticulously manicured yard and necked for a while. He was all hands, and I was too tired to fight. He definitely wanted more than he was getting. We had been through this over and over, and I didn't know how much longer I could hold him off. But he was patient, I have to say. It was nice being with him because he was so laid back about most things, and we had always just clicked.

It was time to gather up our stuff, though, and call Mommer an' 'em to come get us. I was so tired I could hardly make it up those steps one last time. The ladies dressing room was upstairs, of course, and that's where all the girls changed and hung their formal dresses up. *What a lovely lifestyle to have,* I thought. *I could definitely do this kind of life, but I'm not so sure about some of the people.* Many of them were so snooty and cocky, and a lot of them I really didn't like. Marty's mother got me home, and of course Mother was perched by the front door, waiting. Luckily we weren't late, or she would have been on the warpath. Marty was still terrified of her because of her look that could cook the flesh right off your bones. I had to hang onto his arm to keep him from bolting at the mere sight of her. He gave me a little peck on the cheek and was gone.

"Well, did you have a good time?" Mother asked.

"Yes, we did, and I am so tired, and my toes are throbbing. Thanks for letting me go, and here, take these and burn them please." I shoved the cruel shoes into her hands as I headed for bed. "But they did look marvelous with that dress."

"Well, tell me how it went," Mother persisted, wanting details. "Was it wonderful? Did you get pictures? Talk to me, dammit."

"It went great," I said through my exhaustion. "It was wonderful. Got pictures coming, so get your wallet ready. I felt like the princess that I am, and now I am one burned out princess. Good night, Mother."

I did my routine: peed in the dark, got my pajamas out, threw them on the floor, sat down on the floor, put them on in the dark, crawled in the bed beside Diane, and whispered, "Thank you, Sis."

"Shut up and move over," was her response. "If you messed up my dress, I *will* kill you in your sleep. If you're lucky." She just had to play tough guy. *Meanie!* She really did have a soft underbelly that was not often exposed, but I knew it was there. I slept like the dead.

For a while.

Chapter Sixteen

There were people everywhere. They were all dressed up and socializing, and at a distance, they appeared to be having fun. As I walked through the crowd, I saw that their eyes were all black with mascara, and tears of blood ran down their faces. I could hear Mother crying from a distance, so I scanned the crowd for her. I was getting frantic as I looked at all the faces: they began to contort as if they were melting. I could still hear Mother's cries, and I became terrified. I called out to her in desperation. Suddenly, I was awake in my bedroom, calling out and crying. Diane was gone, but it was still the middle of the night. I got up and saw a light on down the hall. I pushed open Mother's bedroom door, and there were Mother and Diane, and Mother was indeed crying.

"What's wrong?" I asked, still shaken by my dream. "I was just dreaming about you. There was a crowd of people there too. But I couldn't find you in the crowd, and I could hear you crying, everybody was crying. There was blood, and—"

"I know," Mother sobbed. "I had the same dream, except there was a casket. I opened it and you know who was in there, don't you?

"Sarge."

"Yes," Mother said through more sobbing. "He opened his eyes and said he loved me and to tell you good-bye and that he loved you."

"Okay," I said. "That's weird. Is Madam Alexander still blinking?"

"No," Mother said, starting to gain her composure. "She stopped just a short while ago. I am dreading the call from Sarge's family now. I have no doubt that he is gone. So, tell me about your dream. It sounds like we were in the same dream, but mine went further. Oh God, I hope you aren't cursed like me."

I told her what I remembered of my dream, and I could tell as I looked at her that she knew exactly what I was going to say.

"Well," I said after, "there's nothing we can do for now but try to get some rest, huh? Mind if I sleep in here on the day bed?"

"That would be good," Mother said. Her eyes were swollen from crying, and mine were burning from heartbreak for her and for Sarge's family. He used to spoil me, since I was the baby. I felt real attached to him and hated to think about him suffering and never being able to see him again. And although he was a good friend of the family, and we all loved him, I still wondered why Mother was taking it so hard. She was totally distraught, even though she was no longer crying.

Diane said as she was returning to her bed, "Ya'll are a couple of freaks. I'm outta here."

"Ol' tough girl cover up," I said to Mother when Diane had left. "I bet she goes in there and cries her eyes out."

"Yeah, probably," Mother replied as she turned out the light. "I don't think I can sleep at all, but we'll try."

We did manage to sleep pretty peacefully for the rest of the night. We got up together when Daddy got home. He usually didn't work on weekends, but occasionally he had to. It was

Sunday morning, and this was going to be one of the rare exceptions for 6 a.m. Mass. As we waited for the phone call, I realized that between Mother and Madame Alexander, we probably knew before his family did that Sarge had passed. But we still had to wait it out. We didn't want to upset his family by calling too soon. We knew in our hearts that he was gone, so our grieving process had started.

As Mother headed into the kitchen to start making breakfast, I followed her. "I want you to teach me how to make biscuits, Mommer," I said, trying to distract her from her sorrow.

"Oh hell, chile," she said wearily. "Maybe some other time. I am not in the mood."

"Oh come on," I said gently. "It'll help get our minds off other things, ya' know?"

"We've been through it before," she said as she started gathering the ingredients. "Don't you remember?"

"Not really," I said a bit sarcastically. Most of Mother's cooking was not from written recipes. She wasn't taught that way, and she rarely had to resort to a book. Cooking for her was more of an organic process, one that was absorbed and refined with years of trial and error experience. "Let me write it down this time, if possible. You sure didn't make it easy to learn before. Just hang on till I get a pen and paper."

"Okay, but hurry the hell up," she said. "I need to get these bad boys started. I don't have time for this."

"Okay. Ready," I said.

Mother started to work her magic. She had an old wooden bread bowl that her father had carved out of an oak tree. It was probably sixty years old or older then, and I still have it to this day. "Take off your rings," Mother said, "and wash your nasty little hands."

That done, she said, "Now get this bowl and put about this much self-rising flour in it." She made a brief, cryptic gesture.

"And how much flour would that be?" I asked, again not without some sarcasm.

"Hell if I know," she said, already exasperated. "Several hands full. I don't measure anything, you know that."

"How could I forget? Okay, just keep going."

"Throw in some baking powder," she continued, "then get three fingers of Crisco, and work it in with your hand. Squeeze it through your fingers until it looks right. You work it in the center of the flour, and pull in more flour as needed from the side."

"I had forgotten how impossible this was going to be," I muttered.

"Tough shit," she quipped, taking her turn with the sarcastic tone. "Now shut up and listen. Pour buttermilk in with one hand while you work it with the other hand, squishing, patting, till it looks about right. Then start working in more flour from the sides until it starts to form. Keep pulling in flour and kneading until it feels right."

"Dear Lord," I sighed hopelessly.

"I agree," she said. "Now, don't overwork the dough, or the biscuits will be tough. Feel this? Feel how soft it is, and smooth, but still sticky inside. If you poke it with your finger, see how it does? Do it."

"Yeah, I see. But I don't see how I can ever reproduce it."

"You can't," she explained. "You just have to do it a few hundred times to get it like you want it. No two people do it the same. Your Grannie's biscuits are the best, and I have never been able to make them like hers. Now, flop it out on a floured surface, wax paper is good. Get your rollin' pin and roll it out like you want 'em. Get your biscuit cutter, flour it too, and cut your biscuits. If you want, you can just pull them off in hunks. Then dribble some buttermilk on top. They can sit for a little while before you cook them."

"Great. Thanks. No problem," I said, tossing a paper that had almost no writing on it into the trashcan.

Mother grinned and said, "Anytime."

"Next time we'll try milk gravy or fried chicken," I said. "Maybe I can make a little more sense out of that."

"We'll see. They are easier to do. I'm gonna make gravy now if you want to learn."

"No, I think I'd rather go lick the cat's butt," I said, resolved that it would only be another exercise in futility to try and learn how to make milk gravy. "But thanks for asking."

Mother just let out a cackle and said "We don't have a cat."

"I'll find one," I said as I left the kitchen.

The dreaded phone call came after breakfast, and the whole house became solemn. Daddy woke up to the news that Sarge was indeed gone, and he took it hard too. They had been friends for many a year. Sarge's family had asked if he would be a pallbearer, and of course he agreed. He would have to take off work to do it, and that was rare for Daddy. I dreaded all the commotion associated with funerals. I didn't do well at them at all; I was too tender-hearted. Mother didn't think she could handle it either, seeing the wife and four kids grieving, so she said that we would go to the funeral home prior to the visitation and see him.

"Please don't make me go," I said. "Please, I am begging you. I can't handle it, and I shouldn't have to."

But Mother insisted. "Sara, Diane, you, and I will go before anybody gets there. End of subject." I knew what that meant. I had learned to accept that term long ago.

"All right," I said, ready to change the subject. "I'm going to Beth's for the day. Are ya'll going to Uncle Jack and Aunt Bessie's?"

"I guess we will. Don't we always? Why don't you come with us?"

"Because I can't take it anymore," I said, trying to get my way on this one. "It's the smells and Betty Jo...It's just too depressing."

Betty Jo was Jack and Bessie's youngest daughter. She had caught rheumatic fever as a child, and it had fried her brain to the point of severe mental retardation. She was physically and mentally helpless, and she looked hideous. Her tongue was huge from where she just sat and rocked and chewed on it nonstop. She screamed a lot when she was happy. She screamed when she was mad, hungry, whatever. She just screamed. She had the mind of an infant in a woman's body. She couldn't walk or feed herself or do any basic personal care, so she wore diapers. I had learned to stay out of her reach, because if she ever got a grip on you, you couldn't get loose. She'd rip out your hair, tear your lips off or whatever, though she was obliviously innocent. Poor Uncle Jack and Aunt Bessie were burdened with this giant baby until the day they died. They refused to put her in a nursing home, so they designed a room for her. After they died, she did have to go to a nursing facility, and she did not live long after that. Still, she did live to be in her upper sixties, which shows what good care she got most of her life.

"I know. I don't blame you," Mother said. "I guess you're getting old enough to go your own way, but within limits. The rules are: no boys here with you, and you do not stay here alone. EVER! And you know why on both counts."

"Trust me, I know," I said. "I'll go to Beth's, and we'll stay there." I immediately ignored Mother's first rule and called Marty to tell him the good news: we could have some alone time. But then the more I thought about it, the more nervous I got about the pressure I'd get from him to go all the way. *We will just have to play that by ear*, I thought. Deep down, I was scared shitless of doing it, even though some of my friends had and said it was no big deal. Still, I was scared.

Mother and Daddy left. I waved good-bye, and shortly after that, Marty drove up in his momma's big-ass, fancy Buick. When he got inside he gave me a kiss, and I saw that he looked like he had been on a weeklong drunk. And he smelled weird too.

"What's wrong with your eyes?" I said, more a demand than a question. "You look so different."

"I don't know, just tired I guess," he said as he looked away. He had been acting strange lately, and here it was again: real secretive and distant. "So do we have some private time? No chance of anybody busting in on us?"

"You never know," I said. "I do have brothers and sisters, you know So, I don't think you should get too excited. I'm not ready for that anyway." He gave me a dejected, but resigned look.

"I'm just not ready, and you're acting like a stranger. What's going on? Who have you been hanging around with? I think you're getting in over your head with drugs or something."

Good grief, I do sound like Mother!

"I've just been smoking some pot, that's all," he said defensively. "Everybody is doing it. Except you, that is."

"What do you mean 'everybody'?" I retorted. "Maybe your new long-hair friends do, but mine don't."

Then he started running down a list of all the people who were "cool," which meant that they smoked pot. As he rattled off name after name, I realized those very people had been looking different lately. Ratty ass blue jeans with patches, long greasy hair, funky looking shoes. I had been wondering what that was all about. "Aren't you afraid of getting into trouble?" I asked.

"Not really. We're real low-key and quiet about it. Everybody is so cool, and they do their own thing, and let others do the same.

Nobody is judged by how they dress or how much money their parents have. 'Peace, love, sex, and drugs.' That's their motto."

I was having trouble getting a handle on all this. "You're hitting me with too much stuff," I said. "I don't know if we have anything in common any more. You say you love me, but you sneak off and come back all weird and stinking to high heaven. Then you act like I'm the weird one."

"Look, you're being too uptight about this," he persisted. "Once you get used to being around it, you won't be scared any more. Everybody's just laid back, and it's going on everywhere. I've been protecting you from it for as long as I can, but it's time to just face the facts. I'm not quitting, so you might as well get used to it."

"Well, I don't want to be around it. First of all, it's illegal. Second, it smells like dog shit, and so do you." That got a grin out of him. "It's not funny, I'm serious." Now he was laughing. "You're asking a lot of me, and it just doesn't fit into my world right now, and you know it. So go be with your new hippie friends, and leave me alone for a while. Maybe then you can decide what you want the most, me or them. What else besides marijuana have you done? No, don't say anything else."

But Marty wasn't giving up easily. "We call ourselves Freaks. We're the second and third generation of hippies. That just means that we're cool with whatever turns you on. Peace, love, sex, and drugs, and the *best* music. You'll see. It's real people. Real love. Not the snobby assed, high-society bullshit that we did last night. Those people are a bunch of pricks, and I know you know it."

"I can't deny that. I like a few of them, but the rest can jump up my ass." Still, I wasn't going to be persuaded easily. Getting back into the daughter of Noni mode, my voice started dripping with sarcasm. "Freaks, huh? Now that is just precious. They're the ones who have the long stringy hair and no bras, and it looks like their clothes have been spray-painted on, right? Flowers in their hair and those ugly, clunky shoes. What's with the patches on their jeans? I know some of them, and they ain't poor. They look pretty pitiful, and that's comin' from somebody that ain't had much material stuff growin' up. No, you're gonna have to give me some time to think about all this. I don't know what else to say."

"Sure," he started to say, then he started to beg. "But please don't make me leave. I want to be with you. I won't pressure you."

"Sorry, but I'm a little scared at the moment," I said. "I love you so much, but sometimes that's not enough. I need to think about things, like where I'm headed. The sorority rushes are coming up, and I'm sure they aren't into the freak stuff. And I'm not sure what I'm into myself, so please go and give me some time. I have worked so hard to get where I am, and you are asking me to give it all up for you without considering what I want. And in all honesty, I have no idea what I want, except for you and me to be like we used to be."

"Me too. I do love you, and I know I have changed. These people have changed my life and the way I look at things. If you give them a chance, I think you'll understand better and like them a whole lot better than those dickheads we were with last night. Do you know they kept trying to get rid of me last night? They said I didn't deserve you and I needed to get lost and quit trying to mess up your life. They said they have more to offer you than I do and they called me a loser."

"Well no wonder you were looking so weird. I'm glad you didn't leave me there with the lions for long. I felt like I was laid out on the buffet table or something when you had gone missing. And now I know you were getting high. I appreciate that a lot."

"I'm sorry. They pissed me off, and I had to go calm down. Me and Howard and Clark snuck off and got a buzz."

"They get high too?"

"Yeah, but they're not Freaks. It has to be hush-hush for them. I personally don't care what people think about how I look, but they will always be frat boys. It ain't cool with that group. Not yet anyway."

"Whatever. Look, I'm gonna go over to Beth's and I want to see if Willa wants to come. Will you drop us off there?"

He looked at me sadly and said, "I'm not happy about it, but if that's what you want."

"Yes it is, please." I called Willa and she was a go, then I called Beth and told her we were going to come on up. Marty drove us up the street and I'll be dipped in shit! Ted was lurking around the neighborhood on foot again. The SOB always seemed to know too much, like when I was alone, for instance. It must be pretty convenient to work for the postal service and be a peeping Tom. A perfect match.

When we got to Beth's, the girls noticed that I was pretty distant and thoughtful. I told them about Marty and the latest about his new habits and friends.

"I've smoked pot once," Beth said with a sly grin. Willa and I were awestruck, but we were curious and asked a lot of questions until we were somewhat satisfied. "Tommy and his friends do it in his room all the time, and they asked me if I wanted to try some. I didn't really feel anything, but they were all hysterical after smoking a joint. They laughed at everything, including me, so I just went back to my room and turned on some music. They said that you don't usually get off the first time you try it, and sure enough, I didn't. But I'm going to try again when they offer it."

When I got back home that evening, I had a lot to think about. I had been leading a double life, a life that I had held secret for so long. *Talk about highs and lows, honey chile, I got 'em all.* I still wasn't too sure about all that drug stuff, and my mother would kill me if I got caught. I knew I couldn't hide anything from her, and I was afraid I would freak out, as they called it, if she confronted me while I was high. But it wasn't like I had to make up my mind immediately. I was feeling a little less intimidated after talking with Beth. I had to admit to myself, I was curious. I started paying more attention, and the more I saw the Freaks and the hippies, the more appealing they became. They were just so nice, they never bothered anybody, and they smiled all the time.

Beth continued to try to get high with her hippie brother and his hippie friends, and two days later, on the third time, she got off. She called me while she was high, and Willa and I immediately went to see her. Her eyes looked like Georgia road maps, and she thought everything was so funny. Before long, she had Willa and me rolling on the floor laughing too. They called it a contact high. I had heard of it from Marty, but I didn't think it was real…until now. I had never laughed so much, and God knows I needed it.

I think I could try this!

When we got control of our giggle boxes, Beth told us that a lot of people were doing LSD too, and she was going to try it soon. She talked about hallucinating, seeing lots of colors, and laughing your ass off for eight to ten hours straight. *Hmmm…* I had heard some scary stuff about what people sometimes did while on acid, and that felt more intimidating to me. But after listening to Beth's account of her brother and his friends doing it, I had to admit it sounded interesting.

"Let me know how that goes," I told her, not yet ready to jump on the bandwagon myself. "Just be careful and make sure you have a babysitter or somebody with experience watching over you so you don't do anything crazy."

"You and Willa are a lot of fun," Beth said, her eyes brightening so much I thought they might start bleeding. She was still on the verge of losing control and falling into another fit of hysterical laughter. "Why don't ya'll come trip with me? Maybe Annie could come over too. I know she's cool. It'll be far out, man."

Willa looked like she was ready to try anything, but I wasn't so sure about taking LSD. "We'll see," I replied. "Can't we start with some pot? I haven't even done that yet."

"I'll try to get some," Beth said, "but no promises, Tommy says it's not as easy to get as acid. But we'll do something. How about this weekend? My house. Momma works third shift, so it'll be perfect."

OH MY!

"Uhhhh…well, okay then," I stammered.

"I'll be there!" Willa said in a flash. "You call Annie if you want her to come. Where are you going to get enough acid for all four of us?"

"It's real cheap and strong," Beth replied, "and we'll split one either two ways or four ways. I'll talk to Tommy about what we should do. He'll know."

Great! I thought. *This is the brother who has always hated you, me, and everybody else, and beats the shit out of his own mother and sisters.*

"Do you really trust him on that?" I asked.

"Sure," Beth said confidently. "He may be an asshole, but he wouldn't want us hurt."

"You're scaring me now," I said in spite of her and Willa's enthusiasm. "I'm not sure if I'm ready for all this."

"Sure you are," Willa said. "It'll be great. Nobody else will know. We know you have a reputation to worry about."

"I'm not sure I care about that so much anymore," I spoke up quickly. I suddenly felt the need to express some of the thoughts

I'd been having lately about all that. "I've met some real shallow people lately in the sororities and fraternities. I've seen their true colors, and I don't like them."

"Neither do I," said Beth. "That's why I quit."

"I've been to the puppet show, I was a big part of it, and I see the strings now," I continued. "And they keep trying to attach them to me, and I don't handle that well. There is some fun to it, as you know. Beth, you were a part of that too, but I know you didn't get into it too much. I was on my own high and just kinda let it carry me to wherever it would, and now I'm not so sure I want to play the part. The part requires that you play by their rules, which are bigoted and narrow-minded. They even told me that I couldn't dance with my black girlfriends, you know, Debra, Regina, and Rosa. I've known them since third grade, and we have always been friends. So the sorority and fraternity snobs can jump up my ass. The rushing starts for the sororities soon, and I guess I'll go just for shits and giggles. But I doubt I'll be joining anything this year."

"I understand all that," Beth said, still trying to convince me. "Still, why don't you come over this weekend and get high? It will be a lot of fun, and the more the merrier!"

"Yeah, we'll see."

As I walked back home that evening with Willa, I was still scared about the LSD thing, but I had other things in my life to deal with. Like a boyfriend who wanted me to go all the way when I knew I wasn't ready yet. And the visit to the funeral parlor tomorrow with Mother and Sara. I was dreading it, and thinking about Sarge being gone, along with having to face the visitation, put the final kill on my contact high.

Chapter Seventeen

The next morning, Mother, Sara, Diane, and I went to the funeral paahlah. We had figured if we arrived early we would miss most of the crowd, and hopefully Sarge's family as well. We wanted to pay our respects, but I think Mother was just like me—too tenderhearted to face his family in the midst of their sorrow. She still seemed to me overly anxious, and she was showing her sorrow more than she usually did over something like this. I wonder why?

But our sneak attack didn't work. When we arrived, the family was already there viewing the body in private, and it was not pretty. Just about everybody was crying. So we waited in the lobby area until they pulled themselves together. *Just our luck! This is worse than what we were trying to avoid.* We walked in…actually, Mother had to pull me in, and I took one look at the casket and its contents and bolted out the door. She didn't come after me, thank God. She apparently needed closure of some kind, and after a short while, she and Sara and Diane came out. We greeted the family outside the parlor, gave our condolences, and left.

"Well, that was just horrible!" I cried out as soon as we got into the car and the doors were shut. "Why did you make me do that? I did not need to see that."

"I had to, so just be quiet," Mother bit out. I could see she was more than a little upset. "I don't feel like arguing about it. He loved you so much, and you loved him. End of subject." After a moment of silence, she added, "He looked handsome, didn't he?"

"Not really what I was expecting," I said disgustedly. *He looked dead as hell to me, and then some.*

Sara drove us home in silence, except for the occasional sniffle. Mother was trying to hold it together, but she wasn't doing very well. I wasn't either, and I was angry. Just seeing his family standing around the casket, looking at him and crying, was too painful. *I wish I could remember him the way he used to be and not a skeleton with skin stretched over it. I have enough bad dreams as it is.*

I've never understood why people want to see that. Mother had said something about closure, but I just didn't get it.

That's what nightmares are made of.

We got home shortly after noon, and Mother and I both did a face plant. That ordeal was truly exhausting for both of us, especially her. She hadn't slept well in weeks, and when she did she usually had more dreams of death. I had often found her over the past few weeks, sitting in the living room, staring at that damn doll's eyes. Now, as we lay in the bed together, I could hear her crying for a long time, but she eventually went silent, and I knew she was asleep. It was as if I couldn't rest until I knew she was sleeping, and I finally fell asleep too. I woke up hungry as a bitch wolf.

When I got up, Mother was already in the kitchen, sharpening her knife on a brick outside the kitchen door, getting ready to cut up some chicken. No fancy knife sharpeners for this woman. She had been using the same brick on the corner of the house for forty years, till the corner of it was worn flat and smooth. It had been her idea, and not for lack of other options—I'm sure we could have afforded a knife sharpener. But she was used to getting by with so little all her life that she had become a great improviser. And that brick worked like a charm.

"Feel better, Mommer?" I asked, hoping to distract her with kitchen talk again. She grunted what might have been an affirmative response. "Show me how you cut up a chicken. I'll just watch, and you talk me through it. Okay?"

Without argument this time, she started telling me how to bend the joints back in order to cut the legs and wings off. Then she showed me how to cut through the breastbone, then remove the thighs from the body. She was so fast at it that I almost didn't have time to get a little nauseated. Almost…

Too much information for an empty stomach.

I knew I'd better do something before I started dry heaving. I quickly ate some Saltines and washed them down with plenty of sweet tea, and all was better. I had never paid real close attention to how Mother did that, and I hadn't expected my reaction. But I knew I'd better get used to it.

"Okay," I said, feeling my color return, "now that the massacre is over, what next? We're frying the chicken, right? Do I need a pen and paper?"

"No, just watch and listen," Mother said. "Right now all you do is salt and pepper the chicken and put the pieces in a bowl of buttermilk. The longer they sit in it, the better, but we've only got about two hours before Elbert gets up for work. So we'll soak for an hour, then we'll start frying." Looking up from the chicken parts, she asked, "Are you okay, baby girl?"

"I'm trying to be," I said without much resolve. "I didn't handle that grieving thing at the funeral home very well. I'm sorry I ran, but I knew I was going to cry and get everybody around me more upset if I stayed, so I had to get out of there."

"I know it was hard for you too," she said, trying to be gentle. "I guess that was too much for you to take in. But I felt like I needed you there with me. I'm sorry you had to go."

"What else are we having?" I said, trying to change the subject. "I need to learn more about cooking."

"We're having fried chicken, rice, milk gravy, macaroni and cheese, green beans, and biscuits." A standard Southern dinner, in other words.

"How in the world are we gonna get all that done in two hours?" I asked.

"*I* have been doing it for over fifty years. Just watch the master and trust me. I was doing this when I was eight years old. I had older brothers to feed, and then younger brothers, and then a little sister. Mama had to work, so who do you think fed all those mouths while she worked? Without Miracle Hill, we probably would have starved. And we wouldn't have had clothes if Mother hadn't made them by hand for us."

"Well, that must have been really hard," I said.

"Everything was hard then," she said, "but that's all we knew, so we accepted it as a way of life. Ya know?"

"Well, while I'm out of school for the summer, and I want to learn and help. So, Chef Noni, boss me around. What's next?"

"Okay then, you asked for it. We need to make some fresh tea so it'll be done before we start the chicken and stuff. You know how to do that. Then grate some cheddar cheese, open a can of evaporated milk, get out the butter, the macaroni, the rice, self-rising flour, and Crisco—"

"Hold up now! Let me get the tea started," I barked. She chuckled and just kept rattlin' on, but I managed to keep it all in my head. After I started some water boiling for tea and got the various ingredients out, she continued.

"Start a big pot of water boiling, get out two medium saucepans and the lids, plus the gravy bowl. Cook the macaroni, and we'll throw together the mac 'n' cheese casserole."

Chef Noni was more like slave driver Noni. But we got the rice cooked, the macaroni and cheese put together, and the green beans started. The biscuits from hell were on the pan ready for the oven. Now all we had to do was fry the chicken and make the gravy.

What a royal pain in the butt. And she cooks like this two or three meals a day for us!

I was surprised she was still alive, and I hoped my life was easier than hers had been. At least I was going to school, whereas she had to quit in order to feed her siblings and play mother before she was ten. Maybe school really wasn't so bad after all.

"Now for the chicken," Mother said. "Get the big cast iron pan from down there. Wipe it out first, then put it on the stove, and I'll show you how much Crisco to use." *A lot!*

She was getting back into the rapid-fire mode again. "Now get a medium bowl and put some flour in it. Just dump it in and I'll tell you when to stop. Then dump some salt, onion powder, garlic powder, paprika, and pepper in it until I say stop. Then mix it in with a fork. Go ahead. What are you waiting for, a sign from God?"

"Yeah, that would be nice. Can you give me a hint as to how much of each?"

"Not really," she said, starting to get frustrated, "just do what I say and watch. You're being too technical. It's all just by feel, looks, and smell." After I had the flour mix prepared, she said, "Don't put the meat in until you KNOW the oil is ready. Just listen…" She held up her hand to stop me from asking any more questions. "Drop a little piece of skin or batter in there and you'll see it sizzle. See there? That means it's ready. Now, you do this part. You keep one hand dry and one hand wet. Take a piece of breast out of the buttermilk, put it in the flour mixture, and use the other hand to cover it with flour and put it in the oil. Bone side down, and keep going that until the pan is full. Not too full or the sides won't cook right and the batter pulls off. And for God's sake, don't mess with them at all once they're in the pan. Leave them alone until you see the sides getting brown, then we'll turn them. It's that easy. Go ahead and get out those old bread butts from the fridge. We'll put several butt pieces on the platter to absorb the grease when the chicken is done. Don't throw away the bread bags, you know. I use them for everything."

"Yeah, uh huh, I know. Like to barf in when we used to go to Florida," I said sarcastically. David had recently been transferred to another base in Texas, and it was such a relief to know we wouldn't be driving to visit them anymore. "There are still a lot of gray areas to this cooking stuff, but I'll manage."

As we cooked the chicken, people started to show up. I think you could smell it all over the neighborhood. Robbie, Nathan, Chris, and Willa had already been there for a while when Buddy arrived unexpectedly. They were all salivating in the living room, a perfect example of why Mother always cooked for an army. She had to make sure there was enough in case all our little orphan friends showed up. Willa wasn't an orphan, but as she lived next door to us, she was close enough to smell Noni's chicken.

"Ya think I had better add some milk and flour to the gravy bowls?" I asked Mother. "The natives look hungry."

"Yeah, maybe so," Mother said. "Be ready to fix the gravy as soon as the chicken is done, you know. Same pan, same oil. I'll start the biscuits then."

"Can we help?" someone called from the orphanage area.

"No!" Mother and I said in unison. "Actually, yes," Mother added. "Stay in THERE!"

"We can do it, Noni," Robbie said. "Did I ever tell you how beautiful you are?" he asked as he hugged her. Then Nathan got jealous, and before you know it they were trying to win her love, one over the other.

"Ya'll are so full of it!" Mother said. "You're just hungry, and I know you love me for my food. It won't be long, and if it's not good this time it's Maggie's fault. Now move it! OUT! OUT! OUT!"

"Thanks, Mother Dearest," I responded with an edge of nerves that was obvious.

The chicken cooked up just lovely, so time for the gravy. The gravy bowl was full of the evaporated milk/milk blend. The left-over flour from the chicken was scattered into the hot oil, although I had no idea how much that was.

"Now stir it constantly with the spatula," Mother said, "and add a little salt and pepper. Keep stirring until it starts to brown and blend in. I'll tell you when to start adding the milk. Do it slowly or it'll clump, and you keep stirring so you don't burn it. When it gets almost thick enough, it's time to pour it into the gravy bowl, because it thickens some more after you take it up."

I did as she said, and it was beautiful.

By then, it was as hot as forty hells in the kitchen. We didn't have air conditioning. I don't know how she stood it all the time. We set the dining room table, and we let Daddy eat first, as usual. He always got served and seated first. The rest of us were hungry enough to gnaw on the furniture by then, but Daddy had just woken up, and this crowd was a bit much for him just yet. But he always ate real fast, so there wasn't a long wait. We moved in and swarmed over the food like we were all starved. Some of the boys were near starved all the time, except for when we fed them. The food was all very good, and I was relieved. Suddenly, Robbie grabbed my hand, got on one knee, and said, "Will you be my awful wedded wife, to have and hold, if I promise to get rid of your brother, till death do…OUCH!" Buddy cracked him upside the head with a couple of knuckles. He was still overly protective with his baby sister, and he didn't think Robbie's little joke was funny.

"Sure," I said, going on with the joke, "and Buddy, don't hit Robbie like that." Turning to Robbie and grinning, I said, "You just love me for my food."

"Not entirely," Robbie said as he wiggled his eyebrows. "And you won't be around to get in the way 'cause you're married," he said to Buddy.

Buddy gave Robbie a look that would melt glass. "You'd better keep your hands off my sister, understand?"

Robbie just kept smiling but didn't respond.

After we ate, we all relaxed in the living room. As I looked around, everybody was happy, if only for a little while. Mother was laughing; I was too; and the orphan boys had full bellies, rosy cheeks, and smiles on their faces. Willa was coming out of her shell and blossoming before my very eyes as she was entertained by this crazy bunch. We were piled up on the floor, on the couch, and in dining chairs or recliners, with some Ray Charles playing. The noisy chatter ceased as a food coma set in. After a bit, I opened my eyes and everybody had fallen asleep. Willa and Nathan had gone home. I guess we were pretty boring while we were sleeping. Mother was in her bedroom, sound asleep. Madam Alexander was resting peacefully also. All was right with the world.

Now for the clean up.

Oh Lord, what a mess!

I asked the guys if they would help me, and Robbie and Buddy jumped right in. I usually thought cleaning up the kitchen was about a much fun as having a root canal, but we cut up and made it a little more enjoyable. I was with two of the four men in my life who I loved and trusted with all my heart. I had been missing Buddy terribly since he had gotten married, especially because he didn't visit us often anymore.

A knock at the front door at this hour could only mean one person. All *was* good with the world until Buddy opened the door and let Ted in. I felt like a cold blast had entered the house. I remained in the kitchen cleaning up while the guys shot the breeze in the living room. They, of course, had no idea what had been going on with Ted, and it was hard to hide my feelings in front of Buddy. So I kept myself busy until the kitchen was clean and decided I'd go to bed.

As I walked through the living room, Ted's eyes were on my crotch with every step I took. Buddy was oblivious, but I still felt so violated. *Again.* I thought about getting my hatpin, but there were too many witnesses present at the moment. I was saving that for just the right moment, when it would be just me and him. No telling what he would have done if Buddy had known that Ted was the reason Daddy blamed him for the ladder incident. At the time, I still didn't know that either. But other things had certainly come to light for me. Things that remained unspoken. I could hear Buddy ask him how his leg was doing from the dog bite. Ted responded with lies, lies, lies. It sounded like the bite had been bad enough to have to go to the doctor.

Good! Maybe the pervert will get gangrene and his leg will rot off.

As walked out of the living room I knew I had to move fast to pee, get my pajamas on, and get to bed before Ted started his stalking routine. *What in the hell did Sara think he did all these evenings? Somebody's gonna kill him one night, and it won't be too soon.*

I knew it was okay to dress in the light for a change, as long as I could hear him in there with Buddy. But as soon as he left, I went into Mother's room, locked the door, and slept like the dead. I heard Diane come in and go to bed just before I nodded out. He wouldn't try any sicko stuff with Buddy all over him, even though Buddy was clueless. Ted made sure he stayed that way.

Chapter Eighteen

Summer sure can seem to move slowly, especially if you don't have any wheels. Luckily, Beth had wheels part time. Willa and I could always walk or ride our bikes, but distance was limited there too. Willa had really started to open up, and I began to love her dearly. We shared many secrets, and being next-door neighbors, we were together a lot. Her parents worked during the day, so we had the house for a getaway from my parents. We spent most of the summer on their screened porch overlooking the creek that ran behind both our backyards.

She had a younger sister, though, and she gave us a hard time. Tami was always yelling "I'M GONNA TELL!" whenever we were doing something she knew we shouldn't be. And she usually did, unless we paid her. In cash. She would accept favors, but she usually demanded money, which we didn't have much of. But sometimes it was necessary. She was always catching us smoking cigarettes, and of course I always took the blame and didn't really try to hide it, while Willa freaked out and all but ate hers. My mother knew that I smoked, but Willa's would go psycho if she knew that Willa smoked, and she would separate us. So Tami had us in a predicament. I was pretty sure she knew Willa smoked too. We had to really be careful, 'cause we were usually broke. And we knew she'd end up telling on us one day in a fit of anger anyway. She had a bad temper, and she was "the baby," so she was used to getting her way. It was just a matter of time.

"So do you want to come with me to Beth's and try the LSD?" I asked Willa nervously. "God, does that sound awful?"

"I'm not sure," she replied. Now that we were down to it, she was starting to have reservations of her own. "If Mom will let me go, I might do it if you'll do it. I'm scared, though. I know Beth sure was having fun the other day when she was so stoned, but LSD is something else. But it might be a lot of fun."

"I know," I concurred. "I'm scared too, but it seems to be everywhere around us. And if we don't, then all our friends will avoid us so they can get high. But I don't think I want Marty there, though. It would change the dynamics of the girls. Don't you think?"

"Maybe so. Yeah, probably, but do what you want about that. Let's just see if we can go first. We'll have all week to suck up and work like slaves to guilt them into it. We'll have to pay one way or another, you know." Willa always had chores to do, especially on the weekends. I would always help her get done so we could play.

"Just don't mention it to Marty, 'cause he'll want to come, and I want it to be just us girls," I said. "Tommy and his friends will be in their hangout if we need them. Okay? It'll be more fun that way."

"Check. No problem," Wilma agreed.

"So let's get to suckin' up. Mother always seem to know what I'm up to anyway, so I'm just going to tell her that's what we're doing Saturday, minus the LSD part of course. I'm sure I'll have to strike some kind of deal with her and serve her all week until we can escape. You figure out the best approach with your mom, and let's get t'suckin'."

Willa and I laughed and laughed. She had the most contagious laugh. She always closed one eye as she quietly cackled, but you could see her jiggling all over.

We plotted and worked it up all week. It looked like we were a go, but Annie wasn't going to make it. She had some weird family stuff going on. She could never go anywhere and couldn't ever have anybody overnight at her house either. I had seen some bruises on her before, and I suspected her father beat up on her, her sister, and their mother.

But of course nobody talked about it. *More than one family with skeletons…*

One day I finally met Annie's father, and when I looked in his eyes, it was like he mentally slammed me against a wall. He gave off some powerful vibes that left my knees shakin'. I had never felt anything like that, and I would have loved to known what Mother would have felt coming off of him. She had already sensed fear and pain in Annie and warned me about going to her house. Mother saw it long before I did, as usual.

Marty wasn't too happy about my making plans without him, *but that's just too bad, ain't it!?* So Willa and I worked our butts off for our moms to keep things in a positive zone. Mother, of course, was suspicious. She could tell that whatever we were planning was important. We couldn't fool her, but she went with it. She knew we would be only three blocks away. Willa's mother finally said she could go, but sometimes she was bad to pull some nasty trick at the last minute. We had psyched ourselves up, and we were ready. We just had to calm down and control ourselves so they didn't get any more suspicious.

We decided that Friday night would be best, so we packed our stuff, munchies, cigarettes, and music. Beth came and got us in her mother's car, and we went directly upstairs to Beth's room.

"Tommy got what we were wanting. He and some of his friends will be here if we need any support. He called it windowpane acid. He says if we divide it four ways, it'll be plenty for your first time."

"So where is it? I want to see it," I blurted out in my excitement as she unwrapped some foil. I looked down, adjusted my eyes, and said, "You're shittin' me, right?"

"No. This is it. Strong stuff. We'll get Tommy to divide it for us. He has experience and the tools to do it."

"That's real good, 'cause I can't even see the damn thing." I was amazed at how small it was. It looked like a little pyramid, tinted slightly gray, about the size of a Chicklet. "I don't see how would be possible to split it four ways, or how it could be that strong."

"Trust me, it is," Beth said confidently. "I'll take it to Tommy now, and it'll be ready when we are. We need to do it while there's still light in the sky. It'll be amazing! I'll be right back."

She took the little foil package and knocked on Tommy's door. He opened it and was his usual asshole self. "What?!" he demanded.

"Hey, will you please split this for us? We don't have the know-how or the tools."

"Okay. Sure. I'll bring it to you in a minute. I'm on the phone right now."

"Cool, thanks."

Then he slammed the door in her face. She was used to it and learned to expect it. That was just his way.

So we turned on some Beatles and staked out our sleeping spots, party spots, music, and stuff. A knock on the door startled us, but we realized it was Tommy with our entertainment package. The pieces were so small, I wasn't sure I was even seeing them right. How could it be that these tiny little specs of plastic would do anything?

"We need to do it pretty soon while there's still daylight. Wanna go for it?" Beth looked at us and wiggled her eyebrows.

"I guess so, if ya'll want to," I said. "Willa?"

"Okay, then. I'm in." Good ol' Willa was always ready for something new.

"I just dropped, so it's now or never," Beth said.

"Dropped what?" I asked, looking puzzled.

"The acid."

"Oh shit! We'll never find that tiny little thing. Where were you when you dropped it?"

"No. 'I just dropped' means I just took it. Sorry, I forgot that you hadn't been around the lingo. When somebody says, 'I just dropped some acid,' that means they just took it. I took mine, it's your turn now if we're gonna trip together."

"Oh boy. It's really time, huh?" I asked nervously. Willa just grinned and took a gulp of water. "OK."

Where is the little suckah?

I touched a damp finger to it and put it to my tongue. It dissolved so fast I really wasn't sure if I got it or not. We kinda messed around waiting for something to happen, and I actually forgot about it for a while until I got a queasy feeling in my stomach. I looked up at Beth, and her pupils were huge, and she was grinnin' like a mule eatin' briars.

"I feel kinda nauseated," I said to the girls.

"It'll pass. That just means that you're getting off," Beth reassured me. "Let's go outside." As we followed Beth downstairs, I noticed that everything was looking real shiny. I still felt a little queasy, but I was beginning to get distracted by my other senses.

As I looked around outdoors, the sky was so blue, and the clouds had that biblical, billowing look, like I expected God himself to show up in the foreground. I couldn't take my eyes off them. They seemed to shimmer with subtle pink and purple around the edges and yellows in the centers. They seemed so alive.

I had forgotten where I was and who I was with. I managed to pull my eyes away from the sky, and found that the trees and the leaves were also amazing. How could anything be so beautiful? The tree of interest was huge, probably at least two hundred years old. Three adults probably couldn't reach around it. I stood there with my arms spread out, my face plastered on its trunk, in total amazement. This was a living thing, and I swore that I could feel the life in it. Looking up into the canopy made my eyes water with complete fascination. This tree had seen wealth, hardship, war, economic depression, drought, winters, summers from hell, and still it stood in all its glory. *If only it could talk.* I had never imagined the emotions I was experiencing over something as simple as a tree or the sky. I looked around, and my buddies were in their own little worlds too. I started toward them as they looked up at me. All I could say was, "Far fuckin' out, man. I get it!"

We started rolling around in the grass, giggling and staring at the freakin' dirt. Grass and dirt were fascinating, if you could believe that. We thought that was so funny, but it was so true. *The magic of dirt.* So many profound revelations in one afternoon.

"I gotta pee," I said abruptly. "Will ya'll go with me?"

I was having some difficulty walking. The ground was closer than it appeared to be, or something. We started around the front of the house when I felt the hair tingle on my head. As I looked up, I'll be damned if it wasn't Ted across the street, slinking around a tree. That son of a bitch had been watching us. *Damn it all to hell.* I freaked out and bolted into Beth's house, with Beth and Willa on my heels. I was hyperventilating when we got upstairs to her room. Talk about a bummer. I had seen hell and torment in his soul, and I will never forget what that felt like. It was as if we were standing toe to toe, and I was being sucked into a dark vacuum. But I had quickly broken the contact. It was hard to say if seconds or minutes had passed because my concept of time was so distorted, but the volume of information that transpired was incredible.

It took me a long time to get over that encounter and just chill out. We put on some music, which helped. Tommy had some cool black light posters and a black light that he shared with us when the sun went down; he seemed to get a kick out of turning us on to stuff. That helped me recover too. I felt safe upstairs with the girls, and they knew I needed a major distraction. The posters were definitely a distraction, seeing as how they all seemed to be moving in their own worlds. Whoever designed those things definitely knew about tripping! We got a real kick out of everything we encountered, and we laughed until we were weak from it. Poor Willa, all she could do was laugh. At one point we were drawn to looking at ourselves in the mirror. *Oh my God, not a good idea!* But we couldn't stop for the longest time. Until the phone rang. *PANIC!* You'd have thought it was a hand grenade or something.

Nobody wanted to answer it, because we weren't sure if we could talk coherently. All we could do was stare at it like some mentally challenged patients who had escaped from an institution. Finally Tommy rescued us and answered it for us. Thank God it wasn't my mother. I don't think my nerves could have handled anything else that day.

We tripped pretty hard for at least eight hours, not including the coming down period. We weren't able to eat much of anything because food was so weird that we couldn't stop laughing about it. I tried smoking a cigarette, but it felt as fat as a cigar and tasted like shit. However, it was fun watching the trails from the lit end as it moved in the dark. You could almost write your entire name with it in the air before it disappeared. *So strange, yet so cool.* We all knew as we tripped our asses off that our lives would never be the same, for we would be seeing the world through different eyes from now on.

Music was also a new experience. It was as if I had never really listened before that day, and music had always a big part of our lives growing up. But this was something entirely new for me. I could hear every instrument, every note. How did the brain decipher all this information? *Who the hell knew, and who the hell cared?* It was just amazing, and all three of us wanted to do it again. But not that night. We had heard that you don't get off if you do it two days in a row. Besides, we were tired, and our brains felt fried from too much input. We just wanted to sleep, and eventually we did. I had dreams of colorful and happy things, and that was a refreshing change for me.

The first thing I thought of when I awoke was Ted. Had I really seen him? I noticed that Willa and Beth were stirring too, so I asked them, "Did I really see Ted yesterday across the street?"

"Yeah, hell yeah he was across the street," Willa said, "but when he realized we saw him, he started slinking down the street like he didn't notice us. I wonder if he could tell that we were tripping. I mean we *were* hugging trees and staring at dirt, you know."

"Oh, he noticed us all right," I confirmed. "He and I zoomed in up close like and connected mentally. What I saw in his eyes freaked me totally out. I'm sorry I freaked and ran, but that was like some Alfred Hitchcock stuff. I don't care if he knows anything, 'cause I know a lot more on him, believe me."

I had never zoned into somebody's head like that, and I wish like hell it had been somebody else's, 'cause he was one very sick dude. It made me more afraid of him than before, and it reminded me of my mother and her ability to probe people's heads. But it was just too weird for me in Ted's case, especially in my condition at the time.

"I'm as hungry as a wolf, how 'bout ya'll?" I needed to get off the Ted subject.

"Oh, hell yeah," both the other gals chimed in. So we headed downstairs as if we were no different than we were yesterday and attacked the fridge. Beth's mom was still up from working all night at the hospital, and she sweetly assisted us in finding food products ASAP. She was going to be off that night, so she wasn't in such a big hurry to go to bed yet. *God bless her, our angel of mercy!* We ate like a pack of wolves and laughed and enjoyed being together. Life was really good.

Chapter Nineteen

When I got home that afternoon, I was still feeling pretty burned out mentally. Certainly not incapacitated, but a bit slow and fuzzy. I called Marty, and he wasn't too happy that he had missed out on the trip, but we agreed to do it together sometime. I was ready to try some of that pot he had been telling me so much about. He said he would bring some over, and we could take a ride over to a friend's house. I was in desperate need of more sleep, so he agreed to come over around suppertime, and we would figure it out from there.

That evening, we took a ride over to Howard's house. Marty said he was cool, and I had figured as much by his long hair and the way he had been dressing lately. Howard was a rich kid with access to too much money, which seemed to be the case with so many of the Freaks back then, including Marty. They weren't like me in that regard. I didn't have access to money. I had to earn it, and I didn't get much when I did.

When we arrived at Howard's parent's home, we found that he had a hippie pad upstairs. His parents apparently just looked the other way and never even considered coming into that room. It still made me nervous as hell, but they kept saying that everything was cool, baby. Howard lit up a joint, and we passed it around and around while we listened to Jimi Hendrix on a really nice stereo system. The guys started getting off right away, but I just sat there waiting for something to hit me in the head like it apparently had hit them. Nothing happened. I was disappointed that I couldn't feel anything from the smoke, but they reminded me—as if I needed it by now—that it takes a few times before you get off on pot.

"Well phooey," I said, admitting only to myself that I had really wanted to get high this time. I was already starting to like the idea of an altered state of being. I told them all about my first LSD trip and how much I enjoyed it.

"Sounds like you had a really good first one," Howard said.

I could tell Marty was watching me closely, like he was trying to read my mind and emotions. "I was hoping we could spend the night together at the Mullinax's this weekend," he said tentatively. "We could try smoking again, and we'd get to sleep together for the first time."

"Oh really?" I responded, startled by the sudden but not surprising turn to the topic of sex. "And when did this development occur?"

"Rocky, Margaret, and I were talking about hooking up with our dates this weekend, and they said they would love to have us come too," Marty explained. "Just the six of us, so everybody would have a private room. Think you can work that out with your parents?"

"I don't know," I said, really not trying to be evasive this time. I really didn't know if I could get away two weekends in a row. "I spent the night with Beth this weekend already, but I'll try. You know I'm not on any birth control, so if we do *it*, you are going to have to—"

"I've got it covered. Literally," he grinned, and then we all busted out laughing, especially him and Howard. I was rather embarrassed about the whole thing. Up till that moment, Howard was fiddlin' with something, acting like he wasn't listening to us, and I had almost forgotten he was there.

"Let's talk about something else, okay? This is too weird," I said when I got over my embarrassment. "I wish I had gotten off on the pot. Now I smell like dog shit for nothing."

"Keep trying," Howard assured me. "It'll hit you one day soon. Be ready, 'cause when it does, you're gonna laugh your ass off."

"I did that all last night with the girls," I said, smiling at the memory. "My stomach actually hurts from laughing so much. Is it gonna be like that?"

"Not for so long, just for a little while. It's a lot different from acid, not so debilitating."

"Thank God, 'cause we were without a doubt mentally challenged," I replied. "For hours. I started to wonder if I would ever get back to being normal. Not that I particularly wanted to come down, but I started to feel burned out, you know."

"Oh, I definitely know," Howard said. "You're a good head. You'll have fun with pot, I'm sure of it."

"I guess you'd better take me home, Marty," I said when I had finally given up on getting high. "I have some things to do, and I gotta start suckin' up to Mommer again if I'm going to have a chance at next weekend. Can you drive safely like this?"

"Sure, no problem," he said. I knew he had done it before, but I still had to ask. "All I've had is that little bit of pot. Let's go then."

We got back to my house and relaxed in the kitchen with the little TV on while we looked for munchies. Mother had made some strawberry turnovers from some local ripe strawberries.

Oh my God! I gotta learn how to make these things.
"I sure feel hungry," I told Marty. "My mouth and throat feel dry and parched. What's up with that?"

"It's part of the pot smoking deal. It's called the munchies. Or the dreaded munchies. Or the screaming munchies. Or whatever..." He was still pretty high apparently.

"Great, that's all I need, to be starving all the time. God, these turnovers are so good! And I didn't even get off yet, but I sure have the killer munchies. This is bad." I was grinning as I said it. *Another contact high, I guess.* While we ate, we kissed and fooled around under the table, until Mother ran him off.

This weekend was going to be exciting and scary—if I could go at all. I wasn't too sure what to think or do. Margaret called me the next day and formally invited me to come over, and she was quite frank about the sleeping arrangements and the activities. She said that if I had any questions, please just ask. She apparently had some experience in the sex department, as well as the illegal substances department. So okay then, at least I would have some females to interact with who were experienced. Later on in the week, I told Mother that I was going to spend the night with my sorority friends. It was time to start plans for rushing for the high school sororities, and I told her it was most important.

Damn, she fell for it! I think she was just tired of fighting and worrying. After all, I was the fifth child and a real BIG surprise when my parents found out she was pregnant at the age of forty-two.

So that was easy, now if I just don't get caught.

That night, my brother David called with all kinds of bad news about his gang of convicts. Bonnie had been a Type I diabetic for years, but it had rapidly progressed from moderate to severe, with all kinds of subsequent system failures, and she had to be hospitalized. Mack was already in a prison in Texas for hardcore underage criminals. Kathy had been caught stealing some clothes in Texas, but she didn't have to do any time. Sherri and Mandy were okay, but David was totally overwhelmed. They had decided that next summer they would come to visit us, after Bonnie's health got stabilized. *God help us. Again!* Then he asked Mother if she could come down to help for a while. As soon as possible.

She agreed without hesitation, although she dreaded it, and she didn't know what to do with me. I told her I would be fine. I could stay with friends or they could stay with me. *Should be interesting.*

I hadn't been alone for more than a few hours in my life, especially since Ted had been sniffin' around. I had already decided, before seeing him while I was tripping, that I had had enough of his nasty shit. That experience, while scaring the hell out of me, had galvanized my resolve and somehow strengthened me. I wasn't going to be afraid any more. I was going to continue standing up to him, and wound him as often as possible. He'd better hope I didn't have access to a gun, because now I was pissed off enough to shoot him in the nuts. And I would really hate to go to prison over him. *Talk about pissed off.* I was ready to blow the whistle on him or blow him out of the water, one or the other.

Mother had agreed, with reservations, to let me spend the night with Margaret, thinking it was a sorority thing. *Sure.* My nerves started working overtime about the sex thing. I talked to Margaret about birth control, since she was older and more experienced than me, and she offered to help. She recommended that I go ahead and call the health department and get an appointment with family planning. That way I could get on the Pill without my parents knowing, and it was free. *Cool!* In the meantime, we'd have to use condoms. *That should be interesting.*

So again, all week, I went t'suckin' up, so Mommer didn't get pissed and change her mind. She had been known to do that from time to time, and I wasn't taking any chances. I had to reiterate how important this "meeting" was to me and the sorority. Everything seemed to just click into place. Part of me, the scared part, was kinda hoping I could weasel out of it for now, but NOT! So I just went with it.

I may as well get it over with, 'cause worrying about it is gettin' old.

Marty picked me up Saturday evening, and we arrived at the house of sex and drugs with our overnight stuff. It appeared that nobody was there yet, not even Margaret. But Marty knew what to do and where to go. I was scared half to death. I followed him to our room, and he was on me like a duck on a June bug before we could close the door.

Whoa!

"Hold up man! Jesus!" I protested. "I have things to do first, so just get a grip and chill out a little. How do we know that nobody is gonna come bustin' in here, 'cause right now I am about as nervous as a cat in heat? Okay?"

"Sorry," he said without looking it. "But I have really been looking forward to this."

"Well, I'm terrified, but I'm willing if you have the protection that we need. Just tell me that nobody is gonna come bustin' in here. And you'd better mean it!"

"It's cool, baby. The parents are in Atlanta for the whole weekend, and they have already called from down there and said they made it okay. We're cool, okay?"

"Okay, but I'm still nervous. Is there something that will help me relax? Some wine or something?"

"They've got some Seconal," he offered.

"I don't know what that is, but I don't believe that's what I had in mind." The nerves cranked up even more at the mention of yet more drugs. "What have I gotten myself into?"

"Quit worrying. Everything is gonna be all right. Just relax."

"Yeah, uh huh! Why not just knock me out and cover me up when you're through?"

"Because that wouldn't be as much fun. Fun, but not as much fun," he said, grinning. "But I'll take what I can get at this point."

I slapped at his arm and said, "Very funny. Where's the pot? Maybe that'll help me relax."

"I have a doobie rolled right here," he said as he grinned and lit up. He handed it to me, and getting up he said, "Maybe we should smoke it on the porch so we don't stink up the house."

"Good plan. It would smell like somebody tracked dog shit all through the house."

We took the joint outside and burned the whole freakin' thing. I stood there waiting to get off, but to no avail. "Dammit, I still don't feel anything! I think ya'll are pulling my leg about all this, cause I don't feel a thing."

"Don't worry, one day it'll hit you upside the head. Real good."

"I was hoping 'one day' would be tonight. Is there any beer or wine around?"

"Yeah, we have some of both, and their parents have a cabinet full of liquor."

"No thanks on that. I'd like to be at least somewhat aware of what happens. Just some wine would be good. And besides, what's the hurry with the sex?"

"The hurry? The hurry!? Oh please. We've been working up to this for months and months. I know you want to be with me. Do you really love me?" he suddenly asked.

"Of course I love you. I can't imagine being with anybody else. I'm just nervous. You know, the nervous virgin. I'm supposed to be, right?" I asked, trying to calm myself down. "I guess we just muddle our way through this, huh?"

"That appears to be the popular way of thinking. I've never done this either, but I do know what to do. Let's just be like we always are, but this time, we don't have to stop, and we won't have on clothes. Okay? It'll be nice."

"Jesus help me," I muttered. "Well, the lights will need to be off or down real low, or I'll be too embarrassed to live."

"Okay, baby. Anything you want," he said. And I actually believed he meant it.

We went back up to the bedroom, and I started to relax some. The wine helped the anxiety level, and soon we were getting all hot and bothered. It was fun, but all I could think about was the "doing it" part. We finally got to that part, and he apparently knew what to do with the condom. I guess guys practice when they're young so they'll be ready. I dunno, but it went on without a hitch.

The rest was kinda…well…somewhat lacking is the best I can say. I didn't know what all the commotion was about, but I wasn't too impressed when it was over. It left me feeling worse than before. I got the feeling that he enjoyed it wa-a-ay more than I did.

So let's do it again…

Apparently you have to wait a while before you can do that. Well, by then I couldn't have cared less. I had lost interest. But since we had the time and place, we went at it again. Same as before. My immediate thought this time was, *This sucks, get off me,* but I kept it to myself. It would be years before I knew what to do and how. I guess many of us young ladies went through that. It's a wonder we even kept trying, 'cause *damn*, that sucked. I was getting frustrated just thinking about it.

I knew there had to be more to it than that. I thought it was supposed to hurt. NOT! That ought to tell you something about the state of things. During the third and final session, all I could think about was getting me some hippie clothes, bell-bottoms, halter tops, and stuff. My parents were probably going to freak out, but that stuff had more appeal to me. Hell, it appealed more than sex apparently, 'cause here I was having these thoughts while... The weird part was that when we were done at last, I still felt like a virgin.

Bummer, man.

I still felt love for Marty. Always had, always will. I knew we'd figure it out, 'cause we were tight. Especially now that we had smoked dope together and had sex, such as it was. There were new, special bonds between us. But to summarize the whole affair: I'd had better times. What a disappointment. I couldn't get off on anything. Pot, sex...

When it was time to get home, I knew I had to avoid the Noni brain-probing big time. So I decided rather than being defensive to go on the offense. As soon as I got home and put my things away, I went straight to Mother's room and told her I needed to do some shopping. I had made up my mind while at Margaret's to start changing the way my clothes looked. I was tired of being the little sorority princess. I needed to get some hip-hugger bell-bottom jeans ASAP. Also, I wanted some material so I could make some halter tops.

My plan worked, and soon, off we went, two females on a mission. I got my jeans. Now all I had to do is drag them behind the VW to soften them up a bit. Back then, jeans were thick and stiff as a board when they were new. They were dyed dark blue, which would rub off on the crotch of your panties until it washed out. And that could take weeks, maybe months. Mother had a huge box of material scraps that I used to make halter tops for me, Willa, and Beth. I was good with the sewing machine, and soon I had turned several different scraps of material into the latest fashion fad. Of course, Mother almost had a coronary when she saw us girls sporting our new look.

And Ted was rather pathetic. He was running into everything, dropping stuff, stuttering, and for once I didn't care that he was staring at me. Now, rather than being embarrassed and scared, it felt more like a dare with an attitude. Man, were we cool chicks! Far out. Groovy, even.

I started cleaning out the basement and creating a hang out area so we could get away from the parents. We had a stack of mattresses down there to lie on. I put up some black light posters and hung a black light and a lighted Budweiser sign. I moved in my stereo, some ashtrays, a bedspread, and some chairs. We had to be quiet, but at least we could smoke and hang out in private, although Mother kept coming to the door to check on us. I guess she wanted to make sure we still had some clothes on or something.

I continued to make halter tops for me and my friends, and I started collecting patches for my jeans. A little monogramming here and there, some more patches…and before you knew it, we looked like real, honest-to-God hippies. We had to have Earth shoes too. I always preferred a shoe with a heel since I was only five feet, two inches, but they just looked tough with bell bottoms. People who knew me just a month before gave me that "What happened to you?" look. Inside, I was grinnin' like a Cheshire cat. I finally felt like I fit in, and it was with people who were kind and loving. *And high.* Some of the town's finest families were watching their kids change into Freaks. We were actually turned away from stores and restaurants on occasion because we had long hair and were braless.

Later in the summer, we made a plan to meet at the back end of one of Greenville's ritziest neighborhoods. Down near the creek, where the new golf course was to be built. Be there at 7:00 p.m. Girls, bring your bras. All of them. The plan was to build a fire, get high, dance around the fire, and burn our bras.

Sounds good to me!

The problem was getting there and back home within my strict window of opportunity. But I would break a leg to do it, I thought, not realizing how true that could turn out to be. Marty picked me up on the pretense of taking me to another sorority meeting. Fortunately I didn't live far from the rendezvous area. We parked the car at a friend's house, then walked to the creek.

"How are we supposed to get across?" I exclaimed when we got there. "And by the way, that ain't a creek, that's a river, and it's movin' fast!" I could see a camp area and some people wandering around in the woods. Then I noticed a log laid across the river from one bank to the other, and I looked at Marty.

"Yep, you got the idea," he said, seeing the look of "You have got to be kidding me" on my face. "Just don't think about it. It's easy. Don't look down, and don't stop. Keep going until you get to the other bank."

"You're joking right? That's probably twenty feet across."

"It's no big deal. We do it all the time. Just get up there and go."

I don't know why I was so worried, because I was as athletic as anybody I knew, and it really wasn't a problem getting across. The first time. But that wasn't the cause of my concern. What I was worried about was coming back over in the dark while (hopefully) messed up on pot. We got across, and there were Freaks everywhere. Some of them looked like their eyes were hemorrhaging; some looked like you could see all the way to their brains because their pupils were huge. Nothing but black pupils, with no room for the irises. One look told me they were tripping their butts off on acid. As I looked around, there were joints being passed around and a gigantic hookah with a bowl as big as a coffee cup full of pot. *If I don't get off tonight, I never will.* And boy howdy, did I ever! In about twenty minutes, I was toasted. Blitzed. Stoned out of my mind. And loving it!

We lit the fire and let it get big, then we tossed all our bras into it and watched them as they smoked up the air. We laughed, danced, kissed, and rubbed bodies until well after dark. Eventually, it occurred to me that I had to go home to the brain probe. But first I had to get across that freakin' river. I could see it sweeping me away from my beloved and all my wonderful new friends. Actually, I felt like killing him for getting me into this predicament, but I was the one who agreed to it. But I did manage to get back across on my first try, and then I worried all the way home. Paranoia had set in on the incredible high that I had been sporting, and that tends to bring you down pretty fast. I knew my eyes looked like Georgia road maps, and we were late getting back.

OH SHIT! Of course Noni was waiting at the front door.

"You're late! And what's wrong with your eyes? Marty, you were supposed to get her back before ten."

"I know," he said, hanging his head. "I'm sorry Mrs. K."

"Your eyes are red as hell," she said as I tried desperately to avoid eye contact. She always was suspicious of anybody who didn't look her straight in the eyes until they allowed the brain probe so she could decide for real if they were guilty or innocent. I was no different, and I had to come up with something quick!

"I'm not surprised," I said weakly. "I've been crying. We got in an argument. That's why we're late. I'm sorry, Mother, it was my fault."

"Well, don't do it again," she said, still looking at us both suspiciously.

"Okay, Mother. I just want to go to bed, I'm really tired."

Marty said good night, apologized once more for being late, and left quickly to avoid any further questioning. When I got to my bedroom, I realized I was still so freaking high that about all I could do was giggle in the dark. I gathered my pj's, turned off the light, and sat in my usual place in the floor to change clothes. For some reason all this crap just seemed funny to me. I had altered my life, living in fear of being seen or being touched by a pervert I had known all my life. I'd lived in the floor and in the dark, just because Mother Dearest said so.

What is wrong with this picture? And why in the hell am I laughing? After a while I started hearing things outside the house, inside the house, even in my head, and I finally wore myself down enough to sleep. I had to fight the urge to go to the kitchen and find FOOD! I had a crippling case of the munchies. We didn't have microwaves then. It had to be a cold sandwich, chips, or cook something on the stove. *Not!* Thank God the reefer high was less intense than acid and didn't last as long, so I was able to fall sleep within an hour or so…I think. But who the hell knows? I had no concept of time really, but it was real nice. That old knot in my stomach I had been carrying around for years seemed to loosen a bit.

Thine eyes have seen the glory of a whole new world. A world that seemed to fit.

Chapter Twenty

Mother was worrying herself almost sick about having to go to Texas without me, but there was no way I was going with her. The problem was how to do it without me being alone in the house while she was gone and Daddy was at work. Of course, Sara offered for me to stay with her and Ted, but I politely refused, and I think her feelings were hurt. But I really didn't care. I was able to make arrangements to stay with Beth and Willa, alternating each night. I went back home each day to check on things and see Daddy. Since he worked third shift, I just went when he got home from work and then stayed at home on the weekend when he was there all the time.

Ted stayed scarce when Daddy was home. *Imagine that.* Based on the look in Daddy's eyes when Ted was around, I was pretty sure they'd had words about the ladder, and some other things as well. I know Daddy hid the ladder so it would be harder to get out without making a lot of noise, but I still wondered how much of that had to do with Buddy's little incident years before. Poor little Buddy never did anything off color. Hell, I never even saw him in his underwear, and vice versa. He was just a wild man, a practical joker, not a sexual deviant. And boy, did I miss the hell out of him. But his new little wifey-poo didn't like us and refused to share him with us. She didn't like for him to come over and visit, but he occasionally snuck over any way. He didn't look very happy to me, kinda distant and lonely.

Meanwhile, I was thinking about how I could have more time alone with my sweetie while Mother was gone and give the sex thing another try. I was sure Sara and Diane would be policing the area, but at least it wouldn't be as if Noni was around. Nobody was like her. She was wicked perceptive and terrifying to those who defied her—or attempted to. The last thing I wanted was to get caught at whatever it was that I was trying to do by whoever was supposed to be policing. Because regardless of who that might be, I'd still have to face Noni in the end, one way or another.

But I was confident that Marty and I would be able to work out some alone time. There was something major missing from the sex, and I felt like clawing my own eyes out—or possibly someone else's. It was very frustrating stuff for me, and so far I really hadn't felt anything faintly resembling satisfaction. I was okay until we actually went through the motions, then I was so disappointed that I seriously thought about not even trying it again. But I knew I needed to give that another chance too. Actually, I was more interested in getting stoned again than I was in having sex. *Now that was fun!* But this time, no logs over rivers.

Mother had decided to stay in Texas for just a week, and then return at a later date if she was needed. She would try to take care of the house while Bonnie was in the hospital and David was working. Mandy was enrolled in a school for autistics and was doing much better, but someone had to pick her up and be at home with Sherri and Kathy and Mandy to make sure they ate, went to school, etc. Since Mack was in prison, she didn't have to deal with him. The others would be enough to deal with. Fortunately for Mother, they were in school during the day. Supposedly. So far, they had rarely felt the true wrath of Noni—only once actually—and they were in for another surprise if they crossed her. I was looking forward to getting a freakin' break from Sergeant Noni. I had to admit to myself that she had loosened the noose a bit on me lately. So far, I had been her shining star. But she didn't know that I had made a dramatic left turn recently. A turn that would lead me down a dangerous path.

Mother left on a Sunday. Daddy and I took her to the airport, and she showed mixed emotions about leaving. She was excited to go flying away, but worried about what she was being thrown into and terrified for my safety. I assured her that I was going to be fine. She had talked to everybody's mother about me staying overnight with them, so the thought police would be everywhere. *Dammit!*

My feeling was that I probably shouldn't even think about doing any hanky panky at home, but Marty had other plans. I didn't think I could relax if I wanted to, so I decided we weren't going there. He came and picked me up on Monday afternoon, and we went to Howard's to get high. He set me up for the ultimate mind-blowing by putting his Bose speakers at my head, one at each ear. We burned a doobie, and I lay down on the floor with my head between the speakers. It was even better than headphones. He put on Cat Stevens's *Tea for the Tillerman* and turned it up loud. Oh my God! He couldn't have picked a better album for me. (Well, except for maybe the *White Album* by the Beatles.) To this day, I get goose bumps every time I hear something off that album. It was almost like tripping, but without the stomach lurching or the hallucinations, and it didn't last so long.

So now I had new things to do! First of all, I had to have that album! Next, I had to get my own reefer. The main problem was that I had no money. I made a meager allowance from my parents, so I would need to get a job babysitting or something if I was going to have anything of my own.

Things were working out pretty well with me staying at Beth's and Willa's while Mother was in Texas. One night after Daddy had left for work and Beth's mother had left for work, Marty and I planned a rendezvous at my house. He had convinced me over the past few days that it would be the most private place we could find after Daddy had left for work.

We entered the house and went to the basement after turning out all the lights. We had a small lamp downstairs so we could see where we were going and what we were doing. We stood right outside the back door and burned a doobie Marty had brought over. He had no problems getting money. *Rich brat! Lucky me.* We decided it was time to get to know each other better, and we headed for the mattresses.

We figured it would be safe. We could hear if anybody was moving upstairs, and it was late so the chances of that were slim. Diane might come home and she might not. She was old enough to do what the hell she wanted. So we started kissing, and before you know it, out came the condom, and off came the clothes. Once again, I was sorely disappointed (no pun intended), but I still enjoyed the closeness of it all. But it was so quick, I just felt like screaming.

Excuse me while I peel the skin off my face again, but I just ain't feelin' it. We lay there for a few minutes, and suddenly I saw something moving out of the corner of my eye. I snatched my head around, and what did I see? *Those goddamn eyes!* Those ice blue eyes, looking through the small window over the driveway, were taking it all in. It was too late to cover up, but of course I did as I started to scream. I had to tell Marty what I saw, because he was so freaked out about me screaming and crying.

"That son of a bitch sicko!" Marty exclaimed as he tried to put his pants back on. "I can't believe he would do that."

"I know I covered all these windows," I said, no longer crying. "He knew we would be here, and he uncovered them in anticipation. I should have checked them first thing. I'm so sorry."

"It's not your fault that your sister married a pervert," Marty said as he ran over to the door and looked outside. "I worry about you all the time because of him. And he's gone, not a trace."

"I don't think he would hurt me, however I *will* hurt him," I said firmly. *And I have hurt him.* "He just gets his rocks off on peeping in on anybody and everybody."

"I don't care," Marty said as he got more and more agitated. "I'll kill him if I get the chance."

"Be my guest."

"I think I'll turn him in to the police," he said, more thoughtful now. "Let them follow him around. They'll put him in prison."

"No, you can't do that," I implored him.

I can't believe I'm having to say this!

"I'm sworn to secrecy. Why do you think I have a deadbolt on my bedroom door? Huh? Mother won't let us talk about it or turn him in, because of Sara and the kids."

"Fuck that!" Marty retorted. "He needs to be somebody's bitch in prison. Let him see how he likes that."

"Really, Marty!" I said, slapping his arm lightly. "That's just nasty! Anyway, just let it go. We'll just have to be more careful in the future." But I could still see the anger seething in his face. "Please, just let it go. For me, not for him."

"Okay," he said after a long pause, "but if I catch him again, I'm gonna shoot his nasty ass. I'll kill the son of a bitch."

"Shoot to kill then, and for God's sake, don't get caught," I offered. "Then my sister and the kids would be okay with the life insurance. If he goes to prison or is disabled, she's screwed, and that means we're screwed because they'll have to live here or some shit."

"That's fucked up," Marty insisted.

"Believe me, nobody knows it more than I do!" I said. "I just look forward to getting away from here. Away from him. Take me back to Beth's please. I feel like I'm in a fish bowl here, and I am utterly mortified and violated. I gotta get out of here now. I love you so much," I said as he pulled me close. These tender moments were very special. Marty was a dear sweet boy, and I really did love him. And I had to admit, I liked the way he tried to protect his girl.

"I love you more," he responded as usual. "C'mon let's get out of here and get you back before something else happens. I am so sorry, babe."

"It's not your fault," I reminded him. "Let's not talk about it anymore, okay? I am so freaked out right now that I can't stand to think about it. Let's get outta here!"

"Okay, but I'm gonna—"

"Just stop it," I yelped. "Don't say another word. I don't want to know and I don't want to hear." I started to cry again. I was trying to save the big cry for later, but I just couldn't hold it in. I was so humiliated, and the reality of what had just occurred was sinking in. I'm talking crotch shot straight up, wide open beaver shot, then the actual sexual act, *short as it may have been*. How could I ever face Ted again? And would he tell anybody?

Oh hell no. Let him, then I'll lower the boom on him and his little problem...God, just kill me, please.

For the rest of the week, I stayed the hell away from our house. I now believed Ted knew where I was at all times, probably because my sisters knew where I was at all times. Or so they thought. Marty would pick me up, with Beth and/or Willa, and we would ride around and get high in the car. We could actually walk around town smoking doobies, and nobody even knew what it was. We would go to the park and hang out with the hippies and get high. I met some of the nicest people on earth during that summer. Some would play their guitars and sing while everybody sat around mesmerized. All we wanted was to be left alone. We wanted world peace, organic food, great music and drugs, and free sex. Their motto soon became mine as well: peace, love, sex, and drugs.

Of course, the police had long ago caught wind of what was shakin' down in the park, and they started busting everybody. *Bastards! We weren't hurting anybody.* But I knew that if I got busted, my ass would be grass at home. So I didn't go back to the park often, although I loved the interaction with all the good heads there. You could see the look of surprise in some of their eyes when they saw me and realized I had crossed over, and I was now one of them. I was no longer a preppie sorority girl. *Thank God. Bunch of hypocrites and ass wipes.* I had been formally initiated at the river camp when we burned our bras and crossed the log high as a kite. That night marked my rite of passage, and I was changed forever.

Marty got his hands on some orange sunshine LSD, so we planned a psychedelic trip for that week. I wanted to do it while Mother wasn't around: she was too perceptive, and it gave me the willies. So we decided to trip at Beth's, with me, Marty, Willa, and her. With her mother working third shift, we pretty much had free rein. Beth's sister was supposed to be watching us, but she really didn't care what we did. We split the orange sunshine four ways, having heard that it was some powerful stuff. And a quarter was a good trip, especially for rookies such as moi.

So here we went again, except Marty was with us this time and we had some pot. We dropped at about 7:00 p.m. It was still light outside and still hot. We hung out in the yard as long as we could, 'cause it felt so good being outdoors. The trees were magnificent again, as well as the clouds. I could see the wind this time! *Try to explain that one...* The birds were singing, and the ants marched out their missions. As we rolled around in the most luxurious grass, we giggled and told stories—or tried to.

I watched Marty closely, and he was more adorable than ever. I was so in love with him, and that meant we would surely work out the sexual deficiencies. I felt like jumping his bones right there in the yard. When finally I couldn't resist it any longer, we went up to Beth's room and explored each other's bodies far into the night.

Finally! NIRVANA! Thank you, Jesus!

I had my first orgasm, and boy did I want more of that! We could hear the girls entertaining each other, now and again getting really quiet and then an explosion of laughter would erupt. Marty and I laughed at his Fred Flintstone feet till we were weak from hysteria. I swear, they looked exactly like 'em, and he took it well, so we ran with it.

We did the music thing with the speakers up next to our ears. *Oh my God!* We were super high on pot and acid and real glad we didn't have to drive anywhere or talk to anybody else. And glad we didn't do any more acid than we did. I felt so safe there, where I couldn't be seen through a window. I could walk around freely without fear, but I still had a feeling that Ted had been snooping around. Ted was always snooping around. None of us had seen him, though, and I had lots of things to distract me. I saw lots of colors and patterns. Textures and beautiful colors within them. Everything was fascinating, and Marty was as fun as the girls. It felt good, and he fit in just fine. He showed us the ropes too. Turned us onto a lot of stuff that he had already experienced with drugs. I started wanting to draw the things that I had seen, so that's what I did. All the black light posters made a lot more sense now. I spent years drawing patterns with colors, paisley patterns, birds and trees with patterns…you name it, I drew patterns.

Chapter Twenty-One

Mother returned from Texas a couple of days later, on a Sunday afternoon. I was glad to see her, but I knew my freedom was going to suffer. I had gotten a taste of it, and I had really liked it. She was dawg tired when she got home. She said that Bonnie was back home and doing better, and that was good to hear. She and I piled up on her ginormous bed, and we slept the afternoon away like two beached whales.

Later on that evening, I was cleaning up my room and I found the pearl-headed hatpin buried under some stuff on my dresser. *Oh hell yeah! That's what I'm talkin' about. It's time to use this bad boy, and it should be in short order.*

Like a sign from God, good ol' dependable Ted showed up at the front door, just as I knew he would. He knew it was Mother's first night home, and he had come to suck up to her as usual. I opened the front door to let him in and turned to close the door. Quick as an eastern diamondback rattlesnake and twice as pissed off, I whipped back around behind Ted with that needle in my fist. I buried that sucker all the way to the pearl in the left cheek of his ass. I felt my knuckles touch his pants as I turned loose, leaving it right where it was. Intact, as it were. It was the most satisfying thing I had done since the Final Net, definitely more satisfying than sex had been. Well, most of the time anyway. Ted let out a scream that scared even me. All I could do was laugh and say quietly, "When are you going to learn to leave me the hell alone?"

"What the hell was that?" Mother inquired as she almost ran into the living room.

"I dunno, Mother," I said, trying to sound innocent. "Why don't you ask Ted?"

"Ted, what's the matter?" Mother asked, catching on to me quickly.

"I think I must have stepped on a nail or something," Ted replied. "I need to go to the bathroom and look at my foot." To my immense satisfaction, he had tears in his eyes when I looked at him, but I could tell he was pissed.

"Okay, sure. Do you need any help? I'll get you some band-aids or whatever. Let me know," Mother offered.

"Thanks, Nora," he tried to say calmly, but I know it was difficult for him. He was limping toward the bathroom. I followed him as far as Mother's bedroom and sat down on her bed. When she came in behind me, I tried not to look her in the eyes, but she had that way of drawing me in and I couldn't resist. When our eyes met, hers had a little twinkle that let me know she was on to me. Not one word was exchanged at that point. I just curled up beside her after she lay back down, and we watched TV as if nothing had happened. But I was about to burst out laughing. We heard Ted through the bathroom door, cussin' up a storm. I guess he was trying to get that four-inch nail out of his ass. He left without speaking to us after about five minutes. Then she asked me, "What did you do to him?"

"Remember that biiiiiig hat pin you gave me when I was ten?"

"Yes," she said, then it hit her. "No you didn't..."

"Yes, I did. Let's just say I don't have it any more. I believe Ted has it."

"My God! No wonder he screamed so loud. Scared me to death."

"Screamed like a little girl, huh?" I said proudly. "Very effective and very satisfying too. I need more of those." And at last I couldn't help but break out in hysterical laughter. Mother did too, once she got over the shock of what I had done.

"You are truly evil, my daughter."

"No, Mother, I'm pissed. And don't preach. It was just something that had to be done."

I wished I knew where all this was leading, but what I did know for sure was that I'd had enough. I would continue to hurt Ted every chance I got. Luckily, I was terrified of guns, so that wasn't an option. I probably should have started some kind of therapy, 'cause that man was making me nuts. I was becoming more and more like Mother, getting mean. And more aggressive. Like my Daddy used to say, "A woman is the meanest animal alive, because no other animal could bleed for that long and not die."

So look out, Ted, 'cause I mean business.

By late July, I started getting invitations to the high school sorority rushes. *Oh my God.* It was something I used to think I would enjoy, but now I dreaded. I went to a couple of them. The first was the really rich, upper crust group. All of the rushees met the sorority girls at the local mall to hang out and get to know each other. Silly girls. At one point, they gathered around the rushees, holding hands and singing some Kumbaya shit in the middle of the mall. It was some sorority song that was so special they all got teary eyed. *Jesus, please rescue me.* The other sorority wasn't as sappy, but still, it wasn't my game anymore, and they knew it. I didn't get invited again, and at least I didn't have to lie about why I wasn't going to join.

It would soon be time to get ready for school to start. The new and improved moi would be a real shocker to my peers. I made more halter tops and got my jeans in perfect condition with new patches. I got a back-up pair along with a blue jean jacket and sewed some patches on both of them. I also got Mother to buy me some cool shoes that looked good with big bell-bottoms.

Beth was working on getting ol' Bertha to herself, her mother's Chevy Bel-Air tank, as her mother was going to get a new car. I was hoping to ride with her as much as I could when we started back to school. Until now, Willa's older sister Laura Ann used to take us most of the time. Laura Ann was a damn scary ride. She would nearly wipe out every fence, mailbox, and parked car within a five-mile radius of our house, including Diane's little Kharmen Gia that she backed into once. We were often late getting to school as a result of her driving.

Meanwhile, we spent our free time riding around a lot, getting toasted on pot. Every time Mother got a good look at my eyes she would say, "What's wrong with your eyes? Are you on drugs?"

I would always respond with, "Of course not. We've been swimmin' at the Y. They always put too much chlorine in the water." And she bought that for a while. But it wasn't as easy to hide when I had been doing acid. She *knew* something was not right when my pupils were so huge that you couldn't even see the green of my eyes. We started going to concerts as much as possible and would always drop some acid on the way there. We had a lot of fun—or at least what I remember was fun. One concert that stands out in particular was Alice Cooper's Billion Dollar Babies tour. Not a good one to see on acid; I had permanent damage just from that concert alone. Not to mention the many others that we attended. Or sort of attended, as the LSD had a way of making me feel displaced. Another concert I especially enjoyed was the Allman Brothers Band. I got to see them before Duane died, and it was awesome, a definite high water mark for my musical experiences.

One rainy day, Beth, Annie, and I were riding around, getting high, and having a good time with the music blaring. We were pumped; we had us a bag of good pot and a car with gas. What else did we need? One of our favorite songs came on the radio, and we started jiving to "Slippin' into Darkness," by War. Well, just as that chorus started, we were singing, "Slippin' onto…holy shit!" The car hit a crack in the concrete, and we started slippin' into a complete 360-degree spin in the middle of a very busy road. We hardly had time to panic, and the car righted itself, going in the correct direction as if nothing ever happened. *Alrighty then…*

That was probably another one of those permanent brain imprint things. We all had a lit cigarette, a drink, and we were passing a doobie around, singing and jamming, when the car started spinning. But we never missed a lick.

Later I wondered if that really happened, and I asked Beth some years later about it, and she confirmed. I figured since she was driving, she would definitely remember, and she shivered as she recalled it like it was yesterday. There is so much that I don't remember about the '70s, but it really wasn't apparent to me until my friends and I got together when we were older and reminisced. At times I couldn't recall a thing about what the others are laughing hysterically over.

Kinda scary, ain't it?

But I didn't do any more drugs than they did, and maybe not as much. I now blame it on a head injury I sustained in a car accident when I was visiting friends in Chapel Hill, North Carolina, later on in life. I think it wiped out a good bit of memory from those days. Still, what I remember was mostly good.

In August of that summer, Willa asked me to go to the beach for a long weekend with her, her mother, Tammy Lynn, and her Aunt Mary. The family owned a house at Fripp Island, a really plush, high-end resort, barrier island. Mother, surprisingly, agreed to let me go. And, of course, Willa and I dropped some acid right as we were getting in the car to go. Her mother was driving, Tammy Lynn was riding shotgun, and Willa and I were tripping our asses off in the back seat. *What the hell were we thinking?* That had to be the longest five hours of my life up to that point in time. First we had the nausea thing that lasts about an hour, then the lower stomach thing that makes you feel like you have to take a massive dump. Then we got the giggles, we had trouble understanding anybody, and at last we had to pretend we were sleeping for the rest of the trip.

When we finally got there, I felt like screaming with joy. We grabbed our stuff out of the car, found the bedroom we would be sharing, and dumped everything so we could get the hell out of there and enjoy what was left of our LSD trip. Willa showed me around and Wow! There was a pool on the roof with a glass bottom directly over the bar in the kitchen and glass on one side facing into the game room. *Cool!* We had to clean it first, but we didn't mind 'cause at least it got us out of the house. The next day we managed to get enough water in that sucka to have some fun. It was hotter'n blue blazes in August on the South Carolina coast, and this house was on the golf course, not the beach. No breeze whatsoever and the no-see-ums and ravenous blood-sucking mosquitoes would skeletonize you within a matter of minutes. We didn't bring or buy any bug sprays or anything like that. Hell if I know why, but as long as there was a breeze, you were generally okay.

But we didn't care. We were ecstatic about the pool, and when we finally got in to cool off, Willa said, "Go down to the kitchen. I want to show you something. Just look up into the pool floor and watch this."

"Okay," I said, though I really didn't want to get out yet. I did a quick towel off and went into the kitchen where everybody was hanging out. I looked up into the pool and said, "Willa said she was going to surprise us." We all gathered around and looked up. We saw a splash and then saw Willa. NEKKED as a jaybird! She was standing where we could see the bottom of her feet, and she suddenly jumped up, then we saw her come down and do the most beautiful labia kiss onto the glass bottom of the pool. *Holy shit!* Hopefully it would be the *only* labia kiss I would ever see. All of us were stunned, and thankfully it was all women in the group. Tammy Lynn shrieked, her mother shrieked, and all I could do was turn a whole spectrum of reds. I turned and ran up to the roof to find Willa laughing hysterically, and finally I was able to crumble into a fit of hysteria as well.

"Now it's your turn," she said as she got control of her laughter.

"Oh. Hell. No. That ain't gonna happen. That was the most obscene thing I have ever seen, and I thought your mother was going to faint. She did that Southern swoon thing with one hand on her brow while the other fanned her face. It was hilarious! I don't know what was funnier, you or the looks on your mother's and Tammy Lynn's and Mary's faces. And probably mine too."

"Come on, do it," she prodded me.

"No way, chick!"

"Okay then, I'll do it again." And she did, several more times, until her mother came up there and said, "NO MORE, Willa! That's quite enough. We're trying to eat lunch, and now we're all feeling rathah nauseous." Willa and I thought it was funny as hell, but apparently nobody else did. We did some skinny dipping later on in the evening, but no more butt plants on the kitchen ceiling.

The next day, Willa, Tammy Lynn, and I went horseback riding. It was one of those deals where the horses knew the trail and they did whatever they wanted to do, even though we were supposed to be driving. Willa and I burned a big doobie before we left. It was so very hot, and at first we were getting eaten alive by mosquitoes and no-see-ums. But soon we could feel the breeze picking up and figured we must be getting close to the beach. Suddenly, we broke out of some trees and bushes, and there it was. What a beautiful sight, a South Carolina barrier island beach. When the horses saw the water, they took off like lightning, headed straight for the water. They went out pretty deep, to the point where we lifted our feet up so they wouldn't get wet. Then the horses' tails went up, and they started emptying their bladders and bowels at will. When they were finished, they decided to take off at a full trot along the beach, then a gallop. They were running straight for a real wide and pretty high jetty, and I realized there was no way around it, so…

"Uhhh, Willa?" I yelled. "Tell me we aren't going over that."

About that time, the horses really dug in and hauled ass. "We are all going to die!" I yelped. Willa, Tammy Lynn, and I all screamed as we sailed beautifully over the rock jetties, and we continued screaming long after we had landed on the other side. "Holy shit, that scared the hell out of me," I said. Tammy Lynn was crying, and I almost was. "Do we have to go back that way?"

"I am afraid so, my friend," Willa answered. "All you can do is hang on for dear life. These horses have been taking the same path for years, and to them, that's the fun part. I've always enjoyed it, too."

"That's easy for you to say," I said. "You actually have legs to hang on with. Mine are so short that I can barely reach the stirrups, and I feel like I am going to fall off even at a trot. Maybe we can adjust the stirrups."

"Probably can. Let's see," she said as she drew her horse up and dismounted. "They're almost up as far as they'll go, but let's take 'em up all the way. It'll help." I held her horse while she adjusted my stirrups.

When I remounted, I said, "Damn, that is better. I wish we had done that earlier, I might not have had that heart attack back there. Jeez…"

We continued up the beach for a bit, just long enough to get good and relaxed, when the horses all turned around and headed back down the beach. It truly was a beautiful thing. That is, until I felt and saw the horses tense up and start getting all excited. They were communicating among themselves, no doubt saying, "Last one over is a rotten egg!" They knew the drill, and all you could do was hold on tight as they geared up for the big jump. The second time it didn't seem *as* scary. For one thing, my stirrups felt more secure, but also I knew what to expect. It was still one of those sphincter moments when we were in midair, seeing those huge, sharp boulders below us. All in all, it was a hell of a lot of fun, but I didn't think I cared to do it again.

The next day, we walked all over hell and half of Georgia, as Mommer used to say. We started walking all over the golf course and saw some gators. We had already heard about them being all around the brackish waters, and with all the water hazards on the golf course they were everywhere. We kept going until we got to the beach, where we spent the rest of the day. The South Carolina August sun cooked us good. *Jeez…*

Riding back home was a bitch with our raw backsides, but at least we didn't trip on LSD this time. That was such a waste of a good hit of acid. Bummer…

I was ready to see my sweetheart, ready to go back to my little hell on earth. We'd had a large time, but it was time to get ready in earnest to start the tenth grade. Time to introduce our new fall fashion line to the preppies. *They're gonna just love the new nipple effect*, I thought as I drifted off to sleep in the back seat.

The great escape. Sleep.

Chapter Twenty-Two

Coming back home after so much fun at the beach was pretty damn depressing. Marty was still cute and so sweet, though. I was so glad to have him in my life. Kinda like a life raft or something, a hope for some kind of normalcy and maybe a future with him. We got together frequently, with friends and without. He had one buddy named David that he ran with, perhaps too much. David was probably not the best influence, but he seemed like a nice guy. He loved to get too high though. He would smoke reefer till he was just plain stupid. He smoked from the time he woke up in the morning till whenever and wherever he passed out. He chain-smoked doobies every time we got in the car. When we got to where we were going, his famous arrival was to open the door and fall out on his head while smoke billowed out from the open car. He would just lay there until we came around and picked him up. It was a sick combination of funny and pitiful, and to this day, I don't know how much of it was for fun and how much of it was real.

His routine got a lot of the wrong kind of attention that we really didn't need. The rest of us were more in control because we had at least one parent who would beat the hell out of us if they caught wind of us doing drugs. David just had a mother who worked all the time. He also had a little brother and two sisters. His older sister, Ruth, used to run with us sometimes. She was nice enough, but very manipulative, and I wasn't too sure about her motives. We were all starting to dread going back to school, 'cause we were now old enough to do some things on our own and had gotten used to some freedom.

"Who's taking you to school today?" Mother wanted to know. I think she was torn between suspicious and old and tired these days. She was suffering with the symptoms of menopause and had become just plain lazy.

"Beth," I responded as I tried to get out the door quickly before she got a good look at how I was dressed.

"Come here and let me see you." She spun me around and said, "Your titties look so…TOO DAMN PURDY! Where the hell is your bra? You are not leaving this house like that. Go put it on. NOW!"

"Oh, Mother, you know I can't wear a bra with this top," I protested. "It ain't gonna happen. I'm wearing my blue jean jacket. Nobody will be able to see anything any way."

"Well, don't stick your titties out." Which was the exact opposite of what she usually told me to do. "Just keep 'em covered. Heaven help me. And cover up your belly! And don't let your Daddy see you going to school like that. Dear Lord, he would have a stroke." Mother looked like she was about to have a nervous breakdown.

"Don't worry, Mumsie," I tried to reassure her. "I'll just look like everybody else does."

The first day of school was a real shocker for everybody. Many of us had changed and were now Freaks. We looked the part with our worn-out bell-bottom jeans with patches, halter tops, long stringy hair, earth shoes, blue jean jackets with patches, and really red eyes. Whenever Beth could take us to school, we would ride around and smoke a couple of joints before school. If David was with us, we'd smoke about five of them. And I'm talking good reefer too. We would pull up to the front of the school, open the door, and David would do his famous fall into the grass while the smoke billowed out. People would back up and walk off, which we liked because we had the area to ourselves. The talk started right away because everybody knew me and I looked so totally different than before. Of course the sorority bullshit was over after the sing-along in the mall, and I was glad to be done with it. I simply did not like those people anymore.

One thing that hadn't changed was my "thang" with Marty. But that didn't stop me from at least looking around real good now and then to check out the livestock. After all, I was fifteen going on twenty-one, prematurely sexually active, and feeling my hormones. I kept seeing this one guy in particular between classes who made my heart skip a beat. I had noticed him the previous year, and he seemed to go out of his way to run into me then. I found myself doing the same now. He had the most beautiful long blond ponytail…We eventually started talking to each other in short spurts, but only as our class changes would allow. He had learned my name by now, and that made me even more nervous around him than before, because I didn't know his. I finally asked one of the upper classmen I knew and found out his name was Bill. I didn't pay any attention to the last name at the time.

He asked if I was seeing anybody, and of course now I was dating Marty. For almost a couple of years we had tried to hook up, but we were never both single at the same time. *Bummer…* But I was a one-man woman, always have been, and Marty was my first and only. But a girl could dream. I did know that if I ever had an opening, he would be the first to know.

I hated my classes for the most part that year because I didn't like most of my teachers. My first period class was biology with Miss Tripp. I liked that class. Her classroom was joined at the back with Miss Walters, and both teachers were a trip, each in their own special way. Miss Walters had a flask of liquor in her back closet, and by the end of the day, she was trashed. Miss Tripp didn't appear to participate in that, but she really didn't need to. She had a funny speech impediment that kept me in stitches all the time. She pronounced all her p's as f's, and it was a hoot. I think maybe it was due to her huge two front teeth. They were so big she had to rest them on her bottom lip when she wasn't talking. It was especially hilarious as stoned as we were every morning.

Freak that I was, I was now hanging with some of the more rebellious kids at school. If we were craving a cigarette, we could either go to the back of Miss Walter's class and stand by the window or go to the bathroom and sit by the vent. Miss Walters never even noticed that people were lined up smoking at the back of her class, some of whom weren't even her students. We didn't have air conditioning, and keeping the windows open didn't help in that deep Southern heat. It was stifling, especially after lunch when the building started heating up good. No wonder we had trouble concentrating on September afternoons.

None of my new friends were in any of my classes except Willa, who was in Miss Tripp's biology class. Where in the hell did they all go? I felt like I was naked all by myself in my little halter top without any of my other exhibitionist friends around. I had to start wearing my blue jean jacket a lot, especially when it started getting cold. The sororities had chosen their little twits for the year, and of course I had been blackballed. Even though I knew it was coming, it still kinda hurt my feelings. Still, I didn't have to act like anybody but myself, or please anybody but myself any more.

But then I was nominated again as one of the top ten contestants in the beauty pageant. *Oh Lordy, not again...*I was ready to pass the torch, lay down my crown, and play invisible, but I was obligated to do it one more time. Good thing I kept one bra.

I had also been selected for a new duty at school. Every day, Annie and I were to drop off schedules to each classroom during our study hall. I'm not sure why we were chosen, because we were both very bold with our clothing. Or lack thereof. You could hear the guys in each room making growling sounds while the girls made huffy sounds and whispered. Annie and I enjoyed it immensely. We got to show off our figures, and basically it reflected our hippie lifestyle. Back then, it was obvious who was cool and who was straight based on the length of their hair and their clothing. Finally, a style I could afford!

One evening after school, a bunch of us burned a few joints and decided we wanted to go to the Red Lobster to deal with our killer munchies. We piled into Don's family Mercedes limousine, burned a few more joints, and went to get some supper. I had never been there before, because my family never went out to eat. EVER! We were primed for it too. There were seven of us. That time of day it wasn't crowded at all, but in another hour, it would be. Don stepped up and said, "We have a party of seven please." I have to admit we were a bit loud. We had the killer cottonmouth and the giggles, and I know we smelled like dog shit too. The receptionist said, "Excuse me, I'll be right back." We stood there trying to hold it together for what seemed like forever, when finally she returned with an older gentleman. He looked at the group of us and said, "We don't serve your type here. Please leave the premises, or we will call the police and have you escorted out."

"I beg your pardon, sir?" Don said.

"I said we don't serve your kind here," the manager repeated. "Please leave or you will be escorted out by the police."

"Are you serious? We have money. I don't believe you are completely aware of the ramifications of what you are doing, sir. You will be getting a phone call from my father, that I can assure you." He sounded like his father, who was a lawyer, when he got serious. Don's family was loaded, and he was not used to being turned away anywhere.

"We don't want your money here," the manager said as he turned on his heels and walked to the phone as if to call the police.

"Well, you don't deserve our money, so we'll gladly go give it to somebody else," Don replied. Little did that man know we had the mayor's daughter and the son of Greenville's most prominent lawyer in our little group. Marty's dad had been one of Greenville's most successful entrepreneurs before he dropped dead at a very young age. But we didn't want to cause a scene, mainly because we were so high and had drugs on us and in the car. We tucked our tails and piled back into the limo. *But what a turd!* I really couldn't believe my ears. We weren't there to cause any trouble. We were just hungry. As we slowly followed the perimeter around the restaurant in our limo, we saw several of the employees and the manager with their mouths hanging open while they gawked at us. The old man looked a little green and a bit shocked.

We ended up at IHOP. They never turned us down. As it turned out, we were rejected pretty frequently from different establishments during the early '70s, or at least followed around like we were criminals. Looking back, I suppose we really did look pretty scary to the straights. But we were harmless and didn't want trouble. Just peace, love, sex, and drugs.

Don informed his lawyer father about the discrimination deal. He called the manager at the Red Lobster. Upon realizing just who he was talking to, he apologized profusely and asked for us to come back, saying that he would make it up to us. But by then our attitude was, "Screw you, dude," and we didn't go back. I heard later that the manager got canned. I never have been one to discriminate, especially after that experience. I felt so low class, and I was ashamed there was so much discrimination of all kinds around me. The Freaks and hippies were never that way. We were all equal, and I fit right in. Not rich, not poor, just a right fit.

Except that now I had to play beauty queen one more time, and I didn't want to fit into that profile at all. I went shopping and got an outfit. It was not nearly as smashing as the one I got the year before, but nice. Mother, of course, had to inspect me in the dressing room. "Remember, stick your titties out. They look so purdy. Turn around and let me see your butt." She slapped me on the back, "Stand up straight, suck in you tummy, titties out… Yes, this will do fine."

"Mother, please," I complained. "I got it already. I just want to get this over with. I really don't want to do this again."

"Girl, you shut your mouth! It is an honor and a privilege to even be nominated as a contestant. So you hold your head up, titties out, suck—"

"Please stop. I know, I know. I'm sorry, Mother, but I'm nervous and dreading this like the plague. I feel like I'm getting dressed up to have all my fingernails pulled out or something. And this outfit is about as comfortable as a stake up the butt."

"Maggie! That actually was funny, 'cause I know how you feel, but you shouldn't talk like that." She thought about it, and said, "Well, you probably won't win if your heart isn't in it, but that's okay too. It's an honor, so do your best. I'm still so proud of you."

"Trust me, my heart is not in it," I said. "And I really don't want to win again. I don't want the attention, and the other girls are still mad at me from last year. I would rather take a back seat on this."

"Well, run with it anyway. You never had a problem with that before. You were always at the top. You belong at the top, not with these mongrels you have been runnin' with." She gave me the brain probe as she spoke, and that always left me kinda weak in the knees. She knew that I had changed and been up to something lately. I mean really, I had gone from wearing Bobby Brooks skirt/sweater outfits and other stuff I really couldn't afford to making my own tops out of scrap material and wearing holey blue jeans. It was pretty obvious. And some of my friends looked like they'd been dumped off on the side of the road, when, really, they intended to look that way. Two of the white guys we ran with had afros bigger than any black person in town. One of them was Annie's squeeze, Kevin. He was a nice, sweet guy, and my parents were pretty fascinated and at the same time disturbed by his hair. But he was the type they could cut up with about it, and he didn't get mad. You couldn't help but like him.

Chapter Twenty-Three

I needed some play money, so I started working part time at the Plaza Theatre in the evenings. Beth quit high school, which really shocked the hell out of all of us. She went to Greenville TEC and finished with a GED. I begged Mother to let me do the same, but she went ballistic. My buddies and I started cutting school and going over to Beth's house. Our favorite thing was to trip on acid and watch Sesame Street. She started working for a local vet's office while going to TEC. I envied her so much.

Marty started wanting a guitar to play. So what did his mommy dearest get him for no special occasion at all? A Gibson Hummingbird acoustic. Then for Christmas he got a freaking gorgeous gold Les Paul electric guitar with an amp and whatever else he wanted. And he couldn't even play the damn things. He bought me a nice Christmas present too, an opal ring surrounded by little diamonds. That was a shocker. It was the most beautiful thing that I'd ever had. I'd never had anything with diamonds on it, so I was just smitten over that boy. But I was really enthralled by the drawing on the Hummingbird acoustic. I drew it and then stitched it in detail on the front left leg of my bell-bottom jeans. *Yeah, baby, one of a kind.* I gradually added patches all over my jeans as they wore out, except I never covered the art. After a year, I had a pair of jeans that was just patches sewn together, and I wore them as long as possible. I wish now that I had framed them, or at least kept them.

I finally got the beauty pageant runway thing over with. Of course I didn't place, since it was pretty much a popularity contest. I probably got some male votes and the minorities this time, but thank goodness it wasn't enough, and it was over. We were still eating a lot of acid and staying stoned as much as possible. Willa and I wanted a buzz one weekend, and I stole some of Mother's meds out of her purse. She had some good stuff, if you could find it. I didn't know what they were, but I tried one, and it didn't do anything. So I stole about eight of them, and Willa and I took four apiece one Saturday night. I never felt much of anything, and I went home.

I found out later that evening that Willa had passed the hell out from her blood pressure falling too low. Her mother called my mother and asked her what it was that we took. Of course Mother didn't have the foggiest idea what had happened. Then she started looking and realized we had taken her blood pressure meds.

That day changed things for Willa and me. The parents started monitoring us much closer, so we started having to sneak around even more. And just how did we go about that, you might ask? In a typically teenage manner: STUPID!

One night about a week later, I was at Willa's, and we crushed up some purple barrel LSD and snorted it just before eating dinner with her family. Holy shit, did we get off fast! And *real good*. I don't recommend eating baked chicken and English peas while tripping. The way the peas exploded in my mouth was very disturbing. We hurried upstairs to do our homework before we got any higher, if that was possible. I had to draw a paramecium, or what Miss Tripp called a "Faramecium." I was so high that I really didn't know what I was drawing, but I did the best I could. We stayed in her tiny bedroom for probably twelve hours, tripping our asses off. We were too high to even comprehend music or conversation. When I looked out the little window down into the yard, I saw millions of snakes crawling around in the yard. I knew they were a hallucination, but they looked so real. The best I could do was to sit in the dark, take out the contents of my purse, piece by piece, and put it all back. I did that over and over again. We were virtually helpless all night, and then had to be in Miss Tripp's class at eight in the morning. *God help me.*

Laura Ann and her wild-ass driving took us to school after we had been up tripping all night. The school seemed so dark and dismal. The echoes of all the students shoes in the halls just about made me freak out. But I held myself together, made it to Miss Tripp's class, and turned in my Faramecium and sat down. I was still very high, and my pupils were still the size of dimes. I was trying to see just how small I could get when Miss Trip called for the class to look up front. She held up my drawing, and I almost freaked out for sure when I saw it.

"Class, attention," she said in her usual sweet voice. "I want you all to see this veautiful ficture of this Faramecium that Maggie drew. Fass it around and everybody look at the detail of this s'fecimen."

I was relieved she liked it so much, and yet when I noticed everybody staring at me, I quickly turned away, hoping they wouldn't see my dilated pupils. I got an A++ on that picture and an A+ in that class that year. It's amazing what you can do when you like a subject. She kept it on the wall in the classroom for years after that, or so I heard.

Acid was becoming more rampant and more powerful. We were toasted all the time. Another batch of orange sunshine came into town. We had been forewarned that it was the most powerful, ass-kicking, mind-bending acid we had ever seen. So one weekend some friends and I did a quarter of a four-way hit while riding around in the car for hours. Real smart, huh? One of the girls who was with us had never tripped before, and she cried the entire time. Bummer, man.

If it hadn't been for that, the rest of us would have enjoyed ourselves, but I think riding in the car and all the lights were just too much for a rookie. We had to get rid of her, so we took her home for her sister to babysit. Then we were okay, at least until we had to go to our own homes.

Just go to my little hell, turn out the light, get on the floor, put on my jammies, and get in the bed. No problem. But I kept hearing things in the driveway.

Probably dear ol' Ted. I tried not to think about it so I didn't freak out. Finally, I drifted into another state, not really sleep but not normal wake. My mind was reeling, but my body didn't move. I felt like I had the answers to all the world's problems. *Interesting.*

I slept a lot on Sunday, then got up and did my homework with Willa. She missed out on the orange sunshine, but she said she wanted in next time. We were good all day for a change. We rode to school together the next morning, and when we arrived to our usual hangout in front of the school, we noticed that everybody looked real solemn, and some people were crying.

"Hey, man, what's up?" I asked the group.

"Craig is dead," Marty answered.

"Oh my God. How? What happened?" I said as my throat started to close up.

Will spoke up at last. "Several of us dropped half of a hit of orange sunshine up at Ceasar's Head Mountain. You know, enjoying the fall colors and stuff. We took blankets, guitars, drinks, and some reefer, ready to stay for the day. We walked to the falls to cool down, rinse our hands and faces, and climbed to the top to get the view. All of a sudden Craig just took a running leap off the top of the waterfall like he thought he could fly. It happened so fast, and we were so messed up there was nothing we could do but watch. He landed on a big rock in the middle of the falls. It didn't even look real. At first we all thought we were just hallucinating, and that it wasn't real, but he just laid there in a twisted little pile, not moving. We were tripping so hard. Then we panicked, because we couldn't get to him. Me, Mary, Susan, Craig, Jim, and Wendy were there." Will almost broke down again, but then he continued.

"We all were helpless and high, but we finally realized we had to go for help. There were people down below us who didn't know him, and they were screaming and crying at the sight of him, but we couldn't even talk. We kept thinking it wasn't real, that it didn't really happen. But it did. Two of us went to the ranger's station and managed to tell them what had happened, between the sobs and hysteria. We didn't mention the acid part, of course. The others stayed and tried to get to him. He died instantly, so he didn't suffer."

Will's face told the story well. He obviously had been crying off and on all night. They had been good friends. I knew Craig, but not real well. I just knew him from hanging around in the park. So sweet and now so dead. I couldn't help but cry too: the visuals I got from what Will was saying, and the look on everybody's faces, broke me down. I wondered if the others made it to school today. I didn't think I could have, especially not Susan, his girlfriend.

"Well, so much for doing any more orange sunshine," I finally said. "It's too strong. Just a quarter, and we were tripping really hard."

We were all traumatized by the news. As we continued through our weekly routines, we started hearing about others that dropped a whole hit of the sunshine and totally freaked out at an outdoor concert. Some ended up in the hospital and turned to God after total meltdowns. Somebody put his fist through a sliding glass door for no apparent reason and almost lost his arm. Another guy ran face-first into a mirror. It was a reality check for many of us.

We all backed off on the hallucinogens for a while. Reefer was still the drug of choice. At least it was safe, and nobody went crazy on it. Marty had started running with Jack a lot. I liked Jack pretty good. He was nice to me, but I felt Marty pulling away from me and toward Jack. He was spending more time with Jack than he was with me. They would hang out with us at Beth's while we all got high. They both seemed a bit distant, though I didn't think much of it at the time.

We continued to have sex as often as possible. He always had the condom at the ready, but we talked about getting on the Pill. I agreed to go to the free clinic, because I sure as hell wasn't asking Mother Dearest to take me. I wouldn't live to use the damn things 'cause she'd kill me. I made the appointment for February, which was the soonest I could get in. I was going to have to cut school to go, and hopefully I wouldn't get caught. But for now, condoms were the way. I was still having a hard time getting anything out of it, but I loved being close to him, and we would learn with time. At least I hoped so, 'cause it was frustrating as shit to have to finish the job myself after he went home. *Jeez...*

Even then, all I could think about was Ted at the window or something, and that often killed any interest I might have had.

One Saturday in January, I was on the phone to Marty, saying, "I'm going to Beth's if you want to come." What else is there to do but hang out indoors?

"Nah, I am going to Jack's," Marty said.

That cut me like a knife, 'cause it was happening too often lately. Acting all pouty didn't change his decision, but when some of the dudes in our gang started noticing our distance and sniffing around me, he started paying me more attention. But things were different somehow. I could feel a space that used to not be there. I finally made it to the free clinic and got on my pills, even though by then we weren't having as much sex as before. Cold weather made it hard to sneak out or stay in the basement, but I would be ready soon. I tried to fill in the empty space. Sometimes it seemed like old times with Marty, and sometimes it didn't.

One day I went to Beth's, and Marty agreed to come and bring Jack over to hang out. *No problem*, I thought, but I was starting to get jealous of Jack. We were listening to Jimi Hendrix and the Allman Brothers and smoking weed. Out of the clear blue, Jack asked if it would be okay if he shot up. Beth and I were like, "Huh? Whatever."

We'd never been around needles or heroin. So Jack starting getting out his works, and we watched him take the heroin, cook it down in a spoon, draw it up, and put his belt around the top of his arm as he held it with his teeth. He stuck the needle in his vein, pulled blood back into the syringe, and pushed it back in to his vein, then repeated the move. That was when I started feeling sick. I got up and ran to the bathroom and passed the hell out. I woke up with everybody except Jack looking down at me on the bathroom floor and a pounding headache where I had damn near cracked my skull on the porcelain sink.

"You okay?" Marty asked.

"What do you think?" I said as my anger welled up. "That was fucking sick, you know that? Don't ever let him do that around me again. Did you do some too?"

"No," he said. "I didn't know he was going to do that here."

"So that explains a lot, huh?"

"What do you mean?"

"Why you act so different and why you're hanging with Jack all the time. I get it now."

"I won't do it anymore. I'm sorry, Maggie."

"Anymore, huh?" I knew what that meant, and I couldn't even look at him. My heart was crushed, and I still felt like I was going to hurl. I started to cry. Jack finally made it into the bathroom and apologized. I looked up and said, "You will not ever do that again in front of me! And you leave my boyfriend alone. Got it?"

"Yeah, I'm sorry Maggie," Jack said. "I wasn't thinking about it freaking you out like that. I just needed a safe place to shoot up, and I thought ya'll would be cool with it."

"Not cool, Jack!" If I hadn't been recovering from a hard blow to the head, I'd have been up and in his face. I was mad enough to scratch his eyes out right now. "Keep that shit away from Marty."

"Okay. But he does his own thing. I don't have anything to do with what he decides," he responded with slurred words, and that pissed me off even more.

"I mean it, Jack. When I get over this, I'm gonna be fightin' mad, so stay the hell away from me and Marty. Understand?"

"Sure. I'll leave, but I need a ride. Marty, will you take me home?"

"Yeah, come on, let's go."

I looked Marty in the eyes and asked, "Are you coming back?"

"Probably not," Marty said with downcast eyes.

I looked at him and asked, "Are you going to go shoot up?"

"I don't know. Maybe," he said in a smartass tone without looking into my eyes.

"Well you go on then and maybe don't come back."

Then I curled up in the fetal position and cried some more. Beth was real quiet. I apologized when I stopped crying, but she knew it wasn't my fault. She and I were always solid. I couldn't believe how far things had gotten out of control. All of a sudden, I was scared. Scared for Marty and our relationship, scared for Jack, for our generation, and for our friends.

Chapter Twenty-Four

I went for my appointment at the family planning clinic at the health department in mid-February. I had to cut school and spend the entire day in the clinic. It seemed like everybody in Greenville County was there: black and white, Freaks and preppies, and everyone in between. It appeared we were indeed in the midst of a sexual revolution. That was my first pelvic exam. It was right up there with the stake-up-the-butt thing, but I got my pills.

I almost didn't go because I was still mad at Marty and Jack, and I didn't really trust Marty like I used to. I felt him slipping away from me.

Maybe this will help pull him back when he sees that I am trying to do the right thing.

Unfortunately, I got caught skipping school. The school called home, and Mother freaked out. She was waiting at the front door when I came home with my books in my arms. I was acting all studious and innocent, but she knew better.

"Where were you today?" It was not a question, it was a demand.

I knew I was caught, and there was no use lying about school, because that just made things worse. But I still lied about *where* I was. I said I was at Beth's all day, and that Marty and I got in a big fight, and I was too upset to deal with school, and I didn't want to talk about it.

"Well, you do it again and I'm gonna beat the hell out of you *and* ground you," Mother said. "I know you've been skipping school before today, but I didn't say anything. I gave you some slack, and you took advantage of it. But now I'm saying no more! Got it?"

"Yes, ma'am. I'm sorry to disappoint you, Mother Dear," I said with a smartass tone. I don't know why I did that, knowing that it would only make things worse.

"You're damn straight you've disappointed me lately. What has happened to you? You used to enjoy school and stay out of trouble. I don't like those hoodlums you've been running with lately. I think they're a bad influence on you. You're smart, past-president of your class. A beauty queen, for God's sake! And you could've done it again this year if you had been taking care of yourself and not hanging around those bums."

"Big damn deal!" I shot back. "I didn't want to be one to begin with, and I sure as hell didn't want to do it again, so please drop the beauty queen bullshit. Looks don't mean shit to me anymore. Got it?"

That did it. Without warning, she reared back and slapped the ever-lovin' shit out of me. It felt like my teeth were going to fly across the room. I just turned and went to my room, locked the dead bolt, and wept. *Dammit to hell, that hurt!*

I worried about everything from being in trouble at school to Marty to drugs to that asshole Ted to how I was going to hide my birth control pills from Mother. I couldn't even start them for a few more weeks, and now that she was on the warpath, she was probably going to be snooping around in my stuff.

Damn her. She fuckin' knows everything. And of course, she's right. I had given up a world of promise for a guy who looked like he was turning into a junkie, if he wasn't there already. *But I love the little shit, and he's not just some poor boy either. Maybe I can keep him from hanging with Jack and David.* I had been suspecting David of using heroin for a while: he and Jack wore long sleeves in the summer, and that could be for only one reason.

So much to ponder...

Mother agreed to give me an excuse for missing school if I promised that I wouldn't do it again. I mean, what the hell else was I gonna do? After I said, "Thanks, Mother, so sorry, and I won't do it again," she handed over the note.

We'll see how long that lasts, but I'll try. God knows I don't want to be grounded any more than I already am.

When I got to biology class, Mrs. Tripp was looking excited as she announced, "Next week we are going on a road trip to the Flanitarium in Atlanta!" She was smiling with her huge bucky beavers resting on her lower lip. "Everybody has to get a release form signed, and get it vack to me this week, or you'll ve left vehind," she said as she passed out the forms. At least we wouldn't have to attend any other classes that Friday, and we were all glad of that.

The rest of my classes were such a drag, except algebra and gym. Numbers were my deal; they made sense to me. And I was quite athletic, so I liked doing gym stuff, with the exception of track. I could still sprint faster than any girl and most boys, but I hated distance running with my short legs. We girls would always try to get a glimpse of the guys in their gym shorts, which were real short back then, as were ours. That was the style: hot pants, miniskirts, and short-shorts for the youngsters, and bulletproof polyester for the older, cheesy folk.

For the most part, though, school was such a drag, especially knowing that Beth was at home watching *Sesame Street* without us. I tried to stay close to Marty as much as possible, and it worked most of the time. Still, on occasion he seemed to be detained or distracted. We didn't talk about heroin because I was terrified of it, and he didn't want me harassing him about it. I thought he was still dabbling in it, but we didn't go there after the incident at Beth's.

I continued to strut my stuff in my hippie wear, and I loved the hell out of it. The sorority girls were totally disgusted on the outside, but I knew some of them were jealous on the inside. There weren't many female bodies that could rival the one God had given me, and I liked showing it off. That was one thing that kept me entertained at school. Marty was a little jealous at times, but I didn't care.

Step up to the plate and claim your stuff, buddy.

He was still the only one gettin' it, and the only one who ever had. I felt that our relationship was doing okay overall, considering everything we were up against. He was sure enough happy about my getting on birth control, and we would both be glad to not have to deal with condoms any more. They were so awkward and totally disgusting.

Even though I had gotten into the habit of checking all the windows and curtains in the basement, I just couldn't relax down there anymore during sex. All I could see in my mind was Ted's freaky-ass eyes in that window, and I kept looking over at it just in case the curtain fell off or something. There were other windows as well, and I found myself looking from one to the other. If I didn't make the effort to control myself, I could easily get a freaked out about it, and the mood would be ruined.

Unfortunately, the sex still never lasted long enough for me to get too frantic about anything. It was more like a fleeting moment of near-panic, and then it was over. It still didn't give me the satisfaction it was supposed to, but the closeness with Marty was what I craved. I think. I was definitely craving something that I wasn't quite getting, but he had the kindest heart I had ever known, and he seemed so content when we were together.

The trip to the Flanitarium was totally far fuckin' out! Even if we hadn't dropped any acid, it would have been cool. As it turned out, *Oh my God!* Several of us dropped half a hit of blotter acid and burned about five joints in the parking lot at the school before we left, and we sat in the far back of one of the buses. Marty got to go too, because all of Miss Tripp's classes went. It was real nice having more time with him. David, Willa, Annie, and Jack were all there too. We were tripping our asses off, smoking cigarettes, and laughing out loud. I'm sure the straight students thought we had lost our marbles, but they laughed with us too. Or at us. But we never knew the difference. We pretty much had the run of the bus, as Mrs. Tripp was in the other bus.

We arrived at the Flanitarium in Atlanta and filed into the strangest place I had ever seen. The light show was the most beautiful thing I had ever seen as well. I was totally captivated by the technology, the visuals, sounds, and the science of astronomy. I was utterly speechless, which was good, because it was one of those places that you got kicked out of if you talked too much. It was just amazing, and I wondered if it was equally amazing without hallucinogens. Not that it really mattered at the time. We slept all the way home, sitting up. We were pretty burned out from all the stimulation and the drugs, a bunch of little crispy critters.

I got home from school with Laura Ann and Willa. Mother was waiting in the living room of course, cocked and ready. "Did you have a good trip?" she asked me.

"We sure did," I answered with a smirk. The double meaning was rather humorous to me, but she didn't quite catch it. That is, until she saw my eyes. I tried to turn away, but too late.

"What in God's name is wrong with your eyes?" she said as she got up from the sofa and got in my face. "What have you been doing? You're on drugs, aren't you!" She grabbed my arm to spin me around, but I fought her.

"Leave me alone, there's nothing wrong with me," I said defensively, but not convincingly. I tried to shake her off, but it was like trying to shake off a pit bull. Out of the corner of my eye, I saw her lining up her death arm to hit me, and before even *I* realized it, I whipped around and caught both her wrists. *Wow! Kung fu Maggie!* I looked her directly in the eyes and said, "You will not hit me in the face anymore. Got it?"

I couldn't believe it, but I was mocking her. No, worse than that. I was challenging her. And she suddenly realized I was stronger than her. I watched that thought sink in for a moment, and then I turned her loose.

She was too stunned as I walked away to say or do anything. Yet. I headed for the basement, waiting for her to sneak up behind me with a right hook, but she didn't. She let it stew for a short while, then she came downstairs to get me.

"I am ashamed of you, talking to your mother that way," she said, regaining her normal attitude. "Come here! NOW!" I did as she said, but I stopped about six feet from her. She tried to grab me, but I knew her intentions and I stepped back. It quickly became a game of cat and mouse, and I was the mouse. "I mean it! COME HERE!" she screamed at me as I darted around the basement, making sure I kept something between me and her.

"No!" I yelled at her. "Do I look that stupid? There is no way I am going to stand here and let you beat the hell out of me when all I have to do is run around in a circle. Hit me in the face again? No way, Mother Dearest. I have had enough of that!"

She wanted to get the death grip on me so bad that she chased me around and around and around the basement. She got madder with each trip around the stairs. After a couple of minutes, she started grabbing her chest, and her nostrils were flaring, and she was huffing and puffing like a Brahma bull. "Get your ass over here so I can kill you!" She could barely talk between the gasps for air.

Well, that struck me as hilarious. "Why in the hell would I do that, huh? Look at you! You're insane. Now calm down before you have a heart attack." I was laughing at her until I thought about the heart attack part. "You might as well go back upstairs and calm down because I'm not going to surrender, and you're not going to hit me in the face any more. You're going to go upstairs and lie down."

She started for the stairs and quickly spun around, trying to trick me. She almost got me, and we started around the staircase again. After a few more trips around the basement, she was worn down, but she was beginning to see the humor in it all, and then she started laughing. But I still didn't trust her and didn't let her get within six feet of me. She surrendered, I suppose thinking she had better do so before she stroked out. For the first time in my life, I had won a battle with Noni!

"Don't worry," she said as she collapsed on the mattresses in the basement. "I'll get you when you are asleep or when you least expect it."

I remained standing, sensing the psychological advantage it gave me over her as she lay breathless on the mattress. "I wouldn't advise that Mother," I said, emboldened by winning this round.

"I am not going to be hit in the face again by you or anybody else. Ever! If you ever try to do it again, I will find somewhere else to live. And mark my words, you can take care of Sara and the kids, 'cause I will rat on her scumbag husband so fast it'll make your head swim. And you know what else? If I leave, he'll find me. He always finds me. Every damn where I go, I look up and he's there. I even see him when he's not there. He is driving me crazy, and I am gonna crack soon, so as you would say…got it? I have had enough. And remember this, Mother. Legally, you are just as guilty as he is for allowing him to do what he does."

"What did he do this time?" she asked feebly.

"What do you mean, 'this time'?" I could feel the years of frustration pushing me into a tirade. "It's the same ol' shit, Mother, but he's getting worse. He is a sicko pervert, and he needs to be institutionalized and castrated, preferably without anesthesia. He roams around looking in windows all over town, and one day somebody's gonna catch him at it and shoot him. And I hope to God it's not me. But that wild look in his eyes is getting worse, and I wonder if he's getting ready to snap. He's still really pissed about the hatpin, and that's only a small part of it. We have a potentially volatile situation here, and you need to fix it, because I can't take it anymore. I truly don't want to be the one, but sometimes my fear of guns goes away, and I get real tempted to blow his fucking head off. So I'm warning you now: I'm gonna either squeal or shoot him if I catch him one more time."

I let that sink in a moment, then I continued, "You wanna be a live-in Grannie? You wanna be coming to see me in prison? I didn't think so. So get him away from me before something really bad happens. I shouldn't have to live in fear and shame. I live on the goddamn floor in the dark. Did you know that, Mother? I change clothes on the floor, in the dark, so he can't see me. I've gotten real damn good at it, but it's not right, and you know it. I sleep in your room because I can hear him in the driveway under my window all the time. I have even heard him climbing up the side of the house under my window. I can't sleep in there because I am terrified of what he might do, but even more of doing something myself that I will live to regret. I know he's not worth going to prison for, but sometimes I just don't care anymore. Sara would hate me for the rest of my life, and you know she would never admit to any wrongdoing on his part. You know how she is about him. Their innocent children would hate me too, and I love them all. I don't know what they know about all this, and I pray to God every day that he isn't hurting them in any way. Because if I found out that he is, I would have to kill him then."

"Don't say that. Don't even think it," Mother said, starting to look a little sick.

"Don't tell me you haven't thought of it too. I know you have. So do something about it! Cut his nuts off or something. Take care of it. You can do it. I'll be okay one way or the other, but if he ever hurts them, it'll be too late. I'm already damaged because of him, but I don't want them to know anything about the kind of life he lives." *Shit, what am I saying? I'm part of this cover-up too!?*

Mother was speechless. Good idea, because I was a woman on the edge, and she knew not to push me anymore. She had taught me well, and now I was more than ready for battle. She tucked her tail, got up, and slowly climbed the stairs without another word. The queen had been defeated.

The new queen had arrived.

Or so I thought.

Chapter Twenty-Five

My parents and Marty's Mother, Ellen, began getting together on occasion, even though they were from opposite ends of the social spectrum. I guess they figured that they might as well get to know each other since Marty and I were stuck together like glue. It was totally weird seeing them get trashed together. Mother would eat prescription diet pills, which happened to be known to us Freaks as black beauties, and drink liquor and smoke like a fiend. I don't know why she never threw up, but I never saw her get sick. Marty and I would go downstairs to the sex pit and do things while they were upstairs getting trashed. They would stay up half the night and pretty much forget about us in the basement, and eventually Marty would drive his mother home.

March of that year was big for me. I finally got my driver's license when I turned sixteen! After that, the problem was getting the car from Mother, but with some practice, I learned to drive our manual Volkswagen. When Mother was finally convinced I was safe to turn loose in the thing for a while, I mastered driving while smoking a cigarette, a joint, and drinking a beer at the same time. *Aaahhhh, freedom.*

Speaking of which: the second important happening of that month occurred when I started on birth control pills. That was liberating to say the least. It wasn't easy hiding them from Mother and still remembering to take them every day without fail, but I did pretty well with that. If she ever did find them, she never said anything, so it was all cool. Marty and I started screwing like little rabbits, every chance we got. I was conscientious about covering the basement windows, but asshole Ted never gave up. He would come over at night and pretend to check on Mother, then go down to the basement and slink around. As always, he would leave the door open in hopes I would see him down there. But I had learned long ago to not go near that doorway whenever he was around. While he was down there, he would uncover some windows, again in hopes that I wouldn't find them uncovered. It was a game we played for years. It wore me down at times, but I didn't want a repeat of the catastrophe that had occurred before, so I remained steadfast with my routine.

Mother was getting more lenient with me, perhaps because she liked Marty's mother so much. I guess she felt fortunate that, aside from the fact that she had lots of money, she was a nice person too. When her husband dropped dead in his early forties from a massive heart attack, without a will, everything in the estate was split between Ellen, Marty, and Edith, Marty's older sister. Edith was nineteen, married, and living in Atlanta, and I knew her only by reputation. And it wasn't a real good one. The kids had to be twenty-one years old to collect their share, but Ellen gave them everything they ever wanted. If she started running low on money she would just sell fifty or a hundred acres of land to get by for a few more years.

The family owned a thousand-acre farm in Anderson County with a little cabin where Marty and I would go hide out on occasion. We didn't have to worry about Ted when we were there, just the wildlife, 'cause we had sex outdoors almost as much as indoors. It was beautiful, and being a city girl who had spent little time in the wilderness, I found a connection with nature and serenity. I wanted to stay there, but it didn't have a full bathroom or kitchen, so that would be difficult living.

I was having visions of being married to Marty, with babies running around everywhere, and expanding the cabin or building our own house there. Well, that was wa-a-ay down the road, but I hoped that someday we would do just that. But we had to finish school first; that had been made clear by our parents many times. Mother had kept such a tight rein on me for so long, I had become rather claustrophobic. But now I was rebellious. Thank God she was easing up a bit, because I wasn't about to stop.

I was so glad to be on the Pill because it seemed that a lot of girls were getting pregnant and having abortions. The thought of doing that just gave me the creeps. For one thing, my Catholic upbringing had instilled in me a deep respect for life and a natural revulsion to the whole invasion thing. Aside from being a sin comparable to murder, it seemed so violent, crude, and dangerous. There were people performing abortions who had no license to do so, and some of the girls were injured badly. I had heard of one girl who almost died from infection and would probably never be able to have children. One girl we knew had already had three abortions, and she was only fifteen years old.

HELLO?! I won't be doing that!

I kept seeing that gorgeous guy, Bill, between classes. I was almost wishing I wasn't involved with anyone 'cause he was one good-lookin' thang. I knew he was going out of his way to see me, because he was always waiting in the same area. He would look me straight in the eyes and say, "Oh, hi," and my knees would damn near buckle. *Get thee behind me, Satan!* With his beautiful hair in a ponytail and bright blue eyes, he just reeked of pure sex in the most inviting way. He wasn't the football jock kind of hunk—those guys did nothing for me—but he really flipped my switch! I decided to keep him filed away in the back of my mind for now.

Annie and I still delivered the daily schedules to the classes, and that was fun for more than one reason. It got us out of class for a little while each day, and everybody in the high school got to see our nipples and belly buttons…whether they wanted to or not. Our clothes got skimpier and skimpier, and we enjoyed it more and more. Mother had pretty much given up on that issue. We were walking sex goddesses, and to this day I'll be damned if I know why they let us get away with it. The teachers were obviously appalled, judging by the raised eyebrows and huge eyeballs they displayed when we walked into the room.

The hippies and freaks hung out in the bathrooms, or under the wisteria arbor on the lower end of the school campus, and smoked cigarettes and pot during recess and lunch. I think a lot of people were afraid of us because we looked like, well…hippies and freaks. But that was fine with us. I had to be extra careful because everybody at school knew me. I'm not bragging here, it was the truth due to my past exploits as class president, beauty queen, blah, blah, blah. None of that stuff meant anything to me anymore, but I still had to hide when I wanted to be bad. My freak friends thought it was funny, but they helped out so I could get high with them. Of course it was cold as hell in the winter and hot as hell in the summer without air conditioning, but we were guaranteed at least a midday smoke of some kind.

Marty's mother still disapproved of his long hair, and eventually she agreed to buy him an Austin Healey he'd been lusting over if he would get his hair cut. He got it cut, but still not as short as she wanted. He got the Austin Healey anyway. We were still gettin' it on hot and heavy whenever possible and getting high as often as possible. But I could still sense him distancing himself from me, though I didn't dog him about it. I did get pouty sometimes, which occasionally worked: he gave me a necklace with my initials on it, knowing it would make me feel better about our relationship. *Oh, how sweet.* When Mother let me drive the Volkswagen by myself, I would occasionally drive over to Marty's. He sometimes acted funny about me showing up, sometimes not, but I really didn't notice it much at the time.

By the time the school year was over and summer rolled around, it was becoming more and more apparent to me that the rich kids in town were the most vulnerable to weakness with the heavier drugs. The rest of us couldn't afford to be too bad. Our friend Don was the richest, he of the daddy who was the town's most prominent lawyer. His parents let him drive around in the Mercedes limo all the time, and occasionally Don would call us and invite us for a cruise. I know we ruined that limo with pot and spilled drinks, and God knows what he did in the back seats when we weren't there. He had his own new 1973 Mercedes sedan too, and their yard looked like a Mercedes car lot. Everybody in his family had their own, and they had not one, but two limos, which might explain why Don wasn't worried about trashing the one he drove us around in. The first time I got a view of his backyard and all those beautiful cars I was stunned. *What the hell?!* All I knew was that we enjoyed the hell out of it. And the cops never bothered us when we were in the limo. *Tinted windows are wicked cool.*

We were always searching for a good concert, and we heard that Led Zeppelin was going to be playing in Atlanta in late July. Marty's sister Edith, who had become a full-blown junkie, got all of us tickets. I wasn't sure if Mother would agree to let me go, but I didn't care, I would go anyway. Marty's mother would help with that.

My family went to Myrtle Beach in late June. To my surprise, Mother invited Ellen and Marty to go with us. *HOLY...*I rode in luxury Ellen's car. Marty and I were in the back seat while Ellen drove us, and sure enough, I got a little carsick being in the back seat. But with the air conditioning blowing in my face, I managed to not pop.

We stayed at a rundown old house. It was right on the beach, but it was a piece of shit. *Dear ole Dad.* It was embarrassing, but Marty and I had fun. We fell asleep on the same bed by accident one day, and our parents found us and they all damn near had a coronary. This time we were actually innocent. We were tired and dozed off and woke up to the sound of Mother raising hell and pulling me up by one arm. *What the fuck?* We obviously couldn't get away with anything like that again. *Jeez!* My father wouldn't even look at me for two days, and when he did, he told me I was getting fat. I thought *FUCK YOU, BUD*, but I didn't say it aloud. It would have killed him if I said something like that. He was a dear sweet man, but he had a wicked temper.

Not long after we got back from Myrtle Beach, I was invited to go to Clearwater, Florida, with Ellen and Marty in early July, and Mother let me go. Now on that trip, I puked my ass off all the way down there. *How embarrassing...*

Marty and I had a hell of a time scoring some pot in Clearwater. Ellen was now tuned into the pot issue, and she was limiting our funds. I sure as hell didn't have much money, but Marty managed to get $20 out of her. We found some hippies on the beach, and they got us high, so we asked them where we could score some reefer. One guy said he could get us some, so we gave him the $20, but he never showed up with the reefer. *DUMB AS HELL, HUH?* Dumb and way too trusting. Marty went bonzo, and we searched the entire Clearwater area for two days looking for that guy. We were so sunburned and wore the skin off our feet walking around until the sun went down. We never found the guy who took our money, and we never scored any reefer. We occasionally came up on some freaks on the beach who didn't mind sharing with us. So we still had fun, thanks to the generosity of our fellow freaks.

When the sun went down each evening, I would get a chill every now and then, and I noticed my boobs hurt like hell. I reminded myself that my period was late. Very late. But I was on the Pill, and I figured my body was still getting used to the hormones. So young and clueless...

When we got home from Clearwater, I was relieved to learn that Mother had agreed to let me go to Atlanta. Apparently, Ellen had worked things out with her. Edith and her husband Steve were to come pick us up, take us to the concert, and then we would spend the night at their apartment.

The big concert weekend arrived, and our ride picked us up on Saturday morning. During the drive to Atlanta, Marty told Edith that my period was late. And of course I said, "I'm on the Pill, so it's fine."

"How late are you?" she asked.

"Oh, a month. Or two," I said, trying but not succeeding to sound sure of myself.

"Oh shit!" Edith exclaimed. "Why didn't you tell us earlier? There's a doctor here in town who can take care of that for you. If we had known, we would have gotten the money from Mother." Edith Diane was freaking out, and before long she had Marty freaking out too.

"It's okay," I insisted. "I've been taking the Pill every day, so I should be fine. Besides, that is a service I don't believe I would be interested in, but thanks anyway."

"Okay," she said. "But just think about it, and don't wait too long to decide. We'll help you."

"Thanks, I'll let you know if I need help," I said. Marty was starting to squirm all over the place, and I assured him that everything was fine. We were going to see Led Zeppelin's Stairway to Heaven tour, and I didn't want our weekend spoiled by worrying

When we got to the Coliseum in Atlanta, we got separated from Edith and Steve for a while. The crowd was huge and more than a little unruly, and we couldn't manage to stay together. We should have gotten our tickets from Edith and Steve before we got near the gate. It was pretty terrifying being pushed around like a bunch of freakin' cattle. Cops were everywhere, searching everybody and hauling them off to jail, and they were even were airlifting cars that were parked illegally. It was mayhem. *Holy shit!* Marty and I were holding a few joints, and I didn't know what Edith and Steve were holding, hopefully nothing more than we were.

Luckily, Marty and I weren't harassed by the cops. We looked a bit more normal than many of the attendees. It was some of the freakiest shit I had ever seen, a small-town girl going to Hotlanta. The concert was mesmerizing. Joints were going up and down every aisle, more than you could possibly smoke. The cops appeared to be ignoring it, probably because it was everywhere, and they were apparently more interested in busting larger quantities. We were totally ripped from all the reefer by the time Led Zeppelin started playing, but at least we weren't tripping. I think I would have freaked out totally if we had been. They played all the popular ones, "Whole Lotta Love," "The Lemon Song," and of course they ended with "Stairway to Heaven." *What a rush!* My hair was standing on end, and my titties were fucking killing me.

What the hell? No, I don't want to think about it. It can't be. It's just not possible.

We got back to the apartment, and Marty and I had our own private bedroom for the night. It was so cool to not have to worry about getting caught or getting up early. Of course we had that pesky little thought in the backs of our minds about being pregnant, but we pushed that aside for the time being. I figured the worst that could happen is that we would have to get married and live with one of our families until we finished school. That was fine with me if it came to that. As long as I was with Marty, nothing else mattered.

But I couldn't be pregnant! I had taken my pills religiously; I hadn't missed a single day. *Maybe my body is just freaking out since I've never taken the Pill before and I'm only sixteen.* But I had already skipped two periods and was waiting for the third.

If I don't start in a few days, I'll have to fess up and go to the doctor. Mother's gonna kill me, pregnant or not. Just knowing that I was guilty of having sex would be enough for her to skin me alive.

It was a quiet trip home the next day. We were all a little tense, and I knew it had a little something to do with my predicament. I was in denial still, so I was handling it better than they were, for the time being anyway. I was too young and stupid to really grasp the implications. When we got home, we were totally wiped out from all the excitement and traveling. They dropped me off at our house, and I did a face plant in the bed without even changing clothes. Mother and Daddy got back from Uncle Jack and Aunt Bessie's, and they were tired too. That worked out good, 'cause we didn't have to talk a lot. I didn't know why I was so tired. *And STARVING!* But the nap won out over food.

This summer had been a fun one, full of surprises and new experiences, great music, a lot of travel, beautiful southern beaches, and great drugs. But I had been hearing more and more about young guys dropping like flies from heroin overdoses. Greenville had been labeled the number one city in the country for heroin and syphilis. *Nice, huh?* So much for going downtown, unless you want to get mugged, score some heroin, or find a prostitute. Also, I could feel Marty slipping away. I stopped by his house one day to take him something, and he had a weird look on his face. He had some friends there with him, but he said, "We need to talk."

"Okay, what's the matter, babe?" I asked him.

"Nothin'," he replied, not looking at me. "I just think we shouldn't see each other anymore. It's just not working out."

"You call that nothin'?" I shot back. "I can't believe my ears. Marty, what happened? We have had a great summer, and—"

He cut me off at the knees and said, "Just go. We aren't seeing each other for a while, okay? Just go."

I knew that the waterworks were about to spew, and he had said these things in front of David and Howard. Not one of them could look me in the eye.

"It's all about heroin, isn't it?" I accused him, but he still wouldn't look at me. "It is, isn't it? I can tell, because ya'll are so fucked up, and you're pissed because I stopped by and messed up your buzz. Marty is the only one of you with a girlfriend. You guys," I said, pointing at Howard and David, "don't have to hide anything from the girlfriend. So you know what? That's fine, because I am better than that. And so are you. All of you are better than that. I will not stoop to that level, with you or anyone else. As much as I love you, I will not go there, and I will not allow it around me anymore. So take your heroin and your little junkie asses and go fuck yourselves! Go fuck each other, 'cause I don't give a shit. One day you'll understand, if you live long enough."

"Bye," Marty said, as he opened the door for me.

I knew if I turned around, I would cry in front of him. I also knew that I was going to cry a river, but not until I got out of there. And that's exactly what I did. I cried until the well was dried up. Thank God I didn't have to go to school the next day.

Chapter Twenty-Six

Mother knew before I did. She heard me crying all night, but she didn't bother me. She had a dream, and it wasn't good.

While I had been in Atlanta at the concert, Diane had delivered Mother some shocking news. She was getting married to Michael, but that was not the shocking part. She was also five months pregnant! Mother was fine with that. We all knew they were headed for marriage anyway, but holy shit, a baby in three or four months!

God, I'm going to be an only child for the first time. I missed Buddy so bad that I couldn't even stand to think about him, and now Diane was moving out as soon as they could find a place to live. Mother was telling me all this at breakfast, and I sat in a daze with my eyes swollen almost shut. Then she looked at me and said, "I know you and Marty broke up, and I also know that you haven't had a period in a while."

Leave it to Mother to hit you right upside the head with it. All I could say was, "I'm fine."

"How many periods have you missed? Have you been with Marty in that way?"

"NO!" was my first reaction. I was freakin' the hell out, and I couldn't look at her.

"Don't you lie to me. I know better. I can see it in your eyes, and I know how you feel about him. You have been gaining weight, and your titties are bigger."

"Just leave me alone!" I said, trying to sound strong, but only sounding weak.

"No, I won't," she said. "You are going to the doctor as soon as I can get you in, preferably today. So don't leave the house."

Sure enough, we were going to the doctor's office within the hour. I was about to have a heart attack or throw up or both. I was shaking so bad that Mother had to pull me out of the car. At least I didn't have to wait all night in anticipation. I don't think my heart would have survived.

We walked in the door, Mother gripping my arm, and Dr. Smith came out himself to get me. He took me back to a room, had me strip down and put on the gown, and helped me onto the table. I had been through this several months ago at the health department, but I was so nervous. I knew in my heart what he was going to say. He laid me down and did the pelvic exam, looked me in the eye, and said, "You, my dear are pregnant. About four and a half months."

"There's no way!" I exclaimed. "I've been taking the Pill every day. I haven't missed a one!"

"Well, honey, sometimes they don't work," he explained. "Different things can change their effectiveness." We talked about everything, about when I had started taking the Pill and when I'd had sex. After hearing my account of the details, he said, "I think that maybe you rushed it a little, before the Pill could take effect. I'm very sorry. I'll go get your mother. Do you want me to tell her?"

"Yes, please. She is going to have a coronary, so be prepared."

"It's okay. I've known her for years. I'm sure she already knows."

Mother and Dr. Smith walked in a few minutes later. She had a look on her face that I had never seen. He had already told her obviously. He told us it was too late to have the fetus terminated, that it could kill me. Mother begged him to find a way.

"I don't want it terminated," I said without hesitation. "Otherwise I would have done it by now. I just couldn't do it. I won't do it."

Dr. Smith said, "Well, there are options for you and the baby. You could go to an unwed mother's home and give it up for adoption, or keep it and you know the rest."

Mother Dearest interrupted and said, "Oh, hell no. I am too damn old to be raising another kid. No, ma'am. You're on your own with this. We'll talk about this later. Elbert is going to just die. This is just terrible, terrible news."

I sat there quietly, with my wheels turning a million miles an hour. I had always thought that Marty and I would be together forever.

And now he dumps me out of the blue. For heroin. Maybe it's because of this. God, I hope the baby is okay and he wasn't on heroin when it happened. I hope I wasn't doing any acid when it happened.

I knew I wouldn't be doing any more anything for a long while.

"Come on," Mother said rather briskly. I had clearly been in a daze, not hearing anything they had said for a while. We went home, and I went straight to my room and locked the door. I didn't want to see Daddy's face or hers. I really didn't want to see anybody except Marty. I knew he'd come through for me.

Mother called everybody in the upstate of South Carolina, I do believe. All the family, God knows who else. I would obviously start showing soon, so the word was going out. *The little whore is pregnant!* That is exactly what some of them would think, even though I had never been with anybody but Marty in my life. Now several of us were pregnant, so we could get through this together: Diane, Janet, Mary, and now me.

Marty will straighten up and fly right when he finds out.

That night, I stayed in my room. I called Beth and told her, and she proved her true friendship and tried to support me with kind words. I was about to call Willa next when her mother came over mad as a hornet, looking for Willa because she hadn't come home and hadn't called. She was so mad she looked like she could pinch somebody's head off. She didn't believe me when I told her that I had no idea where Willa was and that I was about to call her on the phone. Mother gave me the eye darts, and I told her again and again, "I DON"T KNOW WHERE WILLA IS!" I was scared for her, and I didn't know what to do.

Then Willa's mother told us they were moving to Charleston. That was a shocker.

Oh no, my buddy is leaving me at a really bad time. I started to cry some more. I called everybody I knew, but nobody had heard from her. Suddenly I realized that I was more worried about Willa than myself. I finally cried myself to sleep. Marty never did call, and I knew he knew by now.

The next day, he finally came over to see me. We rode around in silence for a while, and then he asked, "What happened? Why did this happen? I thought you were on the Pill."

"I am. I mean, I was. The doctor said that they don't always work. I never skipped a day, but we may have rushed it a little. Other than that, I just don't know. I'm sorry, but I didn't know what was going on either."

We got back to our front yard, and he got out to walk me to the door. I turned to him and asked, "Well, what are we going to do? You know, we could live in the cabin and fix it up. Or we could live with somebody until we finish school."

"We? This is your fucking fault. Why didn't you do something about it before it was too late? How do I know that it's even mine at all?"

The pain in my heart felt as if he had thrust a dagger through it. I clutched my chest and choked out nothing but sounds, trying to say, "Because I love you and I couldn't do that" When I got my breath, I yelled, "How could you say that? I have never been with anyone else!"

"Yeah, how do I know that?" He gave me a look that could kill, straight into my eyes.

"Please believe me," I stammered, feeling myself falling apart. "You are the only one. Ever. Please don't leave me. I can't go through this alone."

I reached for his arm as he started to turn away. He tried to push me away from him, but I was so desperate for him that I latched on. All I wanted was for him to hold me and tell me it was going to be okay, but instead, he flung me off with a shove. I stumbled backward and fell in the front yard. He turned and walked away, got in his Austin Healey and drove off while I lay in the dirt for God and everybody to see. I lay there clutching my chest, trying to catch my breath again, and then darkness took me.

Chapter Twenty-Seven

"Come on. Get up. Let's go inside. We don't want anybody to call the law," I vaguely heard Mother say. I opened my eyes to see her bending over me in the yard as she pulled me up to my feet.

"He left me," I moaned. "He's gone. He just pushed me down and left."

"What did you expect?" she asked.

"What?" I asked, truly not understanding. "Why would you say that? You don't know what we had together. We, we—"

"Yeah, HAD, as in ain't any more. Don't you get it? He's history."

"What makes you say that?"

"I just know. Now we've got to figure out what to do with this baby."

"I'm having the baby, Mother."

"Of course you're having it, but surely you don't expect to keep it."

"Well, yeah," I wailed. "Of course I do."

"And where do you think you and the baby are going to live?"

"I was hoping to stay at home, Mother. Marty will come around. You'll see."

"No way," she said emphatically as she led me into her bedroom and sat me down on her bed. "I am too damn old to take care of another baby, and your Father is having a nervous breakdown right now, even in his sleep. And Marty *ain't* comin' around. You need to just get it through your head. Besides, I'll shoot the son of a bitch if he does."

"I'm not asking you to keep the baby, Mother," I implored. "I just need a place to live until I can get on my feet, or until Marty decides he wants us."

"No, Maggie," she said with finality. "I said NO. You have shamed me and your Father, and we will not be your babysitters. You are too damn young to have a baby, and you have to finish school. He's not coming back, okay? You have to make something out of yourself. We had such high hopes for you. You have let us down and embarrassed us in front of our family and the entire community. Go to your room, and stay away from your Father when he gets up. I truly don't know what he might do or say. Now get out of my sight." I got up and pretty much crawled to my room and cried some more.

The police showed up later and asked if we knew anything about Willa's disappearance. They called me into the living room and asked me a bunch of questions. I told them I didn't know where she was, and I really didn't. They finally left, and I went back to my room and slept, cried, slept, cried. I cried for Willa and prayed that she was okay. With all that I had been dealing with, I had totally forgotten that she was missing. I really needed her right about now, and I felt a little selfish about that.

I have to find a place to live before the baby is born. I need to call Beth to let her know that Willa is missing. Hopefully she won't freak out.

I could hear Daddy get up for work, so I locked myself in my room and turned off the light. When I heard him leave, I got up to go pee, but of course Mother beat me to it. She finished and went back down the hall to her room, and then I came out. I really didn't feel like facing anybody at the moment. Hell, I couldn't even face myself. As I walked past the basement door, I paused, but then I kept walking to the bathroom. While I sat there, I had wicked thoughts that I was ashamed of. I tried to shake them out of my mind, but they kept hanging there. I was headed back to the bedroom, and I felt the pull of the stairs and the basement. Sometimes when I felt that pull, Ted was down there with his dick in his hand, hoping I would open the door and see him. But this time it wasn't Ted.

I stood at the top of the stairs, turned on the light, and counted the steps going down. *1...2...3....4...5...6...7...8...9...10...11... shit...12...13... That figures... Thirteen fucking stairs, cement at the bottom. Should be effective. What in the hell am I thinking?*

I started backing away from the stairs, and I realized I had been holding my breath the whole time I had stood there. I leaned for the light switch and felt my head spinning, and all kinds of horror flashed through my head as I started to fall. I stumbled down three or four steps and caught onto the rail that had only been up for a few weeks. Thank God Daddy put it up for Mother, or I would have gone all the way down, either taking the steps or going over the side. At that point all I could do was sit down on the steps and collect myself.

I heard, "What do you think you're doing?"

Mother had appeared and was looking down at me. I could tell she knew what was in my head. "Don't do anything stupid, ya' hear? That," she pointed down the stairs, "would definitely be stupid. Come on. Go to bed. I know you're tired. Come on."

I lay down in my bed alone. Diane was now with Michael, getting married. Willa was missing; Marty was gone. *Just me and Junior here, with nowhere to go.*

Hell, even Ted wasn't fuckin' with me lately. I guess he figured I had enough shit in my life, but I had never known him to care before. Of course I had never been in this predicament before. I had a fitful night of anxious dreams, when I could sleep at all.

I kept going back to the basement stairs, every day for weeks. *I could just throw myself down the stairs and hope that I didn't live, and the baby...No, I can't say it or think it.* Often I could hear Mother stirring, as if she was reading my mind again. My days were filled with anxiety, and at night sleep finally came, but the dreams were so disturbing that I woke up exhausted.

Mother had to contact the school and tell them I was not coming back this fall and that I was going to Texas to stay with my brother. I don't think most people bought it, but I didn't care. Beth would come to get me, and we would ride up to the school and park across the road and look for friends. Of course, I was looking for Marty. I saw him a couple of times early on, but after that he disappeared.

After two weeks of hell, Willa finally called and let me know where she was. Her parents blamed me, saying I knew where she was. In the meantime, they were moving out, and they still hadn't heard from Willa. Beth and I went to the house where Willa told us she was hiding. She had been staying with this chick named Beryl. She was babysitting and keeping house while Beryl worked. She told us she had decided to run away when her mother and father announced they were going to split up and move. Beth and I didn't know about her parent's situation until that very day.

No wonder she ran away. Jeeezzz…

Then I told Willa about my situation. She was stunned and upset about it as she said, "You know they're going to take me away, and I won't be here to help you, and I can't do anything to stop them. I'm still sixteen, like you are. Oh, Maggie, thank God you have Beth. I know she'll be good to you. So what are you going to do? What about Marty?"

I had to force the words from my mouth. "Well, Marty has disappeared, and his mother is paying all the hospital bills and covering the OB/GYN visits, but the parents refuse to let me keep the baby. They say they will take no responsibility for us when it comes, and I can't live with them with a baby. I have to either find a safe place for the two of us to live or give it up for adoption. Now, how in the hell am I going to pull that off?"

"Shit!" Willa said.

"Yeah, tell me about it," I replied.

"Please do me a favor. Tell my parents that I called you and I'm okay, but that you still don't know where I am. I will call them soon. I know we have to move away since they're splitting up."

"We didn't know that until today, Willa. That's a real bummer, girl." I couldn't bear the thought of Willa being gone for good. We had become so dependent on each other and had done so much for each other. And I needed her now more than ever.

I couldn't keep the thought of Marty returning out of my head. One day I finally broke down called Ellen and asked her where Marty was. She said he had gone to Myrtle Beach.

"For how long?" I asked her.

"I really don't know. He didn't say," she replied.

"Okay, then. I get it now." It was slowly starting to sink in that he was really gone and that she was not my ally.

We really had a true love, although we were young, we loved each other. He was so sweet and kind to me, until all this shit came down. I said, "Thanks a lot," hung up the phone and called Beth. We could do something together since she had dropped out of school and was getting her GED. That's what I was going to do as soon as the baby came, and then I could get a decent paying job other than the movie theatre. It didn't pay crap, but it gave me a little spending money.

Just when I thought things couldn't get any worse, we found out that David, Bonnie, and their mobsters are coming to visit in a month. Bonnie wanted to come one more time and go to the mountains. She thought she was going to die, and Mother thought so too. She was so young, and I couldn't grasp that she could be dying. Mother must have told them about me too.

I don't think I can handle them right now. I kept thinking about the basement stairs. They still had a strong pull on me, especially now.

"Mother, why?" I asked. "Why are they coming now? You know this is a bad time for all of us."

"Because David said Bonnie want to come and see us while she can. She is dying, Maggie. Mack is still in prison for underage boys, and Kathy isn't coming."

"It's still bad news," I said without hesitation. "Let her die there, for God's sake. She has brought enough grief to us already, and I can't take it right now."

"Too damn bad, ain't it? 'Cause they're coming in just over three weeks, and we're going to Cherokee to see the fall foliage."

"Well screw me blue!"

"What did you say?!"

"You heard me." I walked off as if on a dare. She wouldn't hit me again. I swear to God, I would have cleaned her clock right then if she had touched me. More than ever, I was a woman on the edge. Literally.

Meanwhile, I was getting calls from relatives who were childless, wanting to adopt my child. *Holy Mother of God.* I hadn't even given it up yet. I was still trying to find a way to keep it, but nobody wanted both of us. *They only want the baby.* I decided that if I couldn't keep it, I was not going to be able to sit back and watch someone else raise it. That would not be healthy for any of us, as tempting as it was at the moment. I wanted a family of my own. I wanted Marty to be my husband and take responsibility for us. Even though it was not a planned pregnancy, that is what I had believed would happen.

I was now certain that his dear mommy had convinced him I was out to get his trust fund and that I had gotten pregnant on purpose. I was also certain that his sister had told Ellen I had been missing my periods, and she in turn called my mother. They had it all planned before I knew for sure that I was pregnant. I had been so sure it was the Pill messing with my periods, until my boobs started hurtin' like a son of a bitch, and Edith started freakin' out in Atlanta. It wasn't until then that Mother started questioning me about my periods. *So Edith was the one who got this going between the parents…protecting the family money…*

There was one thing that I was sure of: if I couldn't keep the baby, then nobody I knew could have it. I had family with big houses and money, but nobody wanted me. They only wanted the baby, and they didn't think about how this would affect the baby and me in the long run. They were being totally self-serving as far as I was concerned. Out of all our friends and relatives, only one offered to let both of us stay with them. It was for a questionable period of time, however, and they really didn't have a pot to piss in. She had two small kids and a sorry-ass husband who would come home and beat the hell out of her pretty regularly. They lived in a two-bedroom trailer, way away from town, and I wouldn't be able to get to my little job or school very easily. I couldn't consider that as an alternative.

So back to the stairs. I would sit at the top of the landing and count them over and over. I was afraid that if I flung myself down the stairs, I would live and the baby would die. In my scrambled head, I guess that meant I wanted to die and let the baby live. And that was what I had already chosen for the child anyway. I had chosen life. So I would give life—and keep it.

Subject closed.

Chapter Twenty-Eight

Willa's parents were totally freaked out because she hadn't come home or called them. The police had been combing the area. I told them she had called me and said she was all right, but that I didn't know where she was. Of course they didn't believe me, and they had the police come and interrogate me again. I didn't break, but I told them she said she was safe and was staying with a lady, keeping her kids and doing housework for the mother while she worked. If I hadn't been pregnant, I would surely have taken some drugs of some kind, because that shit was workin' on my damn nerves.

Beth was my running buddy, and occasionally we were joined by Ruth, David's older sister. We also ran with Annie, white boy Kevin with the biggest afro in town, and Mercedes Don. At least I had friends. Annie and Kevin broke up, and he and I would run together sometimes. I always liked him, and for some reason, my mother did too, not that I gave a shit really. He didn't care that I was prego. He thought it was cool and said he would marry me. Such a nice guy, but I couldn't do that to him. We would run together in different groups occasionally, but mostly I just hung out at Beth's and got really good at playing pool. My belly eventually got in the way, but Beth and I could clear a table real quick and beat any guy or gal around at eight-ball.

As the months crept along, I started making my own maternity clothes. Mother had taught me how to sew years ago, and I was getting good at it. I had some very nice new outfits, but they were so "church lady" looking. I made some from cool hippie-looking materials, and I felt so much better in them than the store-bought ones. Some of the guys felt uneasy around me when I started getting big. Beth and I were always on the run, looking for something to get into. We learned of an apartment where a bunch of guys were staying, and we heard that Marty had been over there a lot too. Well, you know, fool that I was, I had to check it out. I had been looking for him high and low, day and night, and eventually he did return from Myrtle Beach or wherever the hell he had been. If our paths crossed, he would speak to me, but disappear very quickly, and he never made any eye contact with me. He would ask how I was doing, but that was it. Quite frankly, he looked almost as lost as I was, and I longed for him to hug me or something, but he just couldn't bring himself to do it. It was like opening old wounds over and over again. Every time I saw him, I hoped he had changed his mind about me. About us. But he didn't look happy at all. I don't know if it was drugs or the pregnancy. Most likely it was both.

Meanwhile, Mother Dearest had set up a meeting with the Department of Social Services about the adoption, along with therapy sessions with both my parents. Mother and Daddy came to the first one with me, but Daddy and I cried throughout the whole thing. The therapist was at a loss. She said, "You don't want to do this, do you? Give up your baby. Do you?"

"What do you think?" I said helplessly. "But it seems that I have no other options. I have to finish school and make something of myself. I have to suffer the consequences of my actions. I have to give this child a better future than I could give it, right?" I turned to Mother and asked, "Isn't that what you wanted me to say Mother? Did I say it right?" I hoped everybody could understand me, because I was yelling while sobbing and snotting all over the place.

She glared at me and said, "Well, it's true. You're too young to raise a baby, and you know it. You would be wanting to go party every night and leave me with it. I know how it goes. You need to finish school, and you can't do that with a baby. You're only sixteen years old, for God's sake. Isn't that right, Elbert?"

Daddy shook his head, but couldn't talk for crying. I couldn't look at him, and he couldn't look at anything but the floor. I had never seen him like that and was wishin' that I hadn't. It still haunts me to this day.

We got back in the car, and all I could say was, "Well, that was fucking horrible, and I won't be going back."

"Yes, you will too. And quit saying that word, or I'll knock the hell out of you."

"NO, MOTHER DEAREST, I WON'T. TRUST ME. I WON'T EVER GO THROUGH THAT AGAIN! And if you think you're going to be hitting on me, think again."

She never hit me again.

By the time Willa came home, her parents had already packed, and they snatched her up and left town before she could come say good-bye to me. They weren't going to take any chances. They thought I was the wild one, but believe me, Willa was a lot wilder than me. She was like the Baptist minister's daughter who goes crazy when she goes off to college because she never had any freedom. That was Willa, and I guess Beth and I were the accessories. About two months later, they dropped her off to see me for about an hour while they were in town. That was the last time I saw her or talked to her for thirty-six years.

Beth and I were bored, so we went over to the apartment where all the hippie guys stayed. We took a bottle of wine and a few joints with us so they would let us in. They all acted a bit strange over there, but I was hoping to run into Marty. They opened the door and let us in.

"Hey, man, how's it going? We just wanted to get a buzz. Hope it's okay." I looked over at the couch and there sat three guys, all passed out. "Whoa, what happened to them?"

Robbie said, "They're fucked up drunk. They passed out a little while ago."

"Frenchie looks like shit. He doesn't look right. Are you sure he's okay?" I asked Robbie.

"Yeah, he drank too much red wine and smoked about seven joints and two packs of cigarettes, then he yakked for a while, and then he came in here. Believe me, he looks better than he did." Robbie laughed and walked into the kitchen. We followed him with our wine to get some glasses.

"Maybe so, but his color is off," I said. I couldn't stop looking at him. I had never seen anybody look like that.

"He'll be fine. He does this all the time," Robbie assured me. So I drank a little wine and took a couple of hits off of a joint. I didn't enjoy it any more. It made me paranoid to smoke pot, and I started thinking about going into labor and shit like that. So I mainly smoked cigarettes, but not a lot of them either. Even they made me feel nauseous sometimes. We were hanging around the kitchen with the guys when Marty and David strolled in. Marty looked at me, then at Robbie as if to say, "What the hell is she doing here?" Robbie shrugged him off.

"We wanted to get a buzz. Do ya mind?" I looked at Marty, and he shook his head and immediately looked at the floor. All I'd seen him do lately was look at the floor. He looked miserable and looked like shit too. I was pregnant as hell, but I looked good. "Don't worry, we're leaving. I don't want to be where I'm not wanted. And by the way, go to hell. And another thing, you might want to check on Frenchie. He doesn't look right. I think something's wrong with him."

Beth and I walked back through the living room, and Frenchie hadn't moved at all. The other guys who were passed out had moved, and one had even gotten up. We split and went to Beth's house. I cried on the way there, but she said, "I was proud of you back there, what you said to Marty. You need to get over him and stay away from him. He's no good for you."

"I know, but it's hard when I'm carrying his baby. He used to be good, before he started messing around with heroin, which I assume he's doing, but I've never seen him do it. I have been so desperate for him to love me. I am so scared Beth. I don't think I can do this alone."

"You're not alone" she said reassuringly. "You have me. I'm not going anywhere. And besides, you have to do it. One way or another, you are going to give birth to a baby. What are the doctors saying? Ya'll are healthy, right?"

"Oh yeah. I am getting the best care in town. We're both healthy as two horses. And I am getting as big as a house. Stretch marks, despite all the lotions and stuff. My body will never be the same."

"Maybe, maybe not. But women have survived this for eons, and you're gonna be all right."

"I know. I guess. But it's so hard, Beth. Thinking about going through all this, then giving the baby away as if none of it ever happened, I don't know if I can survive it. I loved Marty with all my heart. I would have stayed with him forever, if it hadn't been for drugs. I know he's getting in way too deep. I can tell. All of those guys over there are strange. I don't want to go over there anymore. And I've decided that I don't want to see Marty any more. It only makes me hurt, and I can't take the rejection anymore."

"Then don't. Let's play some pool and turn on some Beatles, Joplin, Hendrix, or whatever. You pick."

"Okay. I need something that won't remind me of him. How about some Motown? Wicked Picket?"

"Sure. He's always good."

So we had a fun evening, just the three of us. Kevin came over and helped keep my spirits up. He was good about that. He was a good friend, just like Beth was a good friend. I was feeling pretty tired, lugging all this weight around, so Beth and Kevin took me home. I had fitful sleep that night. Bad feelings. Anxiety. Worry, worry, worry. *Indigestion? What the fuck?* Up and down all night. I dreamed of Madam Alexander blinking her eyes. I think it was a dream anyway. Hell, I didn't even know. The next day, I was still tired and decided that I was not going to go looking for Marty again. I was not going to drink any alcohol or smoke any more pot until "after." I'd only had a little, so I don't know why I had such a bad night. My phone rang. "Hello?"

"Hey, this is Annie."

"Hey, girl. How's it going? What time is it? I am dragging this morning. I had a bad night."

"You're not the only one. They found Frenchie this morning. Dead. He was at the apartment, on the couch."

"This morning? OH MY GOD, Annie!"

"I know. It's terrible."

"No, I mean yes it's terrible. But it's worse. Beth and I were over there around 6:00 p.m. last night, and he and David and Mike were passed out on the couch. I saw him there on the couch. I told Robbie he didn't look good. He looked awful. The last thing I said was for him to check on Frenchie, that he looked sick. He kept saying that he was fine, he did that all the time, and they were laughing about him."

"It was a heroin overdose."

"Shit. I knew something felt wrong over there. They were always sitting around like a bunch of old people. Staring. And they acted weird when we went over."

"Yeah, they're all doing heroin."

"Oh shit. If I had known, I wouldn't have been over there. I guess that means Marty too."

"Probably so. You knew he had been around it anyway, and since he's hanging there, you know he's doing it. He also has the money."

"I guess so. I have never seen it there, and I guess I'm just so ignorant about it that I can't recognize the signs, and they hide it well. But poor Frenchie…How did they find him?"

"Somebody called the cops, but they cleared out everything and everybody before they called. He had been dead about sixteen hours when they got to him. I don't know whose name the apartment was in, but they all split before the cops came and left him there on the couch. Can you believe that? I doubt they'll be back around these parts for a long time. Maybe never."

"Then he was lying there dead all day, slumped over between the two other guys, and they were too fucked up to notice? I knew something wasn't right. I feel terrible. None of us really knew Robbie either. He just appeared one day. Maybe he was their supplier. Who knows? Poor Frenchie. He was what, only seventeen?"

"Yeah. So sad to see what's happening to everybody these days."

"I know, right? Look at me." She got quiet, so I said, "At least I'm healthy and not on heroin. Roll with me, Annie. I'm trying to be positive about something. You know?"

"It's hard when everybody's dropping like flies. You hang in there. You're gonna be fine. You'll see."

"I'm gonna be alone, but I'll be okay. I do have some good friends. Did you know that all my close friends I used to be in the sororities with haven't even called me? Not a one. They are too good for me, you know. Everybody knows, and you know they do, but have they called and asked me how I'm doing? Hell, no. I say fine. I am not like them anyway. I care about people, no matter what color they are, no matter how poor or rich they are. And that makes me a better person than they are, if you ask me, huh? Besides, I know that Peggy has screwed every guy she could get in her bedroom, and she was making fun of me because Randy and I had never done it, and I was only thirteen, for God's sake."

"Damn skrait, girlfriend!" Annie said. "You tell them hoes. No, don't even waste your time. You've always been too good for them. It just took you a couple of years to figure it out. Well, I gotta go to school. I thought I'd tell you about Frenchie before you heard it from the news or something."

"Thanks, Annie. That really sucks. See ya soon, I hope." I waited a little while to call Beth. She freaked out too. I felt so guilty that I threw up. I should've done something when we were over there, but I didn't know what was going on or what to do. I had never seen a fresh dead guy before—or any dead guy unless he was in a casket. They seemed to be real relaxed about him sitting there with blue lips. But I knew he didn't look right. I should have done something. I wondered if I should call the police…NOT!

Well, didn't that group just scatter like a bunch of palmetto bugs when the light is turned on? I know when I'm done. I won't ever go looking for Marty again, so I guess that's the last time that I will see him, unless he makes some miraculous recovery or something. Even then, I won't ever trust him again. To have shown such a tender love for me, but then chose heroin over me and our unborn baby. He cut me deep.

It was a gaping wound so painful that I would never fully recover from it, I finally realized. No matter what the outcome, there would be scars for life.

Chapter Twenty-Nine

Time seemed to fly by, I guess because Beth and I were having a great time. We did what we wanted, and nobody seemed to care. I worked my little job at the theatre and started working at the animal hospital with Beth part-time. Dr. Frazier said I could work there as long as I wanted, after everything was over. He encouraged me to finish school and go to college, and I could work there on the weekends and stuff. He was such a wonderful, kind man, as was his wife Dottie. Life was good, really. If I could just find a way to keep the baby, then life would be really good. I knew I couldn't be a great provider by myself, but there would be lots of love. I just needed a place for us to live for cheap, get me a car, finish school…Yeah right. What was I thinking?

I can't do it alone, but I'll hang on as long as I can and maybe come up with a solution.

Daddy still wouldn't look at me or talk to me. He was losing his marbles at work, and ended up being "retired early." His baby girl apparently had shattered his heart, and he wasn't coping well. Now didn't that just make me feel special?

We were dreading the visit from the family thieves, but it couldn't be helped. So we gathered up all our shit that we didn't want stolen and took it to Aunt Sybil's, Sara's, and Michael's, where we knew they wouldn't be going. Thank God it was only four of them this time because our nerves were so raw. We told them our news, and they told us about Bonnie's medical issues, which were all bad. After a couple of days at home with them, we packed up and went to Cherokee, North Carolina. It was still hot outside, and the leaves were just starting to turn. We stayed in a neat place that had an apartment and also rooms. Sherri and I got the apartment by the pool, with Mother and Daddy. Awkward! I stayed away from Daddy, and he avoided me as well. I really needed somebody to hold me and tell me everything was going to be okay, but nobody was able to do that for me. I had Beth, Annie, Ruth, and my buddy Kevin. I guess because they knew the real scoop, they knew I would survive, but I would have deep festering wounds for life. But I still hoped I would find a way or that Marty would come to me. Even with them being so good to me, I had never felt so alone.

We endured the visit from the family. Actually, it was the best visit we had ever had with them, although Bonnie looked like death. She had lost so much weight and the diabetes had taken a toll on her organs. She apparently still had some good drugs, 'cause she talked like her tongue was three times its normal size. I was pretty much uneventful. I think everybody was in shock seeing me in my predicament. Still, there were no offers for me on housing. We all came back, regrouped, and they left after a few more days. Overall, it was a painless visit except for seeing Daddy and David talking and looking serious and depressed, trying not to let me hear. I just ignored them. I was getting used to doing that everywhere I went.

So I worked hard and played hard, but I still managed to save up a little money. Diane and I both were getting as big as a house, especially her. As time went by, I was getting proposals for marriage from all kinds of guys: old flames, guys who'd had crushes on me from years before, everybody but the one I really loved. My old flame, Randy, even offered to marry me, but I didn't love him anymore, and he had dumped me twice already. Even sweet little Robbie. That was almost tempting, because I knew he would make something out of himself, and I loved him, although it was more like a brotherly love.

I believe they were all really sincere at the time, but they were also too young to think about what it would mean down the road. I'd had many a lonely night to contemplate, but I could never come up with a sound, fair solution. I was mature enough to know that it was not fair to marry a young man I didn't love and not fair to keep a child I could not support by myself. That's how the parents forced me to agree with their plan. The parental units knew that even if Marty wanted to stay with me, we still would need them for at least a couple of years. I personally didn't see why it was such a sacrifice when it meant keeping a child with its family.

I was willing and able to work and didn't mind it. However, I don't think Marty knew what it was like to have to work. He had worked for about a month before, but that was all I was aware of. My brothers and sisters never offered to take me in, except Diane once said, "You know we don't have enough money or room even for ourselves, but we would let you stay if we could." The other siblings never offered or even talked about it, except when Buddy and his wife from hell wanted to adopt the child. I said, "No. I'm sorry, but it won't work." That was hard because I loved Buddy so much, but I couldn't understand his wife, and I knew it would be a major mistake to turn over my child to her. It would be too hard to stand back and watch helplessly. I felt like I had become a mature adult overnight with a somewhat hardened heart.

I spent a lot of time over at Diane and Michael's. We were expecting close to the same time. She was due about a month before me, but she looked like she was going to explode already and had another month to go. They really couldn't take me in. I knew that. They didn't even have good jobs and lived in a tiny one-bedroom apartment, but I knew they would have if they could have. They were newlyweds, and poor ones at that. They didn't need two more mouths to feed. I was coming to the painful conclusion that I was fighting a losing battle. This was where I had to pay for my mistakes, with one big balloon payment at the end. I had already made a few installments, but the deal wasn't sealed yet. Now the deal was starting to look pretty locked up. I had nowhere else to turn. The parents were winning the battle. I had to wonder how much Marty's mother had to do with his reaction. I suspected she had tipped the scale.

I started seeing some of my guy friends, mainly to get out of the house and not wear out my welcome at Beth's. A guy named Jeff kept showing up at our house, wanting to take me out. He was a little older than me, had a big afro for a white guy, and was good lookin', but he kinda gave me the creeps. He begged me to marry him, go out with him, do anything with him, but I couldn't bring myself to say yes. He just made me feel creeped out, and I didn't know why. I would let him visit me at the house, but I wouldn't go anywhere with him. Mother thought he was weird too, 'cause she had already probed his brain, so at least we agreed on something. I kept brushing him off until he stopped coming over almost every freakin' day. I felt bad for him because he seemed sweet, but just a bit too desperate. I guess that was what I was feeling. One day I finally told him that I really wasn't into courting in my predicament, so maybe at a later date we could go out. He said he understood, and finally he seemed to give up. He would call on occasion to check on me, which I thought was sweet, so I agreed to see him after everything was over.

"So are we cool, man?" I asked sincerely.

"Yeah, we're cool," he said as he gave me a little peck on the left cheek. He really was sweet and sexy, if you could get over the stalking part. He appeared to be looking at me like a wolf eyeing its next meal. Kinda made my hair stand up just like his.

"Okay then, bye. I'll see you on the other side," I said while ushering him to the front door.

"Bye and good luck with everything. You sure you won't marry me? I'd take good care of you both," he said.

"I have no doubt that you would. But that would not be fair to any of us." I gave him a peck on the cheek, then I almost shoved him out the door, but I couldn't help it. I almost had a panic attack when those hungry eyes met mine. Jeez, I was freakin' prego and I wouldn't have been surprised if he had a woody. I didn't want to know, so I didn't look. I'd had enough of that bullshit.

Speaking of woodies, here came fucking Ted.

"Who was that?" Ted asked, looking at me.

"None of your damn business!" I walked to my bedroom, and I could hear him chuckling. I guess he was getting a kick out of the way my life had taken a turn. Surely he would leave me alone for a while. Sicko. I heard him slip into the basement, but he didn't shut the door at the top of the stairs, which means he was whacking it down at the bottom of the stairs, hoping I would catch a glimpse of his massive member. I knew the game, and I didn't wanna play. I stayed locked in my room until I heard Mother tell him bye and heard him leave our house through the front door. That was my signal to go to Mother's room.

I opened the door to her bedroom, and…immediate asphyxiation! The smell hit me like a solid wall of shit.

"Oh my God! What in the hell have you been eating?" I asked her with my hand covering my nose and mouth.

Mother started laughing.

"Holy Mother of God," I said. "I can't stay in here. You're just plain rotten. Have you been eatin' deviled eggs? Oh, help me, baby Jesus, I'm outta here." I backed out of the shit cloud and went back to my room feeling a little queasy. She had been in there fartin' up a storm with the door shut and a space heater on. I *do* declayah, it was simply unbearable.

But I couldn't relax in my room, because I felt like those ice blue eyes were on me all the time. I sure as hell didn't want to sit in the dark in my room, and I couldn't breathe in Mother's room. I walked around the house and decided there was nowhere I could go in the house and be comfortable and not feel like I was in a fish bowl. Lace curtains everywhere! So I decided I'd had enough. Again. I went back in to my bedroom, turned on the light, and waited. I was setting a trap. I lit a cigarette, opened the window, and sure enough, Ted's face was about ten inches from mine. I jumped so hard when I saw his face that I almost dropped my cigarette behind the bed. I was trying to not appear freaked out, so I could get close to him. He tried to strike up a casual conversation like he wasn't some sicko freak, which is what I wanted him to do. It was pretty cold outside but he had beads of sweat all over his forehead. His hands were hanging on the bricks under my window with his feet were wedged on the brick of the downstairs window.

"It's hard to beat your meat when you're hanging by your fingertips, ain't it?" I leaned out to exhale and flip my ashes and saw an opportunity that I couldn't resist. As quick as the idea hit, I had already done it. I crushed my cigarette out on the back of his hand, since it was all I could reach without dropping the screen.

He yelped and dropped to the ground, cussin' up a blue streak. "Fuckin' bitch. Blah, blah, blah, blah…"

"You dumb-ass freak. What did you think? Don't you have any idea how fucking weird this is? I am calling Sara right now. If you don't get home in ten minutes, I'm spilling my guts. I'm telling her everything, so get t'hoppin'." I started dialing the phone. For real. She answered, and I saw Ted the Perv haulin' ass down the back of the property, going toward his house.

"Hey. What you guys doing? How are you and the babies?" I asked Sara.

"They're good. I am tired as usual. Ted is working late again, and I am so tired of eating supper alone or holding it till it has solidified and isn't any good any more. The kids keep me from being able to sit down and have a relaxed meal. I'm sorry. I didn't mean to start bitching at you. I'm just glad you called."

"Uh huh. No prob. Ted'll be home soon, right? You okay?"

"Oh yeah, I'm okay. Just whipped, and I'm as hungry as a bitch wolf."

I laughed, but it didn't reach my eyes. I was glad she couldn't see them. I felt so bad for her, but then again I wanted to bust this thing wide open and tell her what a scumbag her husband was. I couldn't do it, though, and I didn't know if I would ever be able to. She worshipped the ground that man walked on.

It probably had something to do with the massive dick he apparently wanted to show off. If she only knew what he did, she'd probably kill him with her bare hands, knowing her.

Within a few minutes, Sara said, "He's home! Gotta go now."

Honey, she just cut me off, like what am I, chopped livah? You'd think the Pope had arrived or something. Very sad. It's amazing what a huge dick can get you. That's the only thing I could figure. God knows I had sure seen it enough to know, and that thing terrified me.

Back to earth…huh? Oh yeah.
"Okay. Take care."
"Thanks for calling." She hung that phone up so fast it was pathetic. I would rather not have a husband than have one like him, so I guess I should be happy. Well, that was a bit of a stretch, but at least I had stopped staring at the basement stairs.

Chapter Thirty

It seemed the F-word had become the most frequently used word in the English language, and it certainly rolled off my tongue with ease these days. It was so versatile it could be used in many ways: as a verb, an adjective, a noun, a participle, or simply an exclamatory expletive. One thousand and one uses. Some people used it every other word, like on the movie Forrest Gump when the hippie announcer had the microphone on stage at the National Mall. Seeing that brought back so many memories. That movie was set a few years before my hippie/freak days, but we looked like that still.

The cops, we usually called them "pigs," had really been cracking down on the drug scene. When I first started smoking pot, we got away with burning a doobie wherever and whenever we wanted; concerts, parking lots, riding around, and walking down Main Street were all perfect places to light up and share. But it had gotten trickier lately, and it wasn't enjoyable to smoke out in the open anymore. It was too risky, and then we would start getting all paranoid, and that was a buzz killer. So we had started going to somebody's house to get high, mainly Beth's.

When we heard the Doobie Brothers were coming to town, we had to go. As we had expected, they were searching people right and left, but they left me alone. I guess they thought I might explode if they touched me. Everybody gave me their stash, and I stuffed it all into my extra-large maternity bra. No problem. So from then on, I carried everybody's stash when we went riding. I didn't get high any more, except for a few hits of pot when I went to a good concert. And this was an exceptional one.

Beth, Annie, Kevin, and I met Michael and Diane inside, and it was rough for poor Diane. She was very close to her due date, and the baby, despite still being in the womb, apparently loved the Doobie Brothers. Every time they played a Doobies record at home, the fetus would start dancing, and you could see her stomach getting all distorted. You could actually see its feet kicking. Now at the concert, the baby was more active than ever. It kicked the whole time and actually bruised her ribs. That child loved the Doobie Brothers for life.

Diane and I looked like we were having a contest to see just how far human skin could stretch. Diane really and truly looked like she was going to explode, and I wasn't much better off, being only a month behind her. It seemed like she didn't deliver until she was about twelve months pregnant, and it turned out she delivered about a month past her due date. God in heaven, we even considered dynamite several times. She couldn't drive because her stomach was so big, and her legs were so short that she couldn't reach the pedals and fit behind the wheel at the same time. So one day I drove her to the only mall in town, and I dragged her all over that place. Up and down and up and down we went, until she couldn't take it anymore. That night, she went into labor. *AT LAST!*

Poor thing, she stayed in labor for about thirty-six hours. I stayed in the waiting room with Michael, and it was the *longest* thirty-six hours I had ever experienced. I was sure that would change soon. She gave birth to a big, fat, beautiful, nine-pound baby boy. He was magnificent, and he was my nephew, and I would be able to hold him whenever I wanted. I knew it wouldn't be the same, but I also knew it would have to do. He looked like a little Sumo wrestler, and I couldn't keep my hands off of him. The more I held him, the more I wanted my own.

God please help me. I am begging you to help me.

It wasn't until then that I started having anxiety over my own delivery. I was due any time now, but it hadn't dropped yet, and I realized I would probably go over the due date like Diane. I had found nobody who I could trust to help me get back on my feet. There were some very kind thoughts, but none I could live with. The single mother's homes would take care of you and the prenatal care, but as payment they wanted the baby to sell to adoptive parents. That's how they made the money to stay in business.

No thanks! I'll just stay at my house, and I don't fucking know beyond that.

Everybody told me not to hold the baby when it came because I wouldn't be able to give it up if I did. And if that happened, we would have nowhere to live and no baby anything. No baby clothes, diapers, bottles…no nothing.

I am doomed to give up this baby. I am in love with its father, a man who loves heroin and his trust fund more than he loves us. I knew it was best that I wasn't with him anymore. Heroin was strong, bad shit, and I would not tolerate it around the baby and me.

When she got home from the hospital with baby Michael, I helped Diane as much as I could. I was as big as the broad side of a barn, but Diane still had me beat in that area. She was relieved for her turn in the delivery room to be over, and I could tell by the way she looked at me that she hated for me to have to go through it and then go home alone. I could see such pain in her eyes when she looked at me, and Michael's as well. I think the two of them cared more about my plight than anybody else in my family. She offered to share her baby with me, and she did so as much as she could. It helped pacify me for a while, and we became even closer.

My prenatal checks were every week now, and things were progressing, but not fast enough for me. I spent as much time as possible helping take care of Diane and little Michael, partly in order to keep my head off things like the basement stairs. There were still times that I considered doing something stupid, but they were rare…only brief, passing thoughts that I immediately rejected. I didn't want to hurt my baby.

On the other hand, if I could just hurt myself so I wouldn't know anything…

In such times of weakness, I wanted to take the chicken's way out. I didn't want to remember any of it, but I wouldn't consider doing anything that might hurt the baby. And that's really what kept me in line.

As my due date got closer, Mother Dearest made me stay at home more, just in case. It turned out that I was just like Diane, and I went a month over the due date. I felt like a caged animal. Daddy still wouldn't talk to me or look me in the eyes. I could feel him looking at me when I wasn't looking at him. He looked like he was dying of a broken heart, and in his eyes, it was as if I had died too. I was now at the pleading stage. I begged my parent's and Marty's mother to help me keep the baby, but they would have nothing to do with it.

One day about a week past my due date, I screwed myself up and made one last pitch to Mother. It was a fastball, high and tight, aimed at the head. I stood at her bedside while she was lying down, using every trick I could think of. "Please, Mother.

Please," I begged. "I don't think I can bear it. Could you? How will you feel later on seeing me suffer? You know that I will end up hating you for this. You know that, right? You think this is the best thing for me, but really, it's best for you. Everything is always for you, Mother. What about me? Huh? What about this child never knowing its family?"

She looked like she was going to give me the right hook after that one, but I stared her straight in the eyes and said, "Go ahead. I dare you." She dropped her arm by her side and said, "Get out. We're not talking about this anymore."

"What will you do if I come walking in here with my child in my arms? Will you kick me out?"

"Hell, yes. You can't stay here with a baby. I can't take it, and your father is losing his marbles already. He lost his job because of you."

Low blow! But at last I knew it was useless. I was defeated. The combination of guilt and insurmountable odds finally broke me. "Okay, Mother. You win. I give up. But I will never, ever forgive you and Ellen and Daddy and Marty for not standing beside me and this child. I am going through this alone, as usual. You have never been there for me through school, the beauty pageants, my presidential speech…nothing. It's if I am not even your child."

"You are my child, but Elbert is not your father."

She dropped that hot potato as casually as if she were dropping something rotten into the trash.

"Whaaatt did you say?" I stammered, frozen in place. "I know I didn't hear that right."

"You heard it right. Sarge was your father. I was in love with him, and Elbert was a whore hound. I was lonely, and I fell for Sarge. I have always loved him."

I had to sit down at once 'cause my head was spinning too fast and I felt dizzy. Dead silence for a long minute. My wheels were turning.

Another fucking skeleton...Oh. Hell. No!

"So that's why you were so upset when he got sick and died. Jesus, Mother, why didn't you tell me before now? This is a fine time to drop that bomb, huh? Does Daddy know, I mean Elbert? Christ, I don't even know what to call him now. That means I have half-brothers and a half-sister. Oh my God!"

"No, and don't you dare say a thing. Elbert is your daddy. He raised you and loves you more than he has anything or anybody. It would kill him if he knew."

That did it. My head was clear again. I stood up as quickly as if I were ten years old and not carrying thirty-plus extra pounds around my waist. I walked over to her bed where she was propped up. "God in heaven! And you think I'm bad? I don't want to hear you say anything about me ever again. You are a fucking bitch!" And then I couldn't resist it. I slapped the ever lovin' shit out of her and walked out. I had wanted to do that for so long, and she desperately deserved it and needed it. I never thought I would see the day, but I had imagined it many times.

That night, I went into labor. I waited until I was sure and there was no doubt. At about 2:00 a.m., Mother came down the hall and said, "You ready to go?"

She always knew everything...She already had on her coat, and our luggage was by the door.

"Yeah, let's do it," I said. I was resolved to my fate, and my baby's, and I just wanted it all behind me now. All the way to the hospital, she kept saying, "Remember, don't hold or touch it, even if they offer it to you, because you won't be able to give it up, and you have nowhere to live and no job. You have to finish school and make something of yourself. You know, right?"

I would just say "Yes, Mother," when I really wanted to say, "Fuck you, Mother!" I had heard it for months, and I was too exhausted to listen anymore.

We drove to Greenville General, went up to the fifth floor, and they wheeled me off alone to do my thing. It felt as if every eye in the place was on me. Looks of pity. They all knew this baby was to be taken away from its mother at birth. Mother had looked pretty anxious too. I don't know if it was fear that I would change my mind, or the fact that she knew the pain of labor and childbirth and was glad it was me and not her. She was pretty selfish that way.

What felt like a week later, but really was only thirty hours later, on January 26, 1974, I gave birth to a big, healthy eight-pound boy. *Ouch and holy shit!* He was going to make someone very happy. I was drugged for most of the worst part of the labor, and afterward as well, so I slept a lot. Thank God 'cause my ass was killin' me. My stomach was smaller, but still puffy and it looked like a bowl of jelly with worms.

I'm ruined. I started to look at what was left of me, and then passed out again. The sitz bath was the best thing I had ever had. *Oh, Lordy, Lordy.*

The next morning, I *had* to go to the nursery. I couldn't not go. I showed them my bracelet, and they brought my son to me. As the nurse approached, I held my hand up for her to stay back. She pulled the blanket open so I could see. And there in her arms was the most beautiful baby I had ever seen. I memorized every part of him, down to his Fred Flintstone feet. *Marty's feet.* The nurse held him out to me, and I backed up so fast that I slammed into the wall, and my eyes exploded with tears. I ran as best I could to my room and locked myself in my bathroom for hours. Everybody kept trying to get me to come out, but I couldn't face the world.

When I finally came out, it was to face a roommate who had her baby in the room, nursing it. Everywhere I turned there were couples with their babies. *Why didn't they just put me in a mental ward?* I probably would have been happier.

Beth and Kevin came to see me in the hospital. They even went to see the baby. Nobody from my family came. *As usual.* I stayed in the hospital, drugged, in baby and mommy hell for three days. I thought about my baby a lot. I thought about Marty, my mother, his mother, and my father, who all of a sudden wasn't my father anymore. I went to see my baby one last time, but he was gone. His new parents had already scooped him up and escaped.

Finally, Mother came and took me back to home hell, where my father was no longer working, and he had yet to talk to me. Mother tried to make conversation, but I wouldn't talk to her all the way home. I felt like somebody was ripping my heart and soul from my body. The pain was unbearable. I don't think I could have talked if I had wanted to. That kind of loss, and the pain that goes with it, doesn't go away.

I had to go to court to formally sign over my child. It was short, but not painless. I had become bitter and hard. I had to live with myself and my parents and without my child and the person I thought was the love of my life. All I had were two pictures of our son—my son—taken the day his new parents came to get him.

I began to hate my parents even more, and most of my family as well. So I became even more rebellious. I got back on the Pill ASAP, and I also got some condoms just in case. I didn't ask if I could go or do, I just went and did what I wanted. I finished my GED within three months, then I enrolled at Greenville TEC in the medical field. The distraction was necessary and welcome.

School was interesting, and I made straight As, working on an associate's degree in applied sciences. Mother had food on the table every day when I got home, and Daddy eventually started talking to me again. It had taken him more than six months, going back to the day he learned I was pregnant. I was straining to reciprocate. He could have talked to me for days, but it wouldn't have made up for the silent treatment all through the fall and winter.

Jeff started coming over again and waiting for me to get home from school. *Every. Day.* I went out with him once to the movies, but he was so distant, and I couldn't get relaxed around him at all. And I was very busy with school. It wasn't like high school. I had to study for hours every night. After all I had lost, I'd be damned if I was going to flunk out of school too. I just didn't have the time or energy to deal with a relationship right now, and I could tell Jeff wasn't who I wanted to have one with even if I had the time.

"Just quit letting him in, Mother," I told her after a few weeks of him showing up every day. "I don't want to see him."

"You know that won't work. You're gonna have to be the one to tell him, not me. I don't want you to go out with him, and you are *not* getting on that motorcycle with him."

"What do you think I've been saying all this time? He's sweet, but he's not normal. And by the way, I don't care what you think anymore. You have no right to tell me shit. And another thing, you really fucked up my head about who my father is. Shitty timing on that one too. What the hell were you thinking? So anyway, leave me alone, or I'm spillin' the beans about Ted. I am feeling very unstable at the moment."

Chapter Thirty-One

Madame Alexander started blinking again. As often as it had happened over the years, I still had to check each time. I would pick her up, turn her upside down, but when I put her down she would start blinking again. All day and night for days. Mother was extremely restless and having death dreams again. When we asked her who, she'd say she wasn't sure yet.

Jeff showed up again on Monday afternoon. I think Mother was expecting him, and she answered the door almost before he knocked. She asked him to wait in the living room and pulled me into her bedroom and shut the door. She said she had experienced a scary brain probe on him and insisted that I *not* get on the motorcycle with him.

"Trust me," she said as she looked deep into my eyes. "I couldn't turn him away, but don't leave with him." For some reason, I agreed with her and found I had no desire to go against her this time.

"Hi, Jeff," I said to him as I walked up to him.

"Hey. You look great," he said to me with a sexy grin, although his eyes never left my feet.

"Thanks. Jeff, listen...I have so much studying to do, and I have to be honest with you, we're not a thing, you know? You and I. It just ain't gonna happen. You're a sweet, handsome guy, but I have been through so much, and I am nowhere near ready to date again or get serious. I'm sorry, Jeff. Please do us both a favor and don't keep coming over. You deserve better. Just go, and I'll see you sometime. Okay?"

"I had to try, but don't worry," he said, still looking at my feet. "You won't be seeing me again. Take care of yourself, Maggie. I'm *crazy* 'bout 'cha, baby." I walked him to the front porch. He leaned down and kissed me on the lips very sweetly. He had a lonely, hungry look in his eyes. He kept them on me until he turned and walked away.

That was the last time I saw Jeff. He went head on with a big oak tree going ninety miles an hour on his way home that afternoon. It was called a suicide. I found out that night when I saw the news. Mother made sure I was in the room when it came on. She sat there with tears in her eyes, looked at me and said, "I'm sorry."

"You're sorry?" I said through my shock. "You knew!? Why didn't you tell me? Hell, I would have gone out with him or something to try to help him. Jesus, Mother! You could have stopped him. I could have stopped him."

"No, that's where you're wrong," she said sadly. I think she liked Jeff, but she didn't trust him around her daughter. "He had a heavy heart, a troubled soul, and it wasn't the first time he had attempted to kill himself. It was just a matter of time."

"Oh, great, so you let me be the one to feel like shit," I replied, my temper flaring again for the...oh, I guess 1,675th time in the last six months. "Thanks a helluva lot. Quite frankly, I wish I had a fast motorcycle right about now. Why do you continue to screw with my head? Just leave me alone. You know, as soon as I finish school, I am outta here."

"I know," she said quietly. "I don't blame you. There are a lot of bad memories here for you."

"You have no idea, Mother Dearest."

"I have my own, believe me."

"Well, I sure as hell hope so. At least that gives me *some* satisfaction," I said bitterly as I left her room and went to mine. I had a really long cry. *Again.* I was so close to the edge myself that I couldn't see a friend was in need, even worse than I was. I knew there was a dark side to Jeff, but I didn't have the strength to help him, and I felt like a total shit-bag. I was so emotionally drained that all I could do was stare off into space. I couldn't concentrate on my studies, and I cried off and on… *How much can one heart stand?*

The psycho doll was still blinking off and on. We figured it would stop after Jeff's little "accident," and it did. But not for too long, a week or two maybe. It started wearing on Mother's nerves, and really everybody's nerves. So we tried to block it out, hoping that it was a false alarm and the doll was stuck in another realm for a while. *Who the hell knew?* So we watched and waited for weeks and weeks.

I had been studying my ass off every night, sometimes with friends from my class. I had met some great buddies at school, and my favorite was a girl named Cici. We would sometimes get high between classes, and we spent a lot of time studying together and quizzing each other.

After one particularly long day of classes and studying, Cici and I finally called it a night. I did a crash and burn. A sound from outside my window interrupted my dreams. I ignored it. Then what sounded like a rock hit my window. I woke up some kinda pissed, cocked and ready to give Ted both barrels of a sawed-off.

If I only had one...

As I ripped back the curtains, my eyes were probably glowing red. But as soon as my mouth opened to let out a string of obscenities, I was struck speechless. It was Marty, and he was bawling his eyes out.

"I have to see you," he sobbed loudly. "I can't stand it anymore. Please come out or let me in and talk to me. I lost the best thing that ever happened to me when I lost you and our baby. I shouldn't have listened. I should have followed my heart. Please talk to me. Please." He was in the driveway, crying to the night and about to wake up everybody in the house and next door too.

"Well, it's a fuckin' fine time to tell me that now. Do you have any idea what I have been through? Alone, I might add. My whole family has disowned me, except Diane. Most of my friends have too. You left me lying in the fucking yard for God and everybody to see. What the fuck, Marty? Some absolute stranger has my baby. *Our baby.* Jesus! I'll let you in the kitchen." I wanted a big piece of him, but he looked too unstable at the moment for me to attack him physically.

"Hell, no," he stammered. "Your parents will shoot me if they see me."

"Very true, but I really don't care."

"Just let me climb up in your window. Okay?"

"Hey, if you can do it, go for it," I said. That short little sucker leaped up and grabbed the window ledge, I opened the screen, and he slithered in.

"Well, I'll be dipped in shit," I said. "You made that look easy."

That got a little smile out of him, but only for a moment. I realized that I wasn't the only one suffering. He looked like he had aged ten years. I figured it was drugs, but he did look pitiful. He looked me in the eyes the best he could because his eyes were swollen almost shut, and he said, "I am so sorry, Maggie. Please forgive me. I have always loved you and I always will, but there were reasons why I did what I did. I know there is no excuse good enough for what I did. I know that now. I would give anything to go back in time and change it all."

"You're not the only one. I have waited a long time to hear you say these things, but Marty, it's too late. I have a hole in my heart the size of Texas. Make that two holes. One has finally started healing, and the other one will never heal. I have a good idea why you did what you did. You were forced, just as I was. Threatened. Am I right? I know I am. Edith told your mother about me missing my periods when we were in Atlanta, and Ellen made you get out before it got any further along."

All he could do was look down with tears pouring out of his eyes and snot everywhere. He just nodded; he had no words to match his misery. I reached out and held him until he stopped crying. We made love one last time, and it was actually the best sex we ever had. I guess because I hadn't had any in so long, and I wasn't worried about the consequences. I was on the pill *and* we used condoms.

We ain't doin' that again! Afterward, I showed him the pictures of our son, and told him about his Fred Flintstone feet. That made him start crying all over again. He asked, "Why aren't you crying? You seem to be handling all this better than me."

"Marty, I have cried for months. Now that it's over, what I feel now is pain, resentment, and hatred. I have cried forty rivers. I've done the walk of shame many times, all by myself like a big girl, in front of God and everybody. I have begged, screamed, even thought of killing myself, but I didn't want to hurt the baby. But I have to admit, I'm glad to see that you really do have a heart and you love me. But it's too little, too late, Marty. I couldn't live with myself and be back with you now. Not without our baby, and he's gone forever. All I have left are scars. Look at my stomach. Every time I look in the mirror, the pain brings me to my knees. I don't know how I am going to live like this for the rest of my life, but I have to. It's not the scars on the outside, it's the ones you can't see. So don't be too quick to judge me, because I am walking a tight rope, and I have nowhere to land but back on my feet. I don't have a big trust fund to fall back on. I have to go to college and learn to make my own way."

Still nothing but silence.

"Don't know what to say to that, huh? What are your plans?"

"I don't know." He just sat there, dripping and stuff. I couldn't feel pity for him, even though he was a victim too. We were too young to know how to handle the mess we had gotten ourselves into. But when it came to the showdown, he had turned his back on me and our child, and that's what brought me to my knees. I would have done almost anything, gone anywhere with him, but the one thing I would never tolerate was heroin. I would not take a back seat to that or expose a child to the repercussions of drug addiction. I knew in his heart he was sorry and that he wished things hadn't turned out the way they did, but they did.

"Well, I do have plans and they are coming along pretty good considering, but they don't include you," I said. I had grown as cold as ice, hard as stone. I didn't know if there would ever be anyone else who could break through all the protective barriers I had put around myself.

He left quietly through the kitchen door, and I didn't give him a last look or thought. I turned around and nearly bumped into Mother. "Jesus, quit sneakin' around like an Indian," I yelped. "You scared me to death."

"That was Marty, wasn't it?"

"Yes, Mother. And things are pretty much what I figured, and I'm pissed all over again, but much worse now. Everything I had suspected has been confirmed, so basically I have been screwed by everybody I ever cared about or loved, and I suspect there's more to all this, but I can't take any more right now. So back the hell up, and shut the fuck up, 'cause I'm feeling really violent right now, okay?"

"Okay. I know."

"You don't know shit. Leave me the hell alone, okay? I fucking hate all of you, and you are nothing but a selfish bitch! I never wanted to be mean like this, but you and Ellen have taken my blood from me, so look out. AND MOVE!" I actually shoved her back into the door so I could get by. She had me trapped, and I knew that feeling all too well. I was shocked at my behavior and nerve. I never would have guessed I could feel this way about my own mother.

I started getting back into the pot scene. Then the pill scene, alcohol, whatever…but never heroin. I found out almost too late that I had been too near it, because everybody kept it hidden from me. It was a hard lesson, but I was now much wiser and more careful than I used to be. I was dating here and there. Then one day I got a call from my old flame, Randy. He asked me to his senior prom. *How appropriate.* So I went. I had lost all my prenatal weight, and I was almost too skinny. But my boobs were bigger than ever. As long as you couldn't see my stretch marks, I had one of those bodies that made most any clothing look obscene. I wore a fitted white dress that crossed between the breasts. Good God, I wish I looked like that now.

Anyway, he and I started dating again. One day he called and asked if I wanted to go see Rickey Godfrey and his band. They played in some local warehouse. Of course I said sure; I love live music. When Randy picked me up, he said, "We have to go pick up Rickey. He's blind."

"Okay, sure." We pulled up to Ricky's house. Randy got out and went up to the door. After a while, he came out carrying some cases and stuff and had Ricky holding onto his left arm. I noticed that poor Ricky was so high he could barely walk, even with Randy helping him. Randy put him in the back seat, and Rickey started talking. "So, Hughes, who's that? I didn't know you had a girl. She smells good."

"Down boy," Randy said with a chuckle. "Maggie and I have dated off and on for years. She was my first sweetheart. We just went to the senior prom together and started dating again. She's never heard you and your band, and I know she'll enjoy hearing you guys."

"That's cool, man. I'm glad ya'll came." That's about all he *could* say. I was trying to figure out how we were going to get him out of the car, into the warehouse, and how in the hell he was going to perform in his condition. He could barely walk or talk. Randy had one glass eye, his left one, and he looked over at me and could tell I was puzzled. He said, "It's cool. He's used to it. Valium, that is."

Randy was a big guy, thank goodness, because he almost had to carry Rickey into the building and up to the stage. Nobody seemed surprised, and they pitched in like it was helping with the dishes or something. I thought to myself, *There ain't no way this guy is performin' anything but snoring.* But Randy sat him up in a chair, got him a cold beer, and Dear God, he started coming to life. The microphone and most of the equipment was set up, except for Rickey's guitar and amp. Within minutes, they started pickin' and tunin'. Then Rickey said, "This one is for Hughes and his high-school sweetheart Maggie."

I could have crawled into a deep hole. Then he started playing and singing "Have You Ever Loved A Woman", and he was gettin' down on it. Damn, he was great! It made my hair stand on end, and I got all teary watching him gettin' into the music. That boy had SOUL! He was clutching the microphone in his hand, standing up, and belting out his entire heart. He took a giant breath and sucked the little foam piece off the microphone, straight down into his windpipe. He was choking to death on stage. He dropped to his knees, trying to cough it out. Everybody was stoned and just stood there paralyzed while he tried to get his breath. I grabbed Randy and started running up to Rickey, which seemed to awaken some others to call for an ambulance.

Just as I got to Rickey, he coughed the foam mic cover up at my feet. It was about the size of a quarter. Rickey finally got his breath, and I handed him his beer. He took two swigs and picked up where he left off in the song. But I was spent. I thought he was going to die in front of us.

What was most weird about that night was that about five years later, I was in the grocery store, miles from the site of the incident, and somebody touched my arm. I turned around, and Rickey said, "Hey, Maggie. I heard your voice and I wanted to say ha-a-a-ay. You were there that night with Hughes when I sucked that damn foam thing down my lungs. Remember that?"

"How could I forget that?" I said as I got over my surprise. "Almost gave me a heart attack. I thought you were a goner."

"Yeah, me too. Thanks for coming up to help me. Good to see ya."

"You too, buddy. Take care." How weird was that? It's amazing what the other senses can do when one of them is lost…

The night after going to hear Rickey, Randy and I finally had the sex I would never give him when we dated. It was sweet, but we both realized the electricity wasn't there. We were just good friends who made a mistake by having sex. Funny, somehow I felt like I owed it to him, but I wished I hadn't given in to him. It changed everything for us. After that, we would talk on occasion. I love him to this day, but I was never "in love" with him, I just thought I was. It was just puppy love.

Chapter Thirty-Two

The word was out that I had finally delivered, recovered, and was available. And it didn't take long. My phone rang off the hook, and I had a date nearly every night. I went to school full time, and I had two part-time jobs. My figure came back quickly through exercise and starvation. I had the hourglass figure you see on occasion, but underneath my clothes, my stomach was fucked. No more bikinis for me. Seventeen years old and scarred for life, inside and out.

I had so many proposals for steady dating and even marriage, it was unbelievable. Even Robbie and I gave it a try, although we only kissed and did a little heavy petting. He had always kidded me about marrying me while we were growing up, but I didn't realize he was serious until now. I had to try him out to see if the magic was there. He seemed too much like a brother, and I couldn't shake that. He just didn't flip my ON switch, it was more like OFF.

There was Allen, who was totally hypnotized by my presence. *So strange.* I dated David, Steve, Tim, Howard, another David, Don...basically just guys I knew from the freak gang or from school. I didn't try them all out sexually, only a few. I did learn very quickly there were all shapes and sizes. There were big ones, little ones, bent ones, soft ones, hard ones, and one absolutely huge one. I was actually attracted to that guy until I saw his tool...more like a weapon.

I looked at him apologetically and said, "I am so sorry, but *that* is not gonna happen." I had been stitched from one end to the other, and even if I hadn't...*Uh-uh, nope.* But I asked him, "May I just admire it for a while?" It was too big to do *anything* with. So I just stroked it a little and admired it. I didn't want to get things out of hand, so to speak, because that was one terrifying weapon he was sporting. Beautiful, but terrifying. I felt kinda sorry for him, because I don't think there were many women brave enough to take that on. *I may be wrong, but oh my God!* I'm talking nightmare or porno star material. He even had Ted beat in the size department. *God forgive me for even thinking about that.* I wish I hadn't...the thought of Ted made me want to hurl.

Between school and two part-time jobs, I had a full plate, and I kept it that way intentionally, so that my head could stay occupied. If it didn't, I caught myself looking at babies and families, almost stalking them to see if the child looked like mine. It was starting to drive me insane, wondering where he was, if he was okay, if he was happy. I would even ask the parents what the baby's age was and birth date. I think I scared a few mothers asking personal stuff like that. I had to force myself to back the hell off before I completely lost it, or before somebody had me arrested. But it didn't stop me from looking and wondering. At least I got to hold D's baby a lot. She shared with me, but when it came down to it, he wanted his Mama, not me.

It really pissed me off when my parents started wanting to keep little Michael. *What the fuck?* They kept him all the time.

Now, tell me this, I thought, *why couldn't they have helped me with mine? Are they feeling guilty? I'm sorry, but I'm a little confused, and I am trying to not take it out on anybody else, but that just cranks my shit right out. As soon as I can, I am getting the hell out of here!*

I continued to meet new people and made some great new friends. I felt like I had to start over for the most part. There were a few old buds who would always be there, but I had lost so many people I *thought* were my friends but really weren't. It was nice to have friends who didn't know what I had just been through. I was tired of the looks I got from old acquaintances, family, and neighbors. Their eyes showed pity, shame, embarrassment, degradation, whatevah…And that didn't help my head any. So I tried to keep my chin up and not show the pain in my heart. I studied hard and worked a lot. Funny, but I actually felt like a normal teenager again, being around people who knew nothing. I dressed to kill and was back on top. *On the outside.*

I kept seeing this guy in my English class who stared at me, and I have to admit, he did trigger something in me. He had long blonde hair, a mustache, and wore glasses. We started sitting together some, talking, and we realized we enjoyed each other's company. His name was Dan, and one day he asked, "You wanna come with me after class to a friend's house? We can smoke us a doobie, have a sandwich or something, and I'll bring you back."

"Well, sure, I guess so," I replied. I had gotten to know him just well enough that my radar was down. After class we got in his car and rode and rode until we came to a house with an apartment in the back of it on the second level. We got out of the car and started up the stairs. He got out a key, and I noticed there was nobody in the house. *Radar up!*

I asked, "Where are your friends? I thought I was going to meet your friends, and you have your own key?"

"Yeah, I stay here sometimes," he answered casually. "I guess they're gone somewhere. It doesn't matter, they don't mind so it's cool." He was looking at me with hungry eyes, eyeing me up and down.

"Well, I don't know, Dan. This is kinda weird. I just went through a bunch of shit, and I'm not too cool with this."

"It's okay. We'll just hang for a little while, and then I'll take you back after we burn one. Come over here while I roll us one."

"Okay," I said, but I lingered behind him, looking around the apartment for signs of who might live here. It looked to me as if it was his place, and perhaps a chick or wife set it up. *Oh shit!* "I think we need to go, Dan."

"I'm almost through rolling this joint. Come here, and let's light it real quick first."

I went over and sat beside him on the edge of the couch while he lit it. It felt a little better having something to do besides pace around the room. We got stoned on the couch, then he started looking intensely at my lips and ran his hand up and down my arm. It felt pretty good, so he started kissing me softly. I didn't resist. Then he got more aggressive, and I started pushing him away, saying, "No, Dan. We didn't come here for this. I can't do this, let's go before things get out of hand."

Then he pushed me down in the supine position and got on top of me. He was a good deal bigger than me, but I was strong.

"Get off of me, Dan. I mean it! Now!"

That's when he ripped my blouse open. The buttons popped off and tore a hole in the front. Well, that really pissed me off. "Son of a bitch! What the fuck is wrong with you? Don't you know the meaning of NO?"

Then he popped the button of my pants. The zipper slid down, and he shoved his hand into my panties and got a good feel as he was pulling my pants down. *Okay, asshole, you wanna play rough? Come and get it!*

I waited until just the right moment…

He managed to get one leg of my pants off and started trying to penetrate me with his arousal.

Wide open shot, nail it!

I kneed him in the fruit basket so hard he wasn't able to make a sound and immediately had trouble getting his breath. The bastard hit the floor head first, and I hit it running. I put myself together as best I could, gave Dan one last hard kick in the ribs that sent him flying even as he was still gasping for breath, and I was out the door before he finished his second crash landing. I ran until I found a pay phone at a little convenience store a good block up the street.

I called Robbie. Thank God he answered. I had to ask the clerk the address, and Robbie was there in fifteen minutes. *Bless his sweet heart.* I asked the male clerk to let me stay in the bathroom until my savior came. It was pretty obvious I had been attacked, so even the clerk got real protective of me. He asked me, "You want me to call the cops, ma'am?"

"No," I said, "I'll just stay in the ladies bathroom until my friend comes, if you don't mind." I described him and his VW Beetle and went into the restroom. I was kinda shaky, but holding it together. After a little while, the clerk said, "Here's that VW you're waiting for ma'am." When Robbie saw me, he jumped out of the car and wrapped around me as I cried. Mostly from being pissed off and embarrassed I had to call him like that. When we got into his car, I told him a little of the story and begged him to take me home and never say a word to anybody. He promised, but when he saw my torn clothes, he was furious.

"Tell me where the bastard is or who he is, and I'll kill him!" Robbie said. He had never been a fighter like Buddy was, but he looked ready. "I'll call the police. You can't let him get away with that." He was almost pleading with me to let him intervene.

"Let's just say that I wounded him severely," I told Robbie. "It pissed me off more than scared me, to be honest. I may feel different later, but right now I'm severely pissed. I considered him a new friend, and he lied to me. He lied about everything. It's my fault for going over there with him. I guess we weren't thinking on the same path when I agreed to go. Just let it go. I'm okay, and he's not doing so good right now, trust me."

"That's my girl. So what…did you ring his bells or what?"

"Yes. No, the answer is hell yes! He won't be using that thing for a while, so let's just leave it at that. Thank you so much for coming for me. I am such a fuck-up and have the shittiest luck, don't I?"

"No, you're not a fuck-up, but you do have shitty luck, and I'm still crazy about ya. What does that say for me?" Robbie said as he cocked a little grin my way.

"You know how I feel about you, Robbie. I love ya like a brother. I couldn't have called and trusted anybody else but you. Please don't make me feel guilty about it all, I don't think I can take it."

"Damn. I was hoping for more than that," Robbie replied. "I've been in love with you half my life, but I couldn't say or do anything 'cause Buddy would have pulled my limbs off and beat me to death with them. I've been waiting for us to grow up all these years."

"I know that now, you sly devil. If we hadn't grown up together, I'd probably feel different about you. I'm sure I would. But you're too close to being family. Like my best male friend, my brother I can talk to about anything, ya know?"

"No," Robbie said, then he laughed. "I don't want to be like a brother. I want you to be with me. You know, like *be with me*?"

"I would give anything to be in love with you. You will make a wonderful husband and father for some lucky lady, but unfortunately that lady will never be me, baby. You understand?"

"I understand, but I don't have to like it. I haven't been looking for a lady. I've just been waiting on you."

"Oh, Robbie, honey!" I said, taking my turn at disappointment. "I didn't think you were serious when we kidded around about it. Why didn't you tell me it wasn't a joke?"

"Because your brother would have filleted me on the spot, and he's my best friend. First, when I realized it, you were too young, then you were involved with that little shithead, so then I thought it was time. The right time, you know, so we could keep the baby, and I would take care of you both for as long as I lived. I would never grow tired of you. Either one of you."

Well, that did it. I fell apart, into at least a million pieces. I almost could have lived with that scenario. "You are the sweetest, best man I know. But that would not have been fair to you. This is my burden to carry, not yours, love. But I thank you from the bottom of my heart. I love you too much to dump something like that on you. You deserve better than me. I am no good for you or anybody else. I am damaged, broken, maybe even ruined, but there will always be a special place in my heart for you, and that you should never doubt."

"Don't ever let me hear you say that again," he protested. "You're a great person, I just wish that we could be more than best friends, you know. I wish you were in love with me like I am with you. Give me a chance, and I know you will love me, and maybe one day be in love with me."

I was truly surprised at his sincerity and persistence. "I really wish it worked that way. Maybe after I get my head on straight, if I ever do, we can try to make it happen. I would love to be so lucky. Right now, though, I want to go home and scrub myself raw. Please don't tell anybody, especially Buddy. Okay? He would end up going to prison for murder if he knew. Okay?"

"Okay, I promise. But don't do anything like that again!"

"You don't have to tell me twice. I am done with men for a while!"

I never saw Dan again. It seems he cut and ran, and I didn't blame him. He probably thought I was going to have the law after him, and I guess I should have. But I felt like it was my fault for going over there to begin with. I was somewhat attracted to him, and I liked him, until I realized he lied to me, and he was just an animal.

Still, when would I learn…

Chapter Thirty-Three

One of my new school friends, Darla, was in the class a year before me, in the same program. It just so happens that she was connected with some hot guys who lived only two blocks from my parent's house. Oh boy! There were two houses side by side, with apartments throughout all full of hot, freaky looking guys. One of them was her boyfriend, Bobby. They were kind of a mix of brainy guys and musicians. They were all super nice. Although they were five to ten years older than us, we didn't mind that. Beth and I would go over there on occasion and party on the weekends with Darla, and through her we met our new friends Sandy and Susan. We seemed to hit it off right away. From them, we caught wind of a new group of guys moving into the apartment next door, so we anticipated that with bated breath.

Beth had the hots for a guy named Eric, and I have to admit, he did something for my hormones too. But you didn't get between a girl and her target, especially when it's your best friend. She was always trying to find him, and I was right along with her. We were making the rounds looking for him one afternoon, but we had no luck in Bobby's building. Then one of the guys said, "He might be next door, the upstairs apartment where the new guys moved in. Don't worry, they're cool. They know all of us and Eric. Just ask whoever answers the door."

"Okay," Beth said. But she was terrified. I told her I would take the lead, at least at first. After what I had been through, I wasn't afraid of much.

"As long as you go with me, I'll ask for Eric," I told her. "Just don't cut and run and leave me standing there alone." So here we went across the driveway and up the stairs to the veranda. I was fearless.

This is a piece of cake, compared to...

The door opened, and there stood a hippie type, his long brown hair pulled back in a ponytail and muscles bulging through his T-shirt.

Dear God, look at those big blue eyes...

All I could do was stand there and stutter.

Damn, I almost forgot what I came over here for! Who the hell is Eric?!

"Uhhh...is Eric over here?" I finally managed to get out of my mouth.

"No, not right now, but come on in," he said as he opened the door wide and smiled like a mule eatin' briars. "I'm Jim," he turned and pointed to his roommates and said, "this is Cliff and Ellis, and you are?"

"Duhhhhh, I'm Maggie, and this is Beth. Bobby sent us over here to look for Eric." I said, but for some reason the words just weren't coming out of my mouth right.

"We were getting ready to burn a joint. Wanna join us?" Jim asked.

"Sure, if it's okay with everybody," I answered back.

"Oh, hell yeah. Come in and cool off. It's hot as hell out there on that veranda, and it's only May," Jim said.

I walked in, kinda like in a trance. I felt so comfortable there. Not threatened at all, as I had felt with Dan. After a few minutes, I started putting things together about who was who. Sandy was dating Cliff, I already knew Darla and Bobby were a thing, but other than that, I didn't know yet. Sandy walked in, and I could tell she wasn't sure what to think of two chicks being on her turf, but she warmed up quickly when she saw that Jim kept looking at me. We didn't stay long. We didn't want to stir up the beehive, just in case there was another queen bee in the nest. That could be bad, and we didn't want any trouble. We left, but we continued to gather information about the new guys next door to Bobby.

I kept running into Jim at the apartments, and Cliff was almost always with Sandy. Beth didn't go over there as much as I did. She would come sometimes to hang, but mainly it was Ruth, my friend Cici, and Darla. I felt more at ease at Bobby's place, just because Darla was usually there, and I knew her from school. I wasn't really trying to find a mate, I just wanted a place to hang and relax. But I found out that Jim wasn't dating anyone.

Hubba hubba. An older man…

Maybe that's what I needed. I hadn't had any luck with the ones my age. They just didn't do anything for me. We got more comfortable with each other pretty quickly, and soon he invited me to go see a movie. *Blazing Saddles* turned out to be funniest movie either of us had ever seen. We didn't stop laughing until long after the movie was over. Something about that guy just flipped my switch, and I couldn't be held responsible for my actions. *Good God in heaven.* We made out in his VW bug like the hormonal freaks we were. When I was around him, my switch stayed in the ON position. Couldn't help it.

We didn't take long to get down to serious business. We were consenting adults, I was on the Pill, and he was the right man with the right tool for the job. We couldn't get enough of each other. He was going to trucking school with his older brother, and afterward he took a job driving to Columbia twice a night, shuttling trailers. I would sneak over there during my school break, wake him up and check out his tools, then leave him to sleep. I should have left him alone to sleep all day, but I couldn't resist. Otherwise I only got to see him on the weekends, and he didn't seem to mind the service terribly. And I was so happy to oblige. It kept a smile on my face: I had finally figured out the sex thing.

It is amazing after all, praise God in heaven! The right man, with the right tools, the right skills, at the right time.

The apartments were always hopping, and with me dating an older man…well, let's just say I thought Mother and Michael were going to have a stroke, but I didn't care. I'd had enough motherin' to last a lifetime. Michael had become my big brother figure since Buddy's wife had pretty much forbidden him to see us. Michael and I had become very close friends, and he didn't want to see anything else bad happen to me. He suffered through my whole ordeal too, so he cared a lot about my welfare. I was actually afraid that he might go over to the apartments and whip somebody's ass, but he didn't. When they met one weekend, he seemed to like Jim, but when he did drive-bys he saw all the activity at the apartments. The place was crawling with long hairs and cowboy boots, and Michael was no fool, so he kept a close eye on me.

About a week later, I took Jim to one of our family get-togethers at Sara and Ted's. Mother was in rare form. She'd been suckin' down the Wild Turkey, black beauties, and Winstons, and was havin' a good ole' time—until I walked in with Jim. We were both dressed pretty ratty, and Jim had a long ponytail down his back, tied with a black velvet ribbon. We approached Mother, the queen, and I said, "Mother, meet my good friend, Jim. Jim this is Nora Keith, my muthah." I introduced him to the whole fam-damily, ignoring the looks Noni was giving me. Jim was eloquent as always. He had been raised well in an educated family, close to the spotlight and rubbing elbows with people in high places. I knew he could handle whatever was thrown his way, and I expected plenty from Noni. She didn't have much to say to him, just "Hello, nice to meet you," but she snatched me up and dragged me into the kitchen and said, "How dare you humiliate me like this? Bringing that stray dog into our family gathering. The nerve!"

"Okay, then," I said nonchalantly. "We'll leave. And by the way, what the fuck is Ellen doing here? And you're too jacked to even talk to right now. Go party, and I'll leave you to it."

"No, I'm sorry," Noni said. "Don't go. I just wasn't ready for the long hair thing."

"Jesus, Mother, at least he doesn't have an afro like Kevin or Jeff. You never said much about that. Give him a chance, I think you'll like him."

So Jim and I stayed for a while. I hung out with the guys out back smoking a joint. Even Ted burned one with us. That was almost too much to digest, but I didn't want to go upstairs where the women were. Buddy had brought his little bulldog wife, and she and Mother now hated each other with a passion. It had become a major source of tension at these little gatherings. The only good part was that we got to see Buddy, but he was as nervous as a whore in church, waiting for the ax to fall at any minute. Mother and Linda got into it nearly every time they were in the same room, and we all had begun to dread these gatherings rather than enjoy them. I floated around playing pool and getting high with the guys and went upstairs to chew on my nails while I walked on eggshells, but at least this time Mother and Linda didn't get into a fight. And by the time Jim and I left, Mother was already warming up to him. *Thank God!*

After a few more weeks, I realized I was getting too involved, too fast with Jim, and suddenly I became terrified. I had been fighting my impulsive defense mechanisms ever since I first met him, and now found I didn't want to do that anymore, at least for a while. I needed a break. So I started dating a little here and there. Ruth introduced me to this hunky guy from Columbia named Bruce. He was a psychologist in a drug and alcohol rehab center. He was so gorgeous, with golden blond hair, light blue eyes, and a great body. He made good money, and we were attracted to each other right away. We dated a few times on his motorcycle, riding up into the mountains. We went to Charlie B's Ranch for an outdoor concert and saw a lot of bands that were popular at the time: the Charlie Daniels Band, Goose Creek Symphony, Billy Preston, ZZ Top, and many more. I had a blast, but Bruce was a stick in the mud. I never could figure that one out. But he sure was purdy to look at, and he gave me the goo-goo eyes a lot.

He came into town to see me about every other weekend, but while I was with Bruce, I kept flashing back to Jim. I realized I was going to have to make a decision soon, because after a while, dating two guys alternating weekends was just not gettin' it for me. It was fun to date around and go hog wild for a bit, but I was already gettin' over it. I had a lot of studying for school, and I still worked two part-time jobs, so every minute of every day was busy. I guess even seventeen-year-olds get tired eventually.

Bruce asked me to come to his pad in Columbia for the weekend, so after thinking it over a bit, that's what I did. Mother almost laid a cow, but I was so tired of her shit that I didn't care.

What the hell? Right? I'll give him another try to see if I'm interested in him long term or not. We hadn't done the nasty yet, but I was into him by then and ready to. He came and picked me up on his monster BMW motorcycle, which really gave Mother the shits. *Don't care!* So off we went to Columbia. I wasn't too crazy about being on a motorcycle on the Interstate, but it was exciting feeling all grown up.

Bruce had a nice bachelor pad condo set-up. He had a roomie who was gone that weekend so we had the place to ourselves. I was getting a bit nervous all of a sudden about being there alone with him, but he had always been a Southern gentleman around me. On went the TV. Football. *Oh yay.* Football had never been a favorite of mine. Bruce got out some brewskies, but I declined. Alcohol wasn't my favorite high.

But not too young to smoke pot. Har har…

We had never talked about smoking pot, but I asked Bruce, "Do you mind if I burn a doobie? I don't really like alcohol." He didn't look too happy about it, but said, "Okay, just do it in the bathroom under the ventilation fan." I used a little metal pipe instead rolling a joint, which kept the smoke factor way down. *Ahhh, niiiice…* So while he was glued to the freaking ball game, my ass was bored, and I kept going into the bathroom to use the vent, and he kept popping beers. I had never seen anybody get so involved with football in my life, except for one time when a guy barfed all over me at the Clemson/Carolina game. I never understood the intensity of the fans, and after that experience, I didn't want to. Bruce was getting louder and louder as he consumed brewskies, and I was getting quieter and quieter.

At least I brought some anatomy and physiology and medical terminology homework with me. What fun…

FINALLY, the game ended and we were snuggling, getting a little worked up. I got up and said, "Why don't I get into the shower and freshen up, and we can go to bed? Sound okay to you?"

"Sounds great," he replied. "I'll get the bed ready and stuff. Here's some fresh towels and washrags. Lemme know what else you need."

"Okay, thanks, doll." When I came out, he was walking around in his boxer shorts, lookin' good. Lookin' confident. He wrapped his arms around me, gave me a big wet beer kiss—*yuk*—as he pulled me close. He asked me softly, "Will you let me make love to you tonight?"

"I thought you'd never ask, babe. I'm yours." So we went into his bedroom, closed the door, and he pounced on me, growling like a madman. We laughed, rolled around, and started to relax some. We got under the covers and peeled off our clothing as things heated up. Then the big moment came for the penetration. *Hello? Hello?!* He sure seemed to be working on something mighty hard, but I'll be damned if I know what it was. I realized that he was going like a little jackhammer, so I asked him, "What are you doing? Is it in?"

Well, didn't that ice the cake? He roared at me, "YES. IT. IS. IN. GODDAMMIT!" He jumped out of the bed and started throwing things: trashcans, records, shoes, whatever was close by. Not really at me as much as in my general direction. He was livid, and I really hadn't meant to upset him. I honestly couldn't tell why he was working so hard while I wasn't feeling a thing. Then I saw him in the dim light as he stomped and cursed and threw things, and suddenly it all made sense. This beautiful, smart man with Hollywood looks, great job, and the *big* motorcycle...had no penis. I'm talking pencil eraser. I was crushed, and he was devastated. Apparently this had happened to him before.

Do ya think? No wonder it took him so long to get up the nerve to ask me. But for the meantime, he was getting more violent by the minute.

"I'm so sorry, Bruce. I didn't mean to upset you."

"Just shut up, you damn pothead," he yelled at me.

"Okay, I deserve that I guess. I'm sorry, but I need to leave. You're scaring me." I started gathering my stuff.

"I really don't give a shit," he yelled. He had suddenly become so hateful. I guess he felt like he was hidden behind the door when God passed out the penises, because he got completely left out. I wondered how he peed without peeing on himself. *I dunno...*

But this beautiful, smart man, a psychologist and drug and alcohol rehab guy, was also a fucking alcoholic and apparently a violent one.

How am I going to get out of this one? Why me? I am such as idiot. While I was trying to figure out what to do, I heard him getting dressed too. Man, I got my shit together so fast, but I didn't know where I was going. I didn't have much money on me; I hadn't needed it.

"Come on, let's go," he said through clenched teeth. "Get your stuff. I'm taking you home."

"Just take me to the bus station," I said. "I don't have any money, though."

"You got a damn deal. I'll cover the ticket," he spit out.

"Thanks. I am so sorry it had to turn out this way, Bruce," I was trying to say to him as he stomped out the door without another word.

So he dumped me off at the really scary bus station in downtown Columbia, South Carolina. He handed me $20, and I shut the door, and he pulled a wheelie as he pulled away in his BMW show car. I had plenty of time to think and then sleep on the way home, seeing as how it took four hours for a one-and-one-half-hour trip. I would call Jim when I got to the Greenville terminal.

Boy, what a letdown that was.

He had promise. Gorgeous, had money, had a career, had stuff...

Goes to show, you just never know.

I realized during that long bus ride that the whole time I was there, all I could think about was sweet Jim. I wanted his hands all over me, not to mention other things. I knew I had hurt him by running off with Bruce, but I was so young, and I'd had a big part of my life totally fucked up. I hadn't wanted to fall in love, and I was headed that way fast with Jim. I wanted to be able to say that I had dated around and played the field. Well, I did, and suddenly I was satisfied with my decision. Jim was the one for me. Nobody had flipped my switch like he did. And it felt like we were already best friends. I just hoped he could forgive me.

Chapter Thirty-Four

"Hello?" A familiar voice answered the phone.

"Jim, hey it's me," I said, and I just couldn't keep the remorse out of my voice. "I'm sorry to call you so early, but I need a favor. I'm at the Greyhound bus station downtown, and needless to say it's a really creepy place to be, even at 8 in the morning. Can you please come get me? I need you."

"I'll be right there," he said without hesitation. "Stay near the ticket area. I'll find you. Are you okay?"

"Yeah, I'm okay and real glad to be home. I'm sorry if I hurt you. I made a big mistake by going to Columbia. Just come get me, please?"

"Give me fifteen minutes," he said. "And stay safe!"

That was an order. Thank God for that man. That was the longest fifteen minutes I'd had in a long time, but I think he made it in twelve, maybe less. He drove up with a patch over his right eye. *What the hell?*

"What happened to you?" I exclaimed. "Why don't I drive? Holy shit!"

He looked pretty rough, but he wouldn't let me drive. On the way home, he told me how he hurt his eye. Just one of those boy stories, something about "Cliff's brother driving an old International Harvester four-wheeler, blah, blah, off the side of the road into a ditch in the middle of nowhere, blah, blah, bent over to look underneath and blah, blah, blah… Damn eye!" I was so glad to be home, and glad he wasn't giving me hell, my mind didn't focus on the details. Until…

That was only the beginning. It turns out he and Ruth had had an interesting night together. She had conveniently gotten stranded at Jim and Cliff's apartment the previous evening. She had it all planned: me in Columbia, and she was going to lay it on my man.

Well, I guess I deserved it, but that heifer was my friend. Was my friend.

They slept in the same bed, and she did her best to come on to him. But he was in excruciating pain with a lacerated cornea and didn't follow through.

He admitted, somewhat later, that had he not been so miserable, he would've tapped it good. Ruth was built like a brick shithouse, had a magnificent set of titties, and enjoyed sharing herself immensely. *Point for me.* I wouldn't have blamed him, but boy, that pissed me off. From that point on, I knew she could not be trusted. I knew she had been into heroin a while back, but she was back on the wagon and had cleaned up well. *Point for her. Don't forget it.*

Within a few days of my return from Columbia, Jim and I were definitely a thang. I knew he was the one for me, without a doubt. A good, honest man. *With all the right tools.* He wasn't rich, but he worked a regular job until he started school in respiratory therapy. At that point, he had to move back in with his parents, which put a major crimp in our love life. But we got by. He was crazy about me, even after knowing about my past, which I had pretty fully divulged. Hell, it couldn't be hidden even if I wanted it to. And I was crazy for him. All the time. I never wanted anyone else again.

I told him a lot about the Ted situation, but I quickly learned the man had one hell of a temper, so I didn't give him all the details. Not yet anyway. He was always very protective of me, and the Ted stuff clearly made him consider extreme violence. I made him take the family oath of silence, and as bad as he hated it, he agreed. The last thing I wanted was him going to jail, and I could tell by the way he reacted to my revelations that he wanted revenge. I also sensed he would be up to the task physically, so I invoked Noni's influence to seal the deal. I explained to him how the sheer force of her will was what kept everybody from taking any action—or even talking about it. And that included Michael, who as a Vietnam vet was a man not to messed with: he was big, strong, in great physical shape, and loved to fight. Jim and Michael had hit it off really good and become fast friends, and I think that helped get Jim's cooperation. He trusted and respected Michael, as well as Noni.

One Saturday I went to see him at his apartment, pulled the VW around back, and got out. I looked up to see him on the veranda. And standing right beside him was Bill, the guy I used to see between classes in high school. The one I had lusted for back then.

Well, I'll be dipped in shit! I realized all at once, as I saw them side by side, that they were *fucking brothers!*

I saw the funny look on the Bill's face as he looked down at me and pointed, turned to Jim, and asked, "What the hell is she doing here?" He almost sounded jealous, like he already knew the answer.

"That's my girlfriend, Maggie," Jim answered, "though I take it no introduction is necessary."

Damn, he's too quick.

"Okay then," Bill said.

"Okay then," Jim said, then he just looked at me, grinning while I squirmed, and said, "Come on up." He introduced us, though it really wasn't necessary. "Bill, this is Maggie, Maggie this is my younger brother, Bill." All I wanted to do was crawl under something.

Well at least we never dated or anything, I kept telling myself, trying to calm down.

Bill said, "Yeah, we used to see each other a lot at school." I know my face probably looked like a too-ripe tomato by then.

"I'm gonna cut out," I said. "I just thought I'd stop in and say ha-a-a-a-ay. Give me a holler later, Jim, if you wanna hang out."

"You know it. I'll talk to you in a little while."

"Okay, bye." Man, I flew outta there like my hair was on fire. *That was a shocker. Never saw it comin'.* I had never seen them together, so it had never occurred to me until…*Oh my God!* Odd, isn't it, that I would be attracted to brothers, even though they weren't that much alike? But side by side, it was obvious.

Well, that's gonna take a little getting used to, but we'll get through it.

Mother had really taken a liking to Jim, thank God, because like it or not, it wasn't going to change anything. Except it did keep the peace. After he "rescued me from the bus station," as she so often reminded me, she loved her some Jim. Jim this, Jim that, Jim, Jim, Jim…She was pissed at me before and after I went to Columbia with Bruce. I felt bad enough for the both of us, but she made me feel lower than cat shit. In her heart, she knew why I had to go, but she was so afraid that I wouldn't "come back to Jim." She was pissed because I hurt "her" Jim.

OK, enough already. I got it, I learned from it, I'm settled. She never knew what had happened in Columbia, of course, except that it didn't work out. And she knew my true love was waiting patiently for me to grow the hell up. *Well, excuse me, but I grew up too fast*. My teenage life had been cut short, and I had the stretch marks to prove it. Not to mention the mental torment that I was trying to recover from. Jim was my savior. He gave me unconditional love, and that was what I needed to survive. He accepted my baggage, skeletons and all. I would have married him in a heartbeat if we weren't in school. And if he was willing.

Mother was having nightmares again, and the psycho doll was batting those eyes like never before. Nothing would stop it. Mother was getting frantic, looking tired from wild nights of bad dreams. "It's Bonnie. I know it is," she said one morning. "I had a dream about her and David and the kids. I saw her through a sheer material, laid out. The kids were crying, all except Mandy, and nobody could do anything with her." She called David, and he verified that Bonnie wasn't doing well at all. We all loved Bonnie, even with all the hell she had put everybody through. You couldn't help but love her. But she sure produced some wicked chilrens. And poor David was a mess.

"We need to get rid of that damn doll. She's cursed," Daddy would say. He knew what it all meant, but he kept a safe distance from the action as much as he could. He had taken a part-time night-shift job recently, and that helped. But he knew to check and make sure that his funeral suit was dry-cleaned and ready, because there would be a funeral soon.

When the phone rings in the middle of the night, you know...you just know. Bonnie had passed away at the young age of thirty-eight. It was a very sad situation, and poor David was left with that mess. He had her body brought to Greenville to be buried with our family. Bonnie wanted to be where Mother was going to be. It was a very sad funeral, and David had already had to endure one memorial service in Texas, then the big one here with all the family. It was truly a sad time. David had come with Mandy only. She didn't know what to do without her mother. Even though she had a rough childhood because of Bonnie, Mandy still loved her and was going to be lost without her. We all grieved for her, David, and the kids. Mack was still in prison and didn't get to go to either service. Bonnie had left David with so much debt, but he loved her with all his heart. He must have loved her to have stuck with her for so long. They stayed with us a few days and then went back to their little hell to try to regroup.

There was a big framed family photo of David, Bonnie, and their children in Mother's bedroom, hanging over the head of her bed. They had given it to my parents years ago, when Bonnie was still healthy and pretty. But Mother noticed that since Bonnie had died, she couldn't see Bonnie's face anymore on the photo. She said it was just a grayed out area where her face used to be. The rest of us could see her fine, but not Mother. She kept this to herself for a long time, because it didn't change anything, and she didn't want us to think she was off her rocker. *No comment...*

Meanwhile, Jim and I were studying hard in the medical field to make good grades and hopefully get good jobs before long. I was a year ahead of him in school because he did the trucking thing for a while, until his truck blew up one night and he took a near-death leap from the cab onto the Interstate. "I cleared both lanes in two strides," he said. He decided then that was enough of truck driving. Thank God it happened at about 2 a.m. and he didn't have to dodge traffic.

School for me was great. I had made great friends, especially Cici. She and I had a lot in common, and she was so much fun. We had a two-hour lunch break every day, so we would smoke a joint, play a set of tennis, eat lunch, and split a pitcher of beer, then go back to class. I still made straight A's. She introduced me to a good friend of hers named Hannah, and the three of us had us some good times. Good people.

Hannah was a little older than us and gorgeous. She was recently divorced and needed to go to Fernandina Beach, Florida, to get some things from their marital house. She asked Cici and me to go with her. So of course we said, "Well, hell yeah!" She rented a U-haul one weekend, and she and I took turns driving while Cici followed in her car. We would switch off driving without stopping the damn thing. We were all so petite, we could just slip into the driver's seat while the other one slipped out. Idiots that we were. Young and foolish, but we pulled it off.

After several hours, we pulled into a gas station to refuel and answer nature's call. Hannah was driving at the time, thank God. We came plowing up toward the gas pump, and heard the most God-awful screeching sound as the truck came to a stop. I turned around and saw Cici flapping her arms and pointing upward and realized what had happened. *Oh my God!* The awning was a bit lower than the U-Haul. I said, "Oopsie daisy." Hannah said, "Oh shit."

I responded with, "Yeah, no shit. Well, shall we make a break for it? Or do you have good insurance?"

"Yeah I do, but dammit to hell," she said. "I'm afraid the whole thing will come down if I try to back out. I guess I'd better get out and talk to the owner."

"Crap! I'll go with you. Let's just hope we can get out without dying."

We did the walk of shame across the parking lot while the onlookers laughed. God knows, I knew how to do that walk. Cici was laughing by then too, but she wasn't about to do the dreaded walk with us. She kinda scrunched down in her seat and waited to see how we were going to get out of this. As we approached the sleazy little gas station in our very tiny hot pants and braless tank tops, the owner came out, all red in the face and with a cigarette hanging out of his mouth. He was shaking his head and said, "Woman, couldn't you see that this thing was too tall for my awning?"

I soon learned that Hannah was a woman who was always in control, no matter what the situation. Positively unfazed and fearless, she replied, "Obviously not, but if you ask me, your awning was too low for my truck to be able to get gas, and I have to get some gas, so forgive me, but I just couldn't tell. And why would you have an awning that a damn truck couldn't fit under anyway? It's just a U-Haul, not a semi. You need a new one anyway. Here's my insurance information. I am in a rush, so let's get this over with. Hopefully, you'll have a better one built next time."

Bubba was visibly and totally surprised at Hannah's demeanor and speech. Realizing this woman had brass balls much bigger than his, he said, "I know it's short. You're not the first one to hit it, dammit. Let's just see what happens when you back up and go from there, huh?"

The whole time, of course, he was looking at my tits and her Barbie doll legs. He cleared the area of people and parked cars, and we proceeded to slowly back up, and the God-awful screeching sound, this time in reverse, made our skin crawl. But the awning didn't fall. So we took off like we were on our way to a fire, with Cici on our tail.

"Well, he did say something about 'go from here,'" I said, laughing. Still no gas, but luckily there was a better place not far from there. Thank God, because we were in Podunk, south Georgia, where you could drive ninety miles and see nothing but pine trees. After we fueled up and went to the girl's room and shook off the thrill of our little incident, we became hysterical. We laughed off and on for hours about it. Actually, for years.

When we finally got to our destination, we were pretty fried. But there was a welcoming party that energized us enough to keep going. Of course, we had to tell our gas station story to all, and everybody got a real kick out of it. We were staying at Jake's house, not at Hannah and her ex-husband's place. Jake told us they had some fresh produce coming in the morning that we would enjoy immensely.

"You know what sprouts three days after a rain? Mushrooms. *Psilocybin* mushrooms. We'll make some tea and have some fun on the beach. Whaddya say, girls?" Jake asked proudly.

"That would be so cool," we all agreed, and right away we were squirming with anticipation. *Tripping on the beach should be a lot of fun, especially with these folks.* They were so nice and easy to get to know. That night, we just hung out on the deck, watched the sun go down, and got to bed early in anticipation of a big day.

Life was really good again. I did miss that Jim, as always. I spent many nights wishing I had met him first, before Marty. Being older, more mature, he could have helped me deal with things better than I did, or maybe prevented it altogether. *I dunno...*Hindsight is always 20/20. But I longed for my son, worried for him. I prayed he was safe and happy, warm with a full belly.

What does he look like now? Does he favor me or Marty the most? Those were always my last thoughts as I lay down to sleep. Just thoughts. One could easily lose oneself in those thoughts. *Guilty am I.*

"Morning, my little beauties. Rise and shine!" Standing in the doorway to our shared bedroom, Jake held up a paper grocery bag full of the prettiest mushrooms you have ever seen. "They are perfect, fresh, and very potent," he said. "We have a full day ahead. Breakfast is in the makin'. After that, I'll start getting these babies cleaned and make a punch with a punch." Jake was most enthusiastic about the day's agenda. "Get those tight little buns up, and let's rock and roll!"

"Shit. What is wrong with him? Is he military or something? It's barely daylight," I mumbled to Hannah.

"No, he's just a mushroom lover," Hannah said. "He was up before the sun, gathering them in the pasture. They sprout overnight, and you gather them in the moonlight, before the sun hits 'em, so they're really fresh and strong."

"Ya'll are shittin' me, right? Does he know what he's doing?" I asked. "The wrong mushrooms can kill you, so I dunno about all this."

"Listen," Hannah reassured me, "I grew up with him in south Georgia, and we have done this many, many times. Trust me, he's the best at this. But if you don't want to trip, that's cool too."

"No, I would enjoy it! I just wanted to know your thoughts on all this, before I do it, ya know?"

Hannah looked at me seriously and said, "I would trust him with my life. And yours."

"Duly noted, my friend. What about you, Cici?" Hannah and I both looked at her through the morning fog. She had yet to speak.

"I've never tripped before, but I can't think of a better set-up than with you guys."

"I'll take that as a yes and a heartfelt compliment, my friend," Hannah replied. "If you're sure, we promise to take good care of you, since you're a virgin to hallucinogenics. Maggie, you're experienced, I believe?"

"More than I like to admit. I'll be fine, but it has been over a year. Or so…"

"Good, then it'll be even better." Hannah got us up and led us to the coffee machine. We sat on the deck and drank it all in, the scenery, the coffee, the smells.

God, what a life. I could definitely live here. Where are those mushrooms? This is gonna be a wonderful day.

We ate a killer breakfast with all the trimmin's. The word got out that I knew how to make milk gravy, so I did. And very well, I might add. We sat around and shot the shit for a while, digesting three thousand calories and about two thousand grams of fat. *Wow.* We got our showers, put on our bathing suits under our little hot pants, and we were in business. David was cooking up his wicked brew. I noticed the smell and had to comment, "That smells like cow shit."

Jake grinned, "That's because that's where it grows. In cow shit. The spores are in the shit, and three days after a rain, they sprout the most beautiful shrooms, as you saw."

"Alrightly then. That explains the smell very nicely, thank you."

"Don't worry. That's why I always cook them real good. Some people eat them fresh, but not me. You'll be fine. After they've made a strong mushroom tea, I'm gonna mix some tasty stuff in there so it'll taste good going down. I've got it down to an art. Trust me."

"He does," Hannah confirmed.

By that time, we had all washed and dressed, and the Master of Mushroom Tea was glowing in anticipation. More people started arriving. Apparently the word was out that the Master had scored. It was not a large crowd, thank goodness, but a few of their close friends. Annie was one who arrived with her baby, Nichole. Nichole was only about a year old and could stand and walk as long as she had a grip on something. She was so sweet, and she seemed like a happy baby. I hoped it didn't throw me into a funk while tripping...you know, the baby thing.

Jake served us up some tall glasses with ice and a purple looking punch. Annie declined, thank God, because someone had to watch the baby, and I would have declined myself in order to do so.

"Down the hatch," Jake declared, and we all turned it up.

"That tastes pretty damn good. A lot better than that cow shit smell," I noted.

"Thanks," Jake said. "But I bet this is a lot stronger, so hold onto your hats, ladies."

Oh boy, was he right about that! *Holy cow...* I immediately got that queasy feeling, then my eyes started feeling funny, and in about fifteen minutes I was flying. Cici had a strange look on her face, but she would laugh on occasion. As we were getting off real good, Nichole took a liking to Cici. She stood at her feet, banging on Cici's legs, screaming gibberish and having herself a good ol' time. But Cici was sitting on the couch looking stricken, and I recognized that look, and said, "Nichole, come over here, baby. Come here and see me." I went over and got Nichole to ease up on Cici so she could try changing seats. But Nichole insisted on torturing Cici.

Any other time it would have been cute and welcomed, but Cici was starting to freak out. She started to cry uncontrollably. I realized that we had to get out of the house right away, and I took the initiative. You never know what might go on in somebody's head when they're tripping, especially their first time. Hannah, Cici, and I walked down to the beach, and the mood instantly changed. We were in awe of everything. *So beautiful.* Cici said, "I don't know what came over me in there, but I couldn't help it. The baby freaked me out something terrible."

"It's okay. The mind is a terrible thing," I said jokingly, and it worked. "But we're out here now, and it's awesome. Let's go play." I headed for the water. Cici followed, amazed at everything. As this was her first trip on hallucinogens, Hannah and I knew we had to help her overcome that first emotional experience quickly.

As we walked down the beach, we saw where somebody had built a sand castle. They had used a lot of water to make it look kinda like melted wax. Or maybe that was the mushrooms talking. But it was really cool. We looked at the water, looked for shells, looked for birds, and even looked for nothing. Suddenly we heard a vehicle come up behind us, and in a surge of paranoia we spun around to find Jake in a Jeep, with the top down. "Get in, ladies, and we'll ride down the beach."

You can do that in parts of Florida. Normally I would not approve of cars on a beach, but in this case, it was really fun. We took pictures that told the whole story when we got home. They were hideous, out of focus, and we looked pretty bizarre, but it was an accurate representation of what was going on. Only the three of us could look at the pictures and know what they showed. And some of them even we didn't know. We laughed for eight solid hours, and it showed in the pictures. We were so sunburned that we looked like tomatoes with teeth, and our hair was flying everywhere, and I have to say it was probably the most fun day I'd ever had in my life. *God knows I was due.* We were so exhausted and sunburned that we took some aspirin, had a couple of licka-made-dranks, and did a face plant by 10:00 p.m.

I didn't even think about all my skeletons and baggage that whole day. Not until those nasty varmints came to me when the lights went out and I was alone. I forced my mind onto another topic. I really missed me some Jim boy. He was my rock, and I prayed that he loved me as much as I loved him. My heart would not survive another wound of this magnitude. *Not in this lifetime.* I should have guarded it better this time, but I couldn't keep him out, no matter how hard I tried. I'd had a hole in my chest big enough to drive a truck through, and he had pulled up in there and parked that beautiful tight ass. And didn't look, at least for now, like he was interested in leaving. *Life was good.*

The next morning we had to drive the truck to pick up Hannah's stuff at her ex-husband's house and be on our way back to South Carolina. He didn't live far from there, so we got there in no time, loaded up her stuff, she said her good-byes, and we left. It very was sad actually. They appeared to still love each other, but they just couldn't work things out. He had retinitis pigmentosa and was already near blind. I don't know if I could have left him like that personally, but they had given it their best, and they had agreed it wasn't enough. A mutual understanding, fortunately without acrimony. They cried, which means we cried, Cici and I.

We switched off driving again so Cici didn't have to be alone the whole trip. God, we were in pain from the sunburn, but thank goodness it wasn't on our back ends. Just our upper body, face, and the front of our legs, a riding-in-the-jeep sunburn. *Whew...* It was a long trip where conversation was limited mostly to a few select expletives, such as, "Shit...Dammit to hell...Fuck, need lotion...Need aspirin...Need a joint...Please kill me," and such as that. We had to unload Hannah's stuff into her parent's garage once we got into town, as she was going to be living there with them for a while. Finally, they took me home.

Chapter Thirty-Five

Jim was waiting for me at my house when I got home. He had been spending the night there a lot lately. He would sleep in my bed, but only when I wasn't there, and sometimes he would sleep on the daybed in Mother's room. I wasn't aware that when I was out with friends, Jim was often at my house, studying and staying with Mother.

When I got there, Mother was relieved, but had "the look of death" on her face. Jim looked kinda ragged too. "What's going on, guys? Ya'll look like shit." Mother turned and went to her room.

Jim looked at me and said, "Psycho doll has been on a marathon, and Noni's having nightmares again. I've been staying here this weekend, and she's been wearin' a damn path down the hall and back at night, all weekend long."

"Oh shit, not again. Please, not again. Did she say who this time?"

"No, she's all shook up and won't talk about it, but she's been on the phone a lot, and she says that nobody is aware of any problems. Whoever it is, it will be sudden. Unexpected." He said. "She's just hoping she's wrong."

"Not good. She's never wrong about that. But it sure is good to see you. I missed you real bad."

"I missed you too, and by the way, you look like a big red chili pepper. You must have had a large time," he said, grinning.

"We had some fresh mushroom punch and spent all day on the beach in freakin' Florida. It just as well could have been Jamaica. I'm surprised we're not in the hospital from sun poisoning, but it still would have been worth it. We had a wicked good time. I was wishing you were there, babe."

"Yeah, right" he said, and his face showed jealousy and humor. "Ya'll are pigs from hell and must be destroyed."

"I know this, my dearest, and rightfully so. But I really was missin' you something fierce."

"Same here, baby. And Noni has had me in a wad, worrying that it might be you this time. She wouldn't talk about it, but she did say it wasn't you. I had trouble believing it until I saw your face. Come here and let me hold you." Jim wrapped around me like cellophane, and he almost whimpered. I know I did. We fit so nicely together, like an old favorite glove. *Feels so right.*

"It's okay, baby," I said into his shoulder. "I'm good. I'm sorry you had to endure the Noni syndrome. It's exhausting, I know. Let me go talk to her. Don't go anywhere. I need to be with you. You know, WITH YOU!"

"You got that right," he said to me with that evil grin of his.

I went into Mother's room. "Okay, Mother? What's the matter? Who are you dreaming of?"

"I can't even say it. I'm not going to say it. But don't worry. It's not anybody in this house. Okay?" She looked up at me, and I could see the pain deep in her eyes, not to mention the fatigue. "Jim was so good to stay with me. He's going to be your husband, you know."

"That's what you keep saying, and that's fine by me. Talk to me, Mother. You're scaring me. Are you sure it's not still Bonnie?"

"I don't think so. I wish it was, but I'm pretty sure it isn't. This is something new and different. I'm so glad Jim was here. Your Daddy had to work all weekend, and I didn't want to be by myself, so Jim said he'd be more than happy to stay. I hope you don't mind."

"Of course not. It's a little weird, but if he didn't mind, and if it made you feel better, that's fine. I know he had a lot of studying to do. I hope you didn't interfere with that."

"No, he studies in the kitchen or in your bedroom. I kept him fed real good for you. Also, a friend of his from school came and stayed too. He slept in your bed, and Jim slept in here. His name was Randy. Nice guy. And a hungry boy too."

"Jesus, Mother. You had two young studs staying with you all night? Why do you get to have all the fun? I'll remember that next time I want Jim to stay over."

"Very funny. He was here to comfort me, and he and Randy have a big exam tomorrow."

"Whatevah…But try not to worry. You need some sleep, and so do I. I am beat."

"You look like it. And you also look like a very ripe tomato. You shouldn't get sunburned like that."

"We had fun. Florida sun is different. We didn't know how bad it was till it was too late. Believe me, we paid for it all the way home. And we're still paying. I need to put something on it. I'm miserable."

"There's some sunburn stuff in the bathroom. I'm sure Jim can help you with that."

"I'm sure. Now go to bed so we can all rest."

She turned with a sly grin. She knew Jim and I had some "business" to take care of, although she would not speak of it.

But she was no fool, and she trusted Jim so much that I really don't think she cared. I went back to the kitchen where Jim was waiting.

"Can you stay for a while?" I asked.

"You couldn't drag me outta here with a Massy Ferguson right now, baby. Let's go downstairs," he said with a wiggle of his eyebrows.

"I need to freshen up a bit, then we'll go down there."

"You'd better hurry up, my little red hot chili pepper, 'cause I feel like a damn missile about to launch."

"Get a grip, and I'll be there shortly. I need for you to put lotion on my back. Hopefully there's still some skin attached. We really fucked up yesterday. All day in the Florida sun…How dumb was that? I never felt a thing until last night when we were crashing, and I noticed that my skin felt about two sizes too small for my body. I knew it was gonna be bad, but I swear, it was worth it."

God, that Solarcaine felt good! It just didn't last long enough. I took more aspirin and got some relief for a while. Jim was almost afraid to touch me, but our needs were greater than the pain. We got to spend some quality time alone in the basement. Mother dared not bother us. Daddy was asleep. Life was good back home. There I lay in the arms of the man who loved me. And he loved me every chance we got, which had become a real problem since he had moved back to his parent's house. As we got dressed I suddenly felt compelled to look over at the little window by the driveway. I was relaxed, enjoying being with my man, and had completely forgotten to check all the curtains and windows. I glanced upward to find those freaking ice blue eyes, and I panicked and yelled, "He's there. He's out there. Oh shit, he saw everything. Oh, God."

We were dressed by then, and Jim hit the floor and the backdoor so fast that I was still trying to get off the bed when he was out the door. I yelled, "No, Jim. Don't do it. He's fucking crazy. Just let him go." I went to the door and noticed as Jim ran by that he had a nice solid piece of strategically cut wooden dowel in his hand that he usually kept in his van for protection. It was probably the equivalent of a baseball bat if you got a piece of it. I yelled again, but there was no stopping him. He was gone in a flash, and so was Ted. Every now and then I heard Jim muttering in a hoarse whisper as he searched the neighborhood. Phrases like "Chicken shit asshole!" and "Come out and face me like a man, you spineless bastard" and "Can't hide forever, fuck face," floated through the night air. At least he wasn't yelling…

It was about twenty minutes before Jim returned, and he was scary mad. Ted was about half again as big and heavy as Jim, but Jim clearly didn't give a rat's ass about that. He'd said more than once, "I'd much rather fight a big man than a crazy man." And right then I could see he was crazy mad. Not crazy sicko like Ted. More like crazy homicidal maniac. "I couldn't find that son of a bitch anywhere. It was like he disappeared into thin air. He is apparently very experienced in the art of escape. But if I get a half a chance, I'm gonna crack his fucking skull. That's what I was hissing at him when I was hunting him, and I meant it. He's not gonna do this shit to you anymore. Fuckin' bastard."

"I'm sorry, Jim. I'm sorry you had to see that. He's been doing that shit all my life, and when I think of him seeing us together, it makes me sick. I can't wait to get out of this damn place. There's nothing but bad memories for me in this house. And in this town. So just let it go. That's what I've been told all my life, and I'm finally numb to it. Although this time, I'm pretty shook up, I have to admit. I should have checked all the windows. I was so glad to see you that I got careless."

"I did check them earlier, knowing you would be back, but the SOB outfoxed me," Jim admitted.

"Welcome to my fucking world."

It was back to school the next morning. I only had three months to go, and I would have my associate's degree in health sciences, with a major in ophthalmology/optometry. Jim still had another year to go in respiratory therapy, with clinicals at the local hospitals. My clinicals included a day shift at doctors' offices in the area. One of them agreed to hire me when I graduated, but he was new and could only afford me part-time to start off. We got along well, and I had no other offers, so I went with it. I just had to finish final exams and graduate. I needed a car too, but I would have to work on that one.

Meanwhile, I was driving our old 1964 VW beetle when it was available. Mother and Dad let me drive the Bug to school, and sometimes I would ride with a friend or with Robbie. One day I had the VW out and about and went to the park just goofing around, where I ran into William, an old friend of sorts. I pulled over, and he said, "I was going to smoke this doobie. Wanna join me?"

"Sure," I said. "I just bought a bag that we can roll one out of it too."

He got off of his bicycle, got in the car, and we lit up his joint. We hadn't had three puffs, when here came a city cop pulling up beside us. We were stuffing that joint out and William was eating what was left of it. The cop stopped, opened his window, and said, "Do you know you're parked illegally? You shouldn't be parked on that side of the road."

Even though we had been parking there like that for *years*...

I said, "I'm sorry, sir, I'll move it right away."

He said, "Okay, and don't do it again."

"Yes, officer," I said, shaking in my boots. He was pulling away when William and his smartass damn mouth said sarcastically, "Have a nice day, officer, huh, huh…"

Well, that did it. The cop stopped, got out, and within minutes, there was another cop car at the scene. They had me out of the car, handcuffed, and were searching my car and my purse… and of course they came up with the bag of pot in there. William was clean and only had his bicycle. But they took us both in, towed my Daddy's little VW, and hauled our dumb asses to jail.

Dear God in Heaven, save me.

The police put us in separate cars. I was dumbfounded. All I could think about was my Daddy's car and how disappointed he would be. I was pretty terrified of Mother's reaction, but mainly I just didn't know what to do. I was now eighteen, so they carted my ass to the county jail like all the other criminals. The cop was talking to me in a sleazy kind of way, starting out with, "You could at least have bought some good weed. That stuff is trash. What's a pretty little thing like you doing with a loser like him anyway?"

"I was riding around and he waved and asked me if I wanted to smoke with him and I said okay. That's all. I've known him all my life, just being around school and stuff. We don't hang together. Just bad timing, bad choice."

"You sure are a pretty thing. Are you in school? Do you work?"

"I am about to graduate from Greenville TEC in a health science program, and I work three jobs."

"What kind of jobs?" he inquired.

"I work in a movie theatre in the evenings and weekends, part-time at a veterinarian's office, and I model for a photographer in town." It was all I could do to keep from crying. "What am I going to do? What happens now? I am finished. I am so finished." Then the tears came.

"You will get a phone call, I guess to your parents. Then they'll have to come get you and post bond to get you out. Then you'll need a lawyer, and then maybe you'll learn your lesson about drugs."

"Oh, I believe I have learned my lesson. If I ever get out of this, I'll never do it again."

Once again, I did the walk of shame in my pretty little outfit. He escorted me into the jail area, and of course I had to walk all the way down past what seemed like a hundred cells to my little cell near the end. The inmates were whistling, hollering, pointing, and laughing as I walked by, saying all kinds of crude things. He removed the handcuffs, shut the door, and looked me up and down, shook his head, and said, "Damn, you're pretty. Um mmm." The way he looked at me made my skin crawl. "If you tell us where you got that shitty weed, we'll get you out of this. Just tell me who and where. It's that easy."

"No way. I'm sorry, but I'm not a snitch."

"Your choice. But it sure would make things easier for you. Think about it."

"No thinking required. I'll take the heat. When can I make my phone call?"

"When we come and tell you. Don't go anywhere, huh?" he said with a cackle as he walked away.

There was a black chick in the cell next to me, hanging on the bars, looking at me, laughing and talking shit. Her hair was matted, and she stunk to high heaven. My guess was that she had been in there a while. She said, "Ooohh, pretty white girl in the pen. What did you do to get you in here?"

"Got caught with some pot. That's all," I answered.

"Shit girl, that ain't nothin'. I stabbed my boyfriend with the scissors. Fifteen times. Caught the son of a bitch in my bed with a ho. In *my* bed with *a ho*! I woulda stabbed her too, but she ran, and he was the one I wanted to kill, so I did it. And I don't regret it. Be messin' around on me. I showed him," she said while she strutted back and forth in front of me, waiting for my reaction.

I made sure to stay out of reach, but I said, "You go, girl. That son of a bitch should not have messed with you. You showed him, didn't ya? You're a woman that don't take no shit! I like that!"

She stuck her hand through the bars to high five me. I hesitated, but I gave her a quick slap. She continued to strut around like a rooster. We had bonded, thank God. I backed away from the bars, and as I turned around and started looking at my accommodations, I became even more distraught. There was a nasty little shitter against the wall, and the walls looked like they had shit and pee all over them, maybe even some blood. The stench took my breath, and I was already hyperventilating from all the adrenalin. Fear had me by the throat.

I am in some deep shit. Again.

The cop who arrested me came to look at his catch off and on. He gave me the sleazy Ted looks. I knew them well. "When can I call my parents?" I asked him.

"Right now. I came to take you to the phone." He unlocked the door and led me by the arm to a holding area. I had already decided to call Diane and let her do her magic. Maybe not get the parents involved. I dialed her number and she answered. "Hello?"

"Hey, D. I am in some deep shit. I am in jail for having pot. I need $200 right away to get me out, and I guess a lawyer too, but for now, I need the money. I have to get the hell out of here. I'm sorry to do this to you. Call Jim, or whoever you have to to get the money quick."

"You're shittin' me, right?"

"I wish I was. Just hurry please. I am freakin' the hell out. Hurry! I don't want to be stuck here all night. Please." I started to cry.

"Okay, don't cry. I'm pretty good at this. I've had to get Michael and his buds out several times. But I don't have $200," D said.

"Do what you have to. I don't care. Mother, Daddy, whatever…"

"Shit! Shit! Shit!" D said. She rarely cursed, but I had put her in a bad spot.

"Tell me about it. Please hurry."

Sleazy Cop took me back to my cell and said, "Now you wait some more."

I waited and waited and freakin' waited.

Another thirty minutes, and I will be stuck here all night. I can't handle that. I don't want to lie down on that cot, I don't even want to sit on it, and I have to pee so bad. I was going to have to pee, audience or not. I used the stainless shitter on the wall, standing up, followed by applause and a whoop-whoop from cells one through one hundred. I guess that's part of their entertainment, waiting for the new criminal to finally break down and use the facilities. Even though they couldn't all see me, if felt as if they could. They all knew what the applause was for. Apparently they had some long-term residents and some frequent fliers.

Here came Sleazy Cop again. This time he opened the bars and said, "You are free to go. Your bail came, and your family is waiting out front."

"Oh God. I'd almost rather stay in here than to face them. Almost."

Here we go again. The walk of shame.

I was getting really good at that. At least this time I was walking out instead of in. All the inmates hollered all kinds of stuff, good and bad. I just turned and said, "It's been a pleasure. Good luck!"

As the door to the front area opened, there stood Mother and Jim. *Oh Lordy, Lordy.* Mother was a little green around the gills—actually, I'm not sure who looked worse, her or Jim.

"What took so long?" I asked them. "I almost had to stay all night."

Mother was beyond being able to speak, so Jim said, "They wouldn't take a check, so I had to get a check written to me and haul ass to the bank. It almost closed in my face, but I got the cash, then flew back here, and they almost closed in my face here too. They let William out hours ago. What the hell happened?"

"I'll tell you later. For now, let's just get out of here. Daddy's car! Oh shit!"

"We know where it is," he said, trying to calm me down. "We'll get it in the morning. D found you a real good lawyer that she knows. She talked to him, and she says it's gonna be okay. Just try to calm down. He'll get you out of this." Jim was trying to reassure me, but I knew his nerves were shot too. Mother had pretty much shut down, but I knew her well, and she would blow eventually. Jim was driving us in Mother's car; I was in the back seat, barely out of reach of the rubber arm, glad to be free. I was rethinking so many things in life, asking myself so many questions.

Am I just that unlucky or plain stupid? Why does God hate me? Why me? Why, why, why?

"We'll have to get the VW early in the morning," I said. "I have clinical tomorrow. Jesus, what did Daddy say? I bet he was livid."

"No, Maggie, he cried. You broke his heart once again," Mother finally spoke. "And you have disappointed us highly… again. When will you ever learn?"

"Sorry, Mother," I said meekly. "I don't mean to be such a disappointment to you and the family. Shit just happens to me. I haven't done anything that everybody else isn't doing. I just get caught, and they don't." Then I heated up. "And where were you when all the good shit happened to me? HUH? Maybe if ya'll had been there for some of that, I wouldn't have turned to drugs. Ever thought about that? And by the way, don't worry, I'll be out of your life as soon as I can, believe me."

I could see Jim squirmin' in his own skin as he drove us home. He was caught between me and Noni. He loved him some Noni. She loved him too, and she would do anything for Jim. He didn't know Noni's dark side yet, but I knew it intimately. She was generous on the outside and totally self-serving on the inside. Once I finished school and starting working the job I had been offered by the optometrist, I was outta here.

When we got home, I went to my bedroom to hide from Daddy. I could hear Jim talking to him in the kitchen. He was taking up for me, trying to convince Daddy that I wasn't a bad person, just unlucky. Jim must have talked to him for more than an hour, and I think it actually helped. He didn't back down from anything Daddy said, and I think Daddy earned some respect for him because he defended me so eloquently. I know Daddy seemed to get over this latest disappointment quicker than he had before.

My plans for escaping were taking shape. As soon as I graduated, Hannah and I were going to share an apartment very close to my new job. I wanted to be away from Greenville for many reasons, the main one being Ted. I wanted to eliminate the convenience factor for him and maybe have a normal life again. *As if I ever had a normal life.* But I also had so many bad memories, so many people who I thought were my friends. The pain of seeing them, seeing places…*too many memories.* It had become unbearable to continue living in Greenville. I was determined to do well in school and graduate. After what I'd had to give up, I couldn't not finish school. I guess that's what I got out of it all: an education and a job. And I met my Jim.

We got up extra early the next day, and Mother and I picked up the VW, I went to clinic, and she went home. Hardly a word was spoken, which was fine by me because I didn't have anything good to say. I had an appointment with the lawyer the following day, so I would have to miss some class time.

The next day, Jim drove me to see the lawyer and waited outside in his van. I dressed conservatively, which I'd had to do since starting my education at TEC. I went up to the attorney's office, and his secretary buzzed him on the intercom and said, "Miss Keith is here."

"Bring her back. Thanks," Mr. Harris said. So I followed her down the hall to his office, opened the door, and he was sitting at his enormous desk with a folder in front of him. "Come on in, Maggie," he said invitingly.

He looked at me as if I had walked in naked. *Oh, Jesus, not another pervert.* He kept looking at my crotch as I walked. *God get me out of here!* His assistant turned and shut the door behind her. Mr. Harris said, "Well now. I see the charges were simple possession. We can work with that, so try not to worry. Tell me what happened exactly." I explained every detail. Then he said, "Tell me about yourself. Are you in school, live at home? Are you dating anyone?"

"I am in school, I do live at home, and yes, I am dating someone. He's in the parking lot waiting for me."

"Why don't you go tell him that I'll take you home when we're done? I have some great reefer in the safe that I got from one of the narcotics agents," he said as he was opening the safe.

Holy shit! I was flabbergasted. "No, thanks. I have to go to my modeling job when I leave here." I held up my hand. "Look, I'm already in trouble because of that stuff. I don't need any more trouble, believe me."

"I'm gonna take care of all that. Don't worry about it. Here take a couple of hits with me, and we'll wrap this thing up." He looked me over again and said, "I'd like to take you to my condo in the mountains. How's this weekend sound?"

"How about not at all," I said. "I told you I am seeing somebody and have been for about two years now. I'm not interested in seeing anybody else. Besides, you're twice my age." I thought that might deflate him a bit, but he kept on trying to entice me with his money, power, and clout.

"Aren't you married?" I asked. "You are wearing a wedding ring after all."

He squirmed a bit and said, "Yes, but we're not doing well."

"Well imagine that," I said sarcastically.

"I know," he replied, and he visibly deflated at bit. "We have a son who is real sick. He needs a kidney transplant, and we haven't located one. The stress has torn us in half. I can't take it anymore. She is losing her mind with worry, and I am too. Anyway, enough of that." He waved his hand in the air as if to erase it all away.

"I am so sorry to hear that," I said sincerely. "I'm sure it is hard to hold things together under that kind of stress." Then I told him about my recent predicament with my surprise pregnancy. I wasn't sure why I did that, other than to take some of the emphasis off his problems. And maybe so he would feel sorry for me and make this all go away. The problem was, I think it made him want me even more. *Jeez…*Anyway, I did take a couple of hits off the joint he'd lit up, and *Oh SHIT!* I was so high I could barely walk out of the building and to the car.

When I did make it to the car, Jim took one look at me and said, "What the hell happened to you?"

I was trying to explain to him, but I could hardly talk I was so messed up. I don't know what that stuff was. "He said it was reefer, but I ain't never had any reefer like that. I think it must have had heroin in it or something." Jim told me later that he had never seen me that fucked up. I had to agree. I thought I was going to barf in the car on the way home. I was way freaked out too, because I had a modeling job I had to go to in a couple of hours, and I prayed I would come down soon. I didn't completely, but somehow I managed to deal with the job anyway.

The trial date was set, and it all proceeded smoothly, with no surprises. Mr. Harris kept his promise to keep it out of the newspaper and have it erased from my records. If I got popped again, however, it would be found. But as far as any inquiries from schools, employers, etc., asking for criminal background checks, nada. I'd have to work two hundred community service hours and pay a fine of $250, but that was it. So as if I didn't have enough jobs, I had to work at the police station several days a week until my hours were done. They put me to work filing arrest tickets. Like forty two billion of them. Toward the end of my sentence time, the police department offered me a job. I thanked them, but declined. The pay was pitiful.

Mr. Harris offered me a job too, serving subpoenas. *Yeah, right...* It paid real well, but that didn't happen. He was still trying to get me to go to some tropical island or wherever with him. Once the trial was over and the sentence was paid, I didn't talk to him anymore. Then all of a sudden, he disappeared from Greenville. Not sure what happened, but I didn't care to find out. I had a feeling it had something to do with their little boy. I did feel for them, and I hoped they found him a kidney and he got his transplant.

Chapter Thirty-Six

I was trying to get school over and done with, work four jobs, and still have some time with my lover. Good thing I was so young, because I had little spare time for sleep. I looked forward with great anticipation to the day I could leave home. Leave Greenville. Leave my sad, wounded past behind me. I tried not to think about it all, I just kept moving. Jim was finishing up his first year in the respiratory therapy program. My class was reviewing for final exams, and I was studying my ass off.

One Monday when we broke for lunch, several of us went to our favorite watering hole and had some beer and sandwiches. Since final exams were so close, we went back to class per our usual ritual, minus the tennis match and the joint. During lunch, Cici told be about her weekend. She had gone to Greensboro with a couple of her friends to see Jethro Tull in concert. One of the girls, Debbie, was really wild and crazy. Unbeknownst to Cici and her other friends, Debbie had brought along about a hundred hits of mescaline. She was selling them both outside and inside the stadium. She had already taken a couple of hits and was acting so dumb and out of control that she got busted before the concert even started.

"I had a bad feeling about her, she was so high and pumped up by the time we got there," Cici said. "Then when she didn't show up in her seat for the whole concert, I knew something bad was going down."

"I know how it is," I told Cici. "I've done some stupid stuff myself, but I was never that wild and out of control. I had a little wild hair from time to time, but I was usually cautious. A lot of good that did me. I got caught at everything I did!"

Cici laughed. She and I had become real close friends, along with Hannah. The three of us had bonded, especially after the Fernandina Beach trip. They had class, they were from nice families, and they thought the same of me. Of course, they didn't know about my cheesy family stuff, and I made sure it stayed that way. I would soon be on my way out of town, leaving it all behind, and there was no need to share most of it with new friends. They knew about the baby, but it didn't seem to change our friendship. Sometimes that bit of information changed the way people treated me. I couldn't decide if they felt sorry for me or thought I was a cold fucking bitch who didn't want my own child, but if so, they never let on. They liked me unconditionally, and it was so good to have friends like that. So unlike most of my old high school and sorority "friends." There was one girl from the sorority days who finally got up the nerve a couple of years later to call me and see how I was doing. I really appreciated that. She knew me well enough to know I wasn't a whore and that I had loved Marty with all my heart. I felt some peace with her and greatly appreciated her reaching out to me like that. The rest of them wouldn't have been caught dead talking to me. And I felt pretty much the same way about them.

We returned to class after lunch, and my professor immediately called to me and said, "Follow me please, Maggie. There's something I need to tell you."

"Okay," I said, and I followed him into his office. He was looking pretty distressed as he sat me down and said, "We got a phone call from your sister right after you left for lunch. Maggie, honey, your Mother has passed away. They need you at home."

"She couldn't have," I said without a shred of doubt. "I would know it, feel it." But as I grabbed the phone on his desk, my hands started to shake. I knew somebody had died, but I also *knew* it wasn't Mother.

I called home, and Sara answered. She was always a strong one like me, and unlike Diane. "Hello?"

"Sara, what happened to Mother?" I asked, unable to keep the fear out of my voice. "They told me she died."

"It was Grannie. Mother's fine. Well, not fine, but no, it was Grannie who died. Come home when you can. I know you're about to have finals and all, but I'm here with Mother. Diane is here, and Daddy's up too. We're okay, so if you need to stay there and finish today, then do it."

"I'll see," I told her. "I don't know if I can concentrate now anyway. I'll talk to my professor. He thinks Mother died. I'm glad it wasn't her, but I'm so sad to see Grannie go."

"I know, we all are. Judy found her on the commode, slumped over. It looks like she didn't suffer, and she was old and had lived a full life. She was watching Lawrence Welk on TV while she was on her bedside commode. Couldn't have been happier, you know."

I went to my professor and explained that it was my Mother's mother who had passed away. He looked relieved and embarrassed and apologized profusely for the misunderstanding. "It's okay," I said. "I only had to panic for a few minutes. You didn't know, so don't worry about it. I guess I'd better go now, but I'll be back tomorrow for reviews. Then I'll probably have to go do family stuff. I'll do the best I can to get finals done on time."

"Don't worry. We'll work it out," Dr. Thomas assured me. "I know you need to be with your family right now. Call me when you know the arrangements, and we'll come up with a time to do your exams if we need to. Now go!"

"Thank you so much, Dr. Thomas. I'll do my best to be here, and I'll let you know as soon as I can," I said as I got up to leave. "I need to tell Cici real quick, okay?"

"Sure."

On my way home, I started to feel the pain of Grannie leaving us. I hadn't been going to see her as much since I started getting into trouble, and especially since starting school. But when I did, Grannie acted like nothing had changed. I felt relaxed around her. But I didn't feel relaxed around Mother's sister and her husband, who Grannie now lived with. They had shunned me, pretty much excluding me from their family, although it was their son who had wanted to adopt my son. *Whatever...* I was glad I didn't agree to let them have him. It would have gotten ugly. They were good people, probably too good to be my relatives. They were Southern Methodist to the core and not the least bit flexible with the rules.

So now we knew why psycho doll had been doing a marathon. Mother was exhausted, and I knew why she couldn't talk about it now. I had been so busy with work, school, jail, and Jim that I kinda forgot about the curse hanging over us. Time for another funeral.

This is going to suck out loud. As I got closer to the house, I started to cry. I knew Mother would be devastated, and I felt very sad too. I walked into the house and noticed the damn doll first thing. She had quieted finally. *The freak!* I understood why Daddy hated that doll. I think it was just Mother's nervous energy coming through the doll, some kind of telekinesis. She had a powerful mojo that you could feel the moment you came in contact with her. Just ask my friends and anybody I ever dated. They were all terrified of her, except for Jim. From the very beginning, I knew he respected her, but he had never shown the slightest hint of fear. That may be another reason why Mother took to him so quickly.

As I entered the house, I could hear everybody in Mother's bedroom, blowing noses, sniffling, talking in choked tones.

Oh God, I don't do well with grieving. I was now convinced I had inherited some of Mother's psychic abilities. Maybe I was an empath or something like that, because I always felt everybody's pain so intensely I could hardly bear it. I'm still that way today, and I avoid funerals if at all possible. I didn't join the group in Mother's room, I just went to my room and started crying and couldn't stop.

So we did the funeralizin', as our maid Elsie used to say. I aced my final exams. It all worked out. Life goes on, but it was empty for a while without Grannie. Mother almost grieved herself to death. We all missed her, of course, but she had been old and ready to go. It was hard to go into Grannie's room after that, and I didn't have any reason to go over there anymore. I didn't appreciate the cold reception I got over there. I grew up visiting that house a lot. Grannie kept me off and on for short periods until I was ten or twelve years old. She was a hoot, and she too had some strong telepathic abilities, at least as strong as Mother's. She was just less intense about it, and she seemed to get a kick out of it as she tended to joke about it and used it to amuse people. Mother, on the other hand, used it to intimidate. Very effectively, I might add.

I graduated from TEC with my AAS degree. It had become time to leave the nest. *Fly, little birdie.* And I flew! I moved in with Hannah, and Jim immediately moved in with us. We were quite a threesome, and we had a lot of good times together.

Mother was actually happy to learn Jim was going to be living with us. She would worry less about me knowing he was there. Jim's mother wasn't crazy about the idea, but he was twenty-two now and working while he finished school, and she didn't make a big deal out of it. She had always been enamored of me for some reason, and she knew how Jim felt about me, so she gave us her blessing in spite of the fact that we were living in sin.

Jim and I went over to Mother and Daddy's one Sunday to gather some more of my stuff. They were getting ready to leave for Uncle Jack and Aunt Bessie's, so Jim and I said our good-byes and went to the basement to get my old stereo, records, bookshelf, and whatever else. We heard them shut the front door and drive off as we were loading up my stuff in my little car. As we were looking around the basement, we heard somebody walking around upstairs in Mother's bedroom, then we heard the rocking chair creaking. We knew the sounds of that house well, having been in the basement sneaking moments together for months.

"They must have forgotten something, or maybe Mother decided to stay," I said matter-of-factly. But suddenly my hair was standing on end, and Jim had a funny look on his face too. We went upstairs to see what was going on, and I called out, "Mother? Daddy?" Nobody answered, but as we entered Mother's room, the rocking chair was rocking and on the cushion of the chair was a ring. As I got closer, I saw it was the ring Bonnie had stolen years ago. I could even smell her perfume.

Jim gave me that deer-in-the-headlights look when he saw what was going on. He didn't know the details about the ring, but he saw the obvious. I had a look of *Holy shit* on my face, and my hair was still standing straight up all over my body. I backed out of the room without touching anything. I wasn't afraid, but I was shocked, because I hadn't seen that ring in a long time, and I knew it was the ring Bonnie had coveted.

"I'll tell you about it later," I said to Jim as we were headed back downstairs. "It'll sound crazy as hell, so don't be surprised."

"It's okay, I'm starting to get used to crazy," he assured me.

"Well, this one is over the top," I said. "Let's get the hell out of here."

When we got back to our apartment, I waited for Mother to call. I knew she would find the ring and know what it was. She would call. We unloaded my belongings, and for a while we didn't talk about what we had seen just an hour ago. At last he couldn't hold back any longer and asked, "What the fuck was that in your Mother's room a little while ago? I felt it, but I've been giving you some time to think it over, and now it's time to talk. I saw the rocking chair, I heard the floor creaking, and I smelled a perfume. It was Bonnie, wasn't it?" Jim had learned a lot about my family while we were together, and he had seen and felt enough of Mother's abilities to figure it out.

"I do believe you are correct. It couldn't be anybody else. That was her ring and perfume. That was her favorite chair too, in her favorite room. I'm waiting for Mother to call and we'll talk about it. She'll have to digest it for a while, but she'll call when she's ready."

And she did call. "Did you and Jim see anything weird in the house when ya'll were here?" she asked.

"Oh yeah! I was wondering when you would call and ask."

I told her what we heard and saw. After I recounted everything we'd seen and heard, she said to me, "I can see Bonnie's face in the picture now. When I got home, that's the first thing I noticed, after the perfume. Then I saw the ring. Do you realize that it has been exactly one year since she died? Diane reminded me of that earlier today."

More goose bumps. "No wonder. No, I didn't realize it had been a year, but she sure got our attention. We didn't touch anything 'cause we didn't want to mess up the mojo for you. But we did feel compelled to get the hell out of there. We were pretty creeped out. Are you okay?"

"Yeah, I'm at peace with her now. I think she was asking me for forgiveness for so many things."

"She put poor David through so much. And she ruined those kids. But he sure did love her. We all did, although I don't know how."

"I know. You couldn't help but love her. But finally it's over. We are at peace."

Chapter Thirty-Seven

I was ready to marry, but Jim had an irrational aversion to marriage. All our friends would ask, "When are ya'll gonna get married?" Jim would shudder and start backing up and shit. He was like, "Ahhh ummm, that's not gonna happen."

Eventually, I got tired of hearing that shit. It not only pissed me off, it gave me no hope of ever marrying the love of my life and having a child. He didn't know it, but he made me cry many times saying that stuff. I knew he was in school, and I was prepared to wait and not distract him from his studies. So I waited patiently. At least he was in my bed every night, without fail. I never doubted him, and I always trusted him. He was worth waiting for, and I was young, only aged beyond my years. He was five years my elder, Buddy's age.

Even without marriage, we had some really good times. We were together *all* of the time, except for when we worked. We enjoyed the same music, the same people, and the same drugs, and we indulged in plenty of them all. But we brought the partying down a notch or two, "only" getting high on weekends when we weren't working. We had good jobs now. For cryin' out loud, we were fine upstanding citizens and taxpayers, and we had to at least be able to act the part. I was working for an eye doctor almost full time and the vet's office on the weekends. I got bored real fast with the eye doctor stuff. Jim worked part-time, which often turned into full time, at one of the local hospitals until he finished school.

And as Mother had always known, I married that man. He finally came around, and in October of 1977, he was officially mine. He seemed as thrilled as I was during the ceremony, even though we had one helluva hangover. Daddy wept through the whole thing from the moment he laid my hand in Jim's. He had to leave before the reception, but he and Mother were so happy and relieved to have me marry Jim.

And there was no way he was slipping out of my claws, I just had to play tough.

Send him home to momma's to live…worked like a charm.

Three years of courtin' was enough, thank you very much. We then had to find our own place to live without a roommate. Hannah was great, but not what we needed to start our married lives together. So we got a little apartment in downtown Greenville. I managed to catch a break and got a good job in a local hospital. My AAS degree got me in the door, but I had to learn a lot of new technology, mostly on the job, some that I was sent to school for.

Not long after Jim and I got married, David announced he was getting married to a lady named Mary, who had three young boys. Our first reaction was, "Dear God, he is a glutton for punishment." Their plan was to marry and move to South Carolina and be with his family.

Dear God in heaven. Sara found them a house just behind hers and Ted's that was big enough to house two adults and six chirrens.

What a cluster fuck that's gonna be.

David's daughter Kathy had married and was living in Houston and had been diagnosed with Hodgkin's disease. Mack couldn't stay out of prison, but he was present for a short time until he once again got caught breaking into some drugstore. He was banned from the state of South Carolina when he got out of prison that time. That was a blessing; we really didn't need him around making trouble.

Sherri was single and on the prowl. I was hesitant to introduce her to anybody, knowing her history of kleptomania and such. But I did introduce her to several guys, and she turned her nose up at and made fun of every one of them. I thought they were nice, good-looking guys. She eventually managed to get a job in a bank, then she met and married a doctor's son. He was a super nice guy with money. She hit the jackpot with him. They had a son and named him Lawrencccce. *Of course!* Our whole family was rather entertained that she would choose a name with an emphasis on the "sss" sound. Maybe she thought that if she said it enough, she could overcome her speech impediment. NOT!

Sherri ended up robbing her in-laws blind. She stole money, jewelry, whatever she could get away with. *Stupid, stupid girl.* She could have had it all. They were loaded. She didn't have to steal ever again, but it was an illness, and I guess she didn't know how to stop. She ended up going to prison for several years for embezzlement from her employer. She lost her dream husband and her son through neglect and abuse.

And she made fun of me all my life? Hello?

Mother kept us posted on where she moved after she got out of prison. The prison system let her teeth rot out, which doesn't seem right somehow, but after five years of incarceration and no dental care, that's what happens, I guess. Hopefully, she had some extra strength Polygrip, because she seemed to move anywhere that had at least two s's in the name: Tuscaloosa, Sarasota,

Corpus Christi, Texassss, then finally Houston, Texassss. *What the fuck?* It was a mystery to us, but it proved to be a good source of entertainment. Cruel, I know, but it was such a comical mystery that it was impossible to ignore.

About a year after David and his new family moved to Greenville, Ted was caught peeping in one of their windows by Mary. David went ape shit and stormed over to Sara's house and unloaded on her. Of course, Sara accused Mary of lying, took up for Ted, and shunned David and Mary for life. Not long after that, they left Greenville and returned to San Antonio with Mary's boys.

Score another one for that blue-eyed motherfucker! What else is that worthless bastard going to do to my family before he gets his?

As it turned out, Mary and her boys were the best things that ever happened to David. It was hard on him to start over with small children, but they bonded quickly. He loved them as his own, and they learned to love him as a father. Mary was an outstanding mother, and it was no surprise to any of us that they all turned out to be good, honest men with wonderful families.

Mack ended up spending his entire life in prison. Literally. He was serving a life sentence for the murders of two women when he died during a gallbladder surgery at age fifty. Kathy died in her midfifties with cancer. Sherri developed congestive heart disease. And Mandy lived in a women's home where she shared an apartment with another autistic lady. They had a caregiver and small jobs to make a little money. She thrived, gray hair and all.

We're all getting older and slower, but what else are ya gonna do?

Jim and I made a mutual agreement about two years after we married to stop the drugs. No cigarettes, no pot, no hallucinogens, no coke. Neither of us had ever considered doing anything that involved a needle. We both finally admitted how bad the drugs were for our bodies, but more than that, we became increasingly alarmed at what drug abuse was doing to young people everywhere. Premature deaths, broken families, school dropout rates…the list of ill effects on our whole society was endless. And I must say, it was easy to quit. We had each other and a bright future, and that was all we needed. We still would occasionally drink alcohol in moderation, but that's been it for many years.

Mother and Daddy passed away in due time. But a few years before she died, Mother finally and sincerely apologized for the way things had turned out. I told Mother on her deathbed that I forgave her, that it was probably best for the baby in the long run. That was a hard one, but I wanted to make peace before she died. She had made the effort to apologize for everything, and I had to reciprocate at last. Then she proceeded to tell me that Elbert was really my father. *What the fuck?* I never figured out why she wanted me to think that I had a different father from my siblings, but in my heart, I *knew* Elbert was my father. We were too much alike. I realized then that I had never really believed that lie, but why… damned if I knew.

And I wonder sometimes why I'm so screwed up?!

Diane and Michael's son was like a son to us. He helped fill in some of the emptiness for many years, and he turned out to be a fine young man with his own wife and son. He became the grandson we would never have. Precious little boy, he was.

Jim stuck with me through some very hard times. There were fifteen years of infertility, misdiagnosed GYN issues, two in vitro fertilizations, three surgeries all female oriented, and finally a total hysterectomy. I was spent and had suffered long enough. At the age of thirty-eight, I thought I was at peace, finally, with being childless. At that point, I just wanted to be healthy and enjoy the most wonderful husband anyone could ask for. The hysterectomy was one of the best things I ever did for myself.

We had good jobs, nice incomes, and we finally built our dream house on a lake. The location was perfect for our jobs, and we thrived as a couple. Jim filled the crater in my chest as well as it could be filled. There would always be a hollow place in my heart, but I had learned to cope for the most part. We tried to take advantage of our blessings and enjoy life. Lakefront living was the best therapy we had found yet. We had lots of company, including nieces and nephews and great nieces and great nephews to spoil. We were approaching retirement age and looked forward to it immensely.

About two years ago, Ted ended up getting shot while peeping in somebody's bedroom window. Imagine that, a seventy-year-old man still getting his rocks off looking in bedroom windows. The cops found him with his dick in his hand and a hole in his head. The son of a bitch was paralyzed, but he lived for a few weeks on a respirator. Diane and I would go to visit, mainly to give moral support to Sara, but she was inconsolable. We would take turns staying there to give her a break, but she would hardly leave. Diane and I struggled with those visits and found ourselves sitting where he could see us, and we just stared at him. We had all kinds of wicked thoughts of what we could do to him, and it was as if he knew it.

After several visits, Diane and I were told that we couldn't see Ted anymore because every time we came, all his EKG and respirator alarms started going off. Everybody would come rushing in to check on him, and it took a few times for them to figure out what the problem was. They told us that he didn't respond like that to anybody else, so we had to agree to stay away.

But we were just starting to enjoy it. When he died, Sara became a recluse. Maybe she finally believed that he really was the pervert he had been accused of being in the past. *Well, duhhh...*

The funeral was just dreadful, and for once I didn't cry. I always cried at funerals, but not that one. It was exceedingly sad for Sara and her adult children, because of the way he died. The kids had their own families by then too. They didn't talk; they didn't even look up. They were devastated, and that was the most pitiful part of the whole affair. Much of the detail was kept as quiet as it could be, but the curiosity and tension among everyone was palpable.

Buddy didn't find out about Ted's little problem until the day of the funeral, when we were gathering in the parking lot at the mortuary. Jim and Michael were talking about the SOB, and Buddy overheard them and demanded to know details. Jim and Michael didn't hide anything from him. Buddy was speechless at first, and you could see wheels turning in his head. He and Ted had been best buddies for years, and Buddy had been totally oblivious to the whole thing. But now he was putting two and two together. Suddenly, he was livid. We thought he was going to blow an artery or something. To this day, he wishes he had known so he could beat the hell out of Ted. He remembered being accused of things as a teenager that he was totally innocent of. It had been Ted doing stuff all along that caused Buddy grief with Daddy. It was all becoming clear, and he was royally pissed off, which made the funeral stuff even more tense and exhausting. We were so glad when it was over and we could leave as gracefully as possible.

When we got home from the funeral, Jim and I just looked at each other for a minute, and I knew he was trying to read me. All I could say was, "Well, that sucked."

"Yes it did," he replied. "After all he put you and Diane and God knows who else through, it was strangely emotional for me to finally have it over with. Talk about a strange kind of closure!"

We made a few minutes of idle talk about the whole damn mess, and then I said, "Enough of that. I can't think about it anymore. Let's go for a quiet boat ride with a tequila-made drink. Or maybe four. Let's take our little Ziggy for a boat ride with us. He loves it so much."

Ziggy was our dog, and we treated him like a baby and spoiled him rotten. We gathered our boat bag, made our drinkie poos, and grabbed some cigars for Jim and some treats for the baby. I was in need of an alcohol buzz, which I rarely did anymore. But it was justified. Jim said he would be the designated driver, so it was the perfect set-up for me to disconnect for a little while. The Zigglet was running around, biting my heels and wanting us to hurry. Jim ran some fuel down to the boat before we loaded everything else up on the golf cart.

The damn doorbell rang.

FUCK! We didn't get away fast enough.

I went to the door, opened it, and there stood a handsome young man with light brown hair and those beautiful green eyes. And holding his hand was the prettiest little girl with ash blonde hair and the same eyes. I looked back at the gentleman, and when he smiled I knew immediately who he was. He asked, "Are you Maggie Keith?"

My knees went weak, I started shaking all over, and I stammered, "Y…yes I am."

He looked me straight in the eyes and said, "Hello, Mother."

My throat closed off and my mind went blank.

With a jolt, reality slammed into my frontal lobe and cognition returned. The little girl looked *just* like me when I was her age. She looked up at her daddy for permission. He shook his head and said to her, "It's okay."

Then she looked at me and said, "Hello, Grandmamma."

Well, didn't my heart just about explode? "He…hello, Sweetheart." My throat wasn't opening up much, and I could hardly speak. "It is so…nice to meet you. Please come in…come in, Son." I held the door open for them.

"What…what is your name, da-a-ahlin'?" I asked my granddaughter as I led her by the hand into the house.

"My name is Chelsea," she said with enthusiasm. "I'm six years old."

I shut the door and turned to look at my son. He said, "And I am Thomas. And you know how old I am." Every time he spoke, our eyes locked like reflections in a mirror.

"You are thirty-eight years old, and I have waited your whole life for this moment, Son." It was all I could do to keep from crying. I knew if I started now, I was going to make an emotional scene, and I didn't want to frighten my granddaughter the very first time we met. "Funny, but that's your father's first name, though he went by his middle name. I have so much to tell you and show you." I desperately wanted to wrap my arms around him and never let go, but I didn't want to overwhelm him too soon.

Then he asked, "May I hug you?"

"Oh, Thomas, I thought you'd never ask." And the dam burst. The three of us clung to each other for the longest time. And when I was able to speak again, I looked at my handsome young man's face and said through tears, "I love you so much. I always have. Never doubt that. I am so happy you found me. I was afraid you would never want to know me, so I didn't force it. I didn't want to upset your life, and I couldn't face rejection. I am sorry for that, Son. But I want you to know, I have longed for this day. Come and meet my husband, Jim. We could never have children, and I have dreamed of this day more times than I could count. He will be so thrilled."

When I introduced my children...*that sounds so good, say it again*...my children to Jim, he was almost overcome with emotion, but he held it together. We sat and talked for a while. It was not nearly long enough, but they didn't live far away, and we were going to visit on a regular basis. Chelsea asked, "Can we go on the boat?"

"Yes, Sweetheart. Anytime your parents say it's okay, we'll go. Do you have time today?" I asked Thomas.

"We would love to," he replied, "but we didn't come prepared. We weren't sure we would find you here, but we'll be back soon. I promise."

"I wish you didn't have to go so soon. Please stay," I begged. "Chelsea, can Grandmamma hold you for a minute? I have missed so much time with you both."

Chelsea climbed onto my lap, laid her little head on my shoulder, and I rocked her and hugged her as long as I could. Thomas was fighting back tears, as was Jim. He had always felt my pain so deeply because he loved me so much. I had gotten past that, and all I wanted to do was look at Thomas, hold Chelsea, and memorize everything about them both. Her little hands, one scraped knee, her eyes that were just like mine, the smell of her hair was hypnotizing. Thomas looked much like his father, with the ashy blonde hair, green eyes that were closer to my shade, and his smile was definitely Marty. But there was something about him that looked like me. Maybe it was my eyes and the high cheekbones from the Cherokee side, but I couldn't put my finger on it. I knew I was staring, but so was he. We seemed to communicate without words, and I could tell he had so many questions, as did I, but we needed private time for all that. I would give him the opal ring with diamonds that his father had given me. I had kept it, hoping I would get a chance to give it to him one day.

Jim studied Thomas's face for long time, and I began to wonder why. When Thomas finally looked at him instead of me, Jim said to him, "You are truly your mother's son. You will find she is a most remarkable woman and the most loving mother you will ever again wish for."

Thomas replied with a smile, "I know that." For a brief moment, he looked puzzled, as if surprised to hear his own words. Then he said, as his still-thoughtful gaze returned to his daughter, "I'm not sure how I know it...I just do."

"I know just what you mean, Son," Jim replied. "I think you're going to find yourself saying that a lot while you're around your mother." I knew Jim was reaching out to him, making him feel welcome and comfortable. Thomas looked pleased, almost relieved.

"When you get a little older," I said to Chelsea, "Grandmamma has some old family recipes to show you, like biscuits and gravy, fried chicken, dressin', and so many more."

"I love biscuits and gravy," she said with glee. "My other Grandmamma used to make me some. She's gone to heaven."

"Oh, oh, honey, I am so sorry she's gone. Well, I tell you what, we'll make some that'll knock your socks off. Whaddya say, Sweet Pea? Of course your parents can come too. We can even go fishing."

"That would be so cool," she said, her little green eyes sparkling. After a period of silence, she looked up into my eyes, got real serious, and asked, "Where have you been Grandmamma?"

"I was lost, Sweetheart, but now I am found. Thank you so much." And I hugged her extra good, again fighting back the tears of joy.

I clung to my precious granddaughter as if she were a life jacket, feeling her heartbeat, breathing in the sweet smell of her hair, touching her flawless, rosy pink skin, cheek to cheek, and suddenly I felt a new connection to the very core of my being. There was a flash of inspiration, or maybe it was a deep-seated race consciousness that awakened, our genes recognizing each other and knowing our kinship down to the very cells in our bodies. I knew the answers before the questions came out…I pulled back and looked at her shining face and asked, "Do you like music?"

She enthusiastically shook her head yes.

Thomas also responded, as if he sensed where this was going, "She does like music, and she *loves* to dance."

Of course she does.

"Well, my baby girl, you and Grandmamma are gonna dance like we've never danced before! And I just happen to have the perfect hairbrushes too."

She looked up at me, puzzled, and said, "Hairbrushes?"

"You'll see, my sweetness. You'll see."

Isn't genetics wonderful?

This was the best day of my life, and I prayed there would be many more.

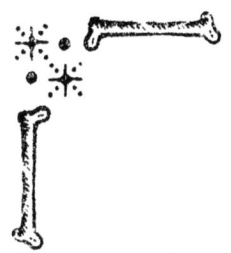

Epilogue

As your life unravels in front of God and everybody, it feels like all you can do sometimes is sit back and watch. It has lasting effects on not just you, but everyone around you. As I aged, I realized I had lost years of my life from grief, fear, and shame. And one day I decided I was not going to give another day to the void. I went for twenty-some odd years without even dancing. I never thought that could be possible. What the fuck was that all about? A broken spirit, I guess. I spent so many years working two to three jobs, taking up all forms of art, gardening, hobbies, and really I believe I needed the constant distractions to keep from going mad. I learned a lot, but now I'm fucking exhausted! I'm also in pain all the time from tearing up my body over the years. Jeezzz...

Watching my parents pass away really sucked. But we were able to forgive each other for so many things before they died, and I am very glad we did. We spent years hurting each other, sometimes by accident, sometimes from spite. But in time we healed and became close again. Once I grew up and got married to my Jim boy, it was easier. He saved my life, no doubt, and gave me something to live for and love for. He is my rock, but he tells me I am his rock. Whatevah...It works. He stuck with me through some real sucky shit, for thirty-eight years so far.

So here we are, hoping to retire within the next five years, with no children, and all of a sudden we have a family? It has changed our lives so dramatically. There are no words to explain the overwhelming joy we feel. It has helped fill that giant hole in my chest—although there will always be scars from the years I missed and can never get back. I am so thankful I have been found and can enjoy life with them from here on out. Now I can help fill the hole in Thomas's chest and little Chelsea's, too, for his adopted mother passed away, and it turns out they were also lost.

Daddy died suddenly, and then Mother had to go to a nursing home. We had to clean out our family home so we could sell it. Talk about sucky! We were going through Mother's jewelry box, and I asked Sara, "Where's that ring Bonnie left in the chair that day, one year after her death? Isn't it supposed to be in the jewelry box?"

Sara said, "Yeah, as far as I know. That's where I saw Mother put it, but that was at least thirty years ago. I don't see it. We'll have to ask Mother when we go see her."

The next day, I went to the nursing home and asked Mother, "Whatever happened to that ring that appeared in the rocking chair from Bonnie that day?"

She was now eighty-seven years old, with white hair and no teeth. She looked up at me with a smirk and said, "She came back and stole it again. She always did love to steal. She let me keep it a long time, though. Now and again, I would think of her and pull it out to look at it. One day I went to take it out, and it was gone. The heifer."

Then Mother laughed. And laughed some more. That was the last time I heard Mother laugh out loud, and I still can see her face as her little green eyes kinda twinkled and wrinkled at the edges as she contemplated and was entertained with the memory. Not long after that, the light disappeared from those eyes. Those eyes that look just like mine, and just like Thomas's and Chelsea's. How I wish they could have met.

So now I'm moving forward. Try to not dwell on the past that can never be changed, and enjoy life. Love like there's no tomorrow, dance like nobody's watching, love your family regardless of the flaws, open your heart, open your mind, and cherish every moment you have on this earth, because you can't get it back.

It's all worth it. Trust me.

Genuine Southern Recipes

Guaranteed Key to Your Man's Heart (Attack)

Food in the South is usually the center of attraction, whether it is for a family get-together, a funeral, a wedding, or just while awake. It is typically high in fat, sugar, and carbs, and that's why it's so damn good. Recipes are handed down for generations and are often the most valuable inheritance you can get. In many cases, they are the *only* inheritance you get. Sometimes you just have a hankerin' for Mommer an' 'em's cookin', and they're not around forever, so you have to learn to cook it yourself. It ain't the same, but with repetition it eventually gets close enough to satisfy your craving. Practice makes perfect, so get on it!

My grandmother and mother never measured anything. Reproducing their recipes is difficult, and it has taken years for me to get it right. A couple of years ago, I started taking notes and measuring ingredients as I cooked their recipes. I can now put them into writing knowing they are as near to the originals as possible.

Please enjoy them. They are delicious and meant to be shared.

Bon appetite!
Ellen R. Rigby
South Carolina

Breads

Biscuits

3 cups self-rising flour
3 teaspoons baking powder
2 teaspoons confectioner's sugar
½ cup Crisco
½ cup of sour cream
¾ cup of milk
(Or you can substitute 1 ¼ cups of buttermilk for the milk and sour cream)

Mix dry ingredients. Cut in Crisco. Mix milk and sour cream together, then add to dry ingredients and mix. When it begins to form, knead it with your hands only a few times. Do not overwork it the dough unless you intend to play hockey with the biscuits. The more you work it, the tougher they get. Dough will be sticky. Dump the ball onto a floured surface. Mash it flat, and roll it with a rolling pin. Fold it over, roll it out, fold again, and roll it till the dough is about ½-inch thick. Use a biscuit cutter or a glass to make pretty biscuits, or just pull off hunks and place them on a greased baking pan. Bake at 450°F for 10 – 12 minutes. Brush with melted butter while hot.

Nummm nummmm!

Cheese Biscuits

2 ½ cups Bisquick
¾ cups of milk
1 heaping cup shredded cheddar cheese
¼ teaspoon garlic powder

Butter mixture for tops after cooking:
¼ cup butter melted
¼ teaspoon parsley
½ teaspoon garlic powder
Pinch of salt

Mix the first four ingredients only. Do not overwork dough!

Scoop out heaping tablespoons of dough onto ungreased cookie sheet. They ain't purdy.

Bake at 12 – 15 minutes on 400°F, or until brown on bottoms. Brush butter mixture on top of each one. Daaaammmn!

Cornbread

2 cups yellow cornmeal
4 tablespoons flour
1 ½ teaspoons baking powder
1 ½ cups buttermilk
2 eggs beaten
2 tablespoons oil or bacon drippings
¼ cup honey optional (if you like sweet cornbread)
Extra oil for skillet or Crisco

Put generous amount of oil (Crisco or canola oil) in iron skillet to coat bottom completely. Place in 400°F oven for 7 – 8 minutes or until oil is really hot. Do not let it smoke. Watch it carefully for it can spatter if it gets too hot. While skillet is heating up, mix dry ingredients. Add wet ingredients. Do not overmix. Combine just until blended. Pour mix into hot grease very carefully, and it will sizzle. Place in oven for about twenty-five minutes or until brown around edges. When edges start to pull away from pan, she is ready.

Dill Dough

(It's not what you think, but is a good substitute)

2 cups self-rising flour
1 cup grated sharp cheese
1 teaspoon flour
1 tablespoon grated onion
1 ½ teaspoons dill weed
¾ cup milk
¼ cup butter softened
1 egg

Mix dry ingredients. Cut in soft butter and cheese. Beat egg with milk. Add onion. Combine dry and wet ingredients. Mix just until blended. Spray loaf pan with oil. Bake at 400°F for 30 – 40 minutes.

MEATS AND STUFF

Southern Style Fried Chicken

1 large fryer cut into frying pieces or breastessess if you prefer (boneless breastesses will cook faster at 375°F)
2 cups all-purpose flour
1 – 2 cups buttermilk (enough to cover meat for soaking)
½ teaspoon black pepper
1 teaspoon salt
1 teaspoon paprika (optional, but adds a lot of flavor)
½ teaspoon garlic powder (optional)
½ teaspoon onion powder (optional)
1 cup of Crisco or canola oil (Crisco cooks batter crispier, Canola is healthier)

Place chicken pieces in buttermilk and soak for at least an hour. Mix all dry ingredients together with a fork. Coat each piece with flour mixture and fry at about 360 – 375°F. Heat oil well before adding meat so it starts to sizzle when chicken is added. Do not turn pieces until they are brown on bottom, and turn only once. Do not disturb the meat unless you want a pan full of batter and naked, greasy chicken. We always used bread butts to drain pieces when done, so start saving them. They work great.

Do not discard oil and crumblies or left over flour if you want milk gravy. See the Milk Gravy recipe in the **Sides section.

Grilled Chicken Breastesses

Chicken tenderloins or breastesses
1 bottle of Italian salad dressing (our favorite is Kraft Sun Dried Tomato Vinaigrette)
¼ cup of soy sauce

Place thawed chicken pieces (we prefer tenderloins), dressing of choice, and soy sauce in a sealed baggie. Use about ½ bottle of dressing, or enough to well cover meat. Marinate for a few hours or overnight. Grill to perfection, either on an outdoor grill or George Foreman grill until lightly browned. Will be moist. Great on salads or with vegetables. Good enough to serve to the in-laws.

Fried Cube Steak

1 ½ package of cube steak cut into manageable size pieces (sprinkle with tenderizer)
1 cup buttermilk
1 cup all-purpose flour
½ teaspoon salt
¼ teaspoon black pepper
¼ teaspoon garlic powder (opt)
1 cup Crisco or canola oil

Soak meat pieces in buttermilk for at least an hour. Mix dry ingredients with a fork. Coat pieces with flour mixture. Fry at 375°F until brown on bottom. Turn only once. Drain on bread butts or paper towels.

Do not discard oil and crumblies or left over flour if you want milk gravy. See the Milk Gravy recipe in the **Sides section.

Eat Without Your Dentures Cube Steak

1 ½ pounds cube steak cut into manageable size pieces
1 cup flour
⅛ cup of oil
½ teaspoon salt
½ teaspoon seasoning salt (Lawry's or we use Johnny's, which you have to mail order)
¼ teaspoon black pepper
32 oz. chicken broth, reserving 1 cup of broth for gravy
2 heaping tablespoons cornstarch
1 onion sliced
1 pound mushrooms
Teeth optional

Mix dry ingredients. Coat meat with flour mixture. Brown on each side in oil. Do not cook until done. Place meat in Dutch oven with a tight lid. Pour chicken broth over meat. Cook for 30 minutes at 350°F. Add onions. Cook 15 minutes, then add mushrooms. Cook another 15 minutes with lid on the whole time. A total of one hour braising time is required.

To make a gravy: Use the reserved broth, mix it with 2 tablespoons of cornstarch until blended. Put Dutch oven on top of stove at medium high heat, remove lid and pour cornstarch mixture into hot liquid with meat. Cook until it bubbles and thickens, while stirring constantly. It will thicken pretty quickly and makes a nice gravy for rice or mashed potatoes. You can omit the onions and mushrooms if you prefer. Cut it with a fork. Delicious!

Poppy Seed Ham Biscuits

½ pound shaved honey ham from deli
1 pkg. Swiss cheese
1 pkg. dinner rolls (rolls are small, rectangular, and stuck together in aluminum pan)
1 ½ tablespoons French's ballpark mustard
6 tablespoons butter melted
1 tablespoon poppy seeds
1 tablespoon onion flakes
2 dashes Worcestershire sauce

Use a long bread knife and slice the whole package of rolls in half, separating tops from bottoms as a whole unit. Leave bottoms in pan and place ½ pound shaved ham all over bottom layer. Place Swiss cheese over ham to cover. Replace tops over cheese. Slice rolls to separate as finger sandwiches. Try not to puncture aluminum pan.

Topping: place mustard, butter, poppy seeds, onion flakes, and Worcestershire sauce in saucepan or microwave to melt butter, stir to combine. Pour over rolls getting, between rolls and on tops. Bake at 350°F for about ten minutes, or until cheese is melted. If you don't make enough, a fight will break out. Better make 2 – 3 pans for a party. One is simply not enough. Trust me.

Quiche for Real Men

4 eggs
2 green onions sliced with tops
1 cup chopped ham or crispy bacon
1 frozen deep-dish pie crust
1 tablespoon Gulden's Spicy mustard
1 bag of fresh baby spinach
1 fresh garlic clove, chopped
1 tablespoon olive oil
1 cup shredded cheddar cheese
½ cup sliced mushrooms
½ cup whipping cream
black pepper
seasoning salt
Grated Parmesan cheese
paprika

Spread mustard all over pie crust , especially edges. Place ham in crust, then ½ of the cheese. Sauté garlic, onions, and mushrooms till almost tender. Stir in spinach until wilted. Drain liquid off and place veggies in quiche. Sprinkle last ½ of cheddar cheese over veggies.

Mix eggs, cream, and salt and pepper until well blended. Pour egg mixture over veggies. Sprinkle paprika and parmesan on top. Place on baking sheet. Bake at 375°F for 35 minutes or until done in the middle. Masculinity will remain intact.

May as well make two while you're at it. Freezes well.

SIDES

Collard Greens

1 mess of collard greens
4 slices of bacon with drippings or fatback
1 medium onion chopped
Salt
Pepper
1 teaspoon of sugar
Wash greens thoroughly, cut off stems and tough veins.

Cook bacon in big pot, keep drippings while breaking up bacon into pieces. Put chopped onion in and cook until tender. Place greens in and pour enough water to almost cover greens. Bring to a boil, cover and reduce heat to medium. When greens are tender, salt and pepper to taste. Serve with cornbread and chow chow, black-eyed peas, and ham for New Year's good luck dinner. Always place a cleaned dime in black-eyed peas for good luck.

Mommer an' 'em's Cornbread Dressing

5 cups cornmeal mix
2 ½ sticks of butter (room temperature)
¼ cup oil
4 – 5 cans cream of chicken soup
3 sticks celery sliced thin
3 medium onions chopped
¼ – ½ teaspoon Sage teaspoon or poultry seasoning
1 can chicken broth
Water
Pepper to taste

Mix cornmeal with water until it makes a soupy batter. Spray baking pan or large iron skillet with oil and cook in 400°F oven until lightly brown. Do not overcook. Break hot cornbread into pieces in a big bowl and mix with butter using a big spoon until butter is melted and pieces of cornbread are workable. Add four cans cream of chicken soup, oil, and ½ can of broth, and mush with hands until pieces starts to get smooth. Add celery, onions, and spices. If batter is still thick, add the last cream of chicken soup and broth. The batter is supposed to look almost soupy. Spray large baking pan or two medium ones with oil. Pour batter into pans, 1 – 2 inches or so thick, but no more. Bake at 350°F for 45 minutes to 1 hour if you can stand it that long, or until the celery is done. The smell is almost as good as the dressing. Makes a large amount, which is what you will probably want to do anyway. Serves 8 – 10 hungry-ass heathens. This is an ole timey recipe. Dressing will be wet when it's hot, like serve-with-a-spoon kinda wet, but it thickens as it cools. Serve with cranberry sauce and giblet gravy. See recipe for that too.

Thanksgiving Giblet Gravy

Giblets from turkey (neck and liver) optional
1 can cream of chicken soup
1 can chicken broth
1 boiled egg chopped
2 tablespoons butter

Cook giblets in water until done. Use just enough water to cover giblets. Can use this as broth in recipe instead of canned broth. Discard neck. Chop liver into small pieces. Add cream of chicken soup, chopped egg, and broth. If gravy is too thin, mix ½ cup of cold water and 1 tablespoon cornstarch until blended. Add to hot gravy. Bring to a slight boil while stirring constantly to achieve desired thickness. Giblets are optional. Good on rice, dressing, and turkey.

Milk Gravy

Drippings from fried chicken, cube steak, or sausage (keep little meat chunks from pan and a little oil)
1 can evaporated milk
Milk
½ – ¾ stick butter
Salt and pepper
¼ cup all-purpose flour

Pick out gravy bowl you want to use. Pour evaporated milk and milk in a 1:1 ratio until bowl is not quite full. This is to achieve the right amount that you want. Sit it close by because it all happens fast.

If you have been frying meats, save little bits and some oil. (If not, just use ¾ stick of butter.) Add butter to pan. Bring pan to medium-medium high heat. Sprinkle flour into melted butter with drippings. If it is dry and clumpy, quickly add more butter. Add salt and pepper while stirring constantly. Don't oversalt, no more than ¼ teaspoon. Stir until flour is blended and starts to brown. Gradually add milk mixture while stirring with other hand. Don't stop stirring. If it looks lumpy, chop and stir until almost thick. Pour into bowl you had chosen. It will continue to thicken after you remove it from heat. It may take a little practice to be perfect, but it'll still be sinful. Serve with hot biscuits, cube steak, fried chicken, rice, mashed potatoes, whatevah. Get out your elastic waist britches.

Hash Brown Casserole

1 large bag frozen shredded hash browns
1 carton sour cream
1 can cream of chicken soup
1 medium onion chopped
Salt and pepper
2 cups shredded sharp cheddar cheese or Colby cheese
1 stick butter

Mix all ingredients except butter. Spray large baking dish with oil and pour ingredients into dish. Dot with butter. Cover with foil. Bake at 400°F, stirring every 15 minutes for 30 minutes. Uncover stir and bake another 15 minutes to brown. Wicked good!

Southern Style Macaroni and Cheese

8 oz. packaged macaroni
1 pound sharp cheddar cheese grated
1 teaspoon dry mustard
3 eggs beaten
Milk
salt and pepper

Cook macaroni until almost tender. If it is too soft, it will be mush. Drain water off, add ¾ of the cheese, mustard, salt and pepper, and eggs. Pour just enough milk to bring level of the hot macaroni. Stir well and heat on stovetop until cheese is melted, cover with foil, bake for 30 minutes on 350°F. Remove the foil, add remaining cheese to top, and bake an additional 5 minutes. Goes with anything, pretty much.

Fried Okra

1 pound fresh okra, smaller pods are more tender, seeds are smaller
1 cup cornmeal
1 tablespoon flour
½ teaspoon salt
½ teaspoon pepper
½ cup oil
Sprinkle of garlic powder (opt)

Wash and slice okra into ¼-inch pieces. Sprinkle with water. Mix dries. Coat okra with dry mixture. Heat oil to medium/medium high heat. Can use deep fryer or pan. Add okra to oil. Do not disturb okra until browns on bottom. Turn once to finish browning. Drain on bread butts. Yummmmm…

Baked Potato Soup

8 – 10 slices bacon, crumbled
1 onion, diced
½ cup all purpose flour
3 (14.5 oz each) cans chicken broth
5 medium baked potatoes, peeled, diced
2 cups half-and-half
1 cup shredded sharp cheddar cheese
1 cup sour cream
1 teaspoon parsley flakes
salt and pepper to taste

In a Dutch oven, cook bacon till crisp, reserve drippings. Cook onion in drippings till tender. Stir in flour, stir constantly for a minute. Gradually add chicken broth, stirring constantly until thickened on medium heat. Add potatoes, parsley, bacon, half-and-half, then cook for 10 minutes. Do not scorch. Stir in cheese and sour cream.

Garnish with bacon, cheese, sour cream, and/or parsley. Some kinda good! Just as good reheated. Makes a butt-load, invite some company.

Fried Green Tomatoes

4 – 5 hard green tomatoes, sliced into ¼ in slices
1 cup cornmeal
1 tablespoon flour
½ teaspoon salt
½ cup oil
⅛ to ¼ teaspoon black pepper
Few shakes of garlic powder (opt)

Mix dry ingredients and roll tomato slices in mix. Fry in iron skillet or fry pan in hot oil until brown. Do not disturb until browned on each side. Drain on bread butts.

SWEETS

Fried Apple Turnovers

4 tart apples, sliced, peels optional
Sugar
Cinnamon
Butter

Cook apples on low with about ¼ cup water until tender, but not mushy. We leave the peels on, but if you peel, they will cook faster. Drain off water, add desired amount of sugar and a dash or two of cinnamon. Add 3 – 4 tablespoons of butter and mix. Turn off heat and let sit. Stir occasionally but don't break up pieces. Let cool. In the meantime, make some biscuit dough (see **Breads** section) or you can use canned croissants. For dough, roll out dough to ¼ inch thickness, and cut into squares. If using canned croissants, unroll triangles. Place 1 heaping tablespoon or so of apple mixture into middle of triangle, fold over in half to form triangle. Pinch all sides closed. Can deep fry or bake turnovers, or cook in oil in pan on top of stove on medium high heat. Turn once if cooking in pan. If cooking in oven, cook on 375 – 400°F until brown. We used to cook them in oil in an iron skillet. Serve with vanilla ice cream. You can also use preserves, peach, raspberry, strawberry, blueberry, or whatevah....

For sugar drizzle on top: Take ½-cup confectioners sugar and add a very small amount of liquid—I'm talking a few drops—which can be milk, orange juice, lemon juice or whatevah… drizzle over warm turnovers.

Lemon Blueberry Muffins

6 oz. lemon yogurt
2 cups all-purpose flour
1 cup sugar
¾ cups milk
½ teaspoon baking soda
2 ½ teaspoons baking powder
¼ teaspoon salt
1 tablespoon lemon juice
1 teaspoon lemon zest
4 Tablespoons butter, melted
2 large eggs
2 cups fresh blueberries, or frozen (do not thaw)
More sugar or cinnamon for topping

Grease muffin cups or liners with spray oil. Combine dries. In a medium-sized bowl, blend eggs, lemon juice, yogurt, milk, cooled butter, and zest. Stir in flour, and mix just until moistened. Fold in blueberries carefully. Do not overmix! Fill muffin cups, sprinkle with either sugar or cinnamon sugar mix. Bake for 15 – 20 minutes or until centers peak and edges are browned. So very good. My husband doesn't share these well with others.

To-Die-For Ole Timey Chocolate Icing

2 sticks of butter
1 box of 10x confectioners sugar
1 bag semisweet chocolate chips
1 cup evaporated milk
1 tablespoon cocoa powder
1 small bag marshmallows
½ teaspoon vanilla flavoring

Melt in saucepan or can use microwave. Mix well with beater. Wouldn't Grannie just roll over in her grave over that?

Killer Chocolate Icing

1 box powdered sugar (4 cups)
1 stick butter
4 heaping tablespoons cocoa
6 tablespoons milk

Combine cocoa, milk, and butter in pan till it melts. Beat in sugar. Take off heat. This is my favorite. It is too good to be this easy. It hardens on the outside as it cools. Good on a cooled Bundt cake, or Duncan Hines Yellow Extra Moist cake. With a Bundt, the chocolate will pool in the middle and is like soft fudge. It will run down the sides, so be careful not to waste any! But you can keep scooping it and re-pouring it over until it starts to cool. Oh my God! This is an ole timey recipe too, but not as sweet as the one above.

Crunchy Peach Cobbler from Heaven

5 cups fresh peaches, peeled, and sliced
1 cup sugar
1 egg, slightly beaten
1 tablespoon lemon juice
1 cup self-rising flour
6 tablespoons butter, melted

Peel peaches and place in big bowl of lemon water. Keeps them from turning brown. After all are peeled, slice into wedges and place in a baking dish, sprinkle lemon juice over slices, and mix to coat. Add ⅛ cup of water, cover and cook in microwave for about 3 minutes to soften peaches. In another bowl, mix flour and sugar. Add in egg and mix slightly. It will look like dry flour and sugar with loose chunks in it. That's what it is supposed to look like. It does not make a batter. Dump flour/sugar mix over peaches. Poke a few holes, pour melted butter over it, and bake at 375°F for 30 – 35 minutes until brown and crunchy on top. Don't swallow your tongue eatin' this one. This is the best cobbler I have ever had, and I have been surrounded by peach orchards for over thirty years. It's also very easy. This recipe doesn't work as well if you try to double it. So just make two separate ones, 'cause this one's gonna disappear real fast.

Miscellaneous Southern Necessities

Sweet Tea

A true Southerner starts out life with sweet tea in their baby bottle, then progresses to the sippy cup as a toddler, then consumption increases in the teens to a gallon a day in some cases. Kinda scary, ain't it? But actually, by then you have developed somewhat of a tolerance and an addiction to caffeine and sugar. It's great! Until you can't have any…then it's Katie bar the door! Do understand that if you just order tea in the South from any restaurant, you will get sweet tea. So if you order unsweetened, everyone will stare at you because they'll know you ain't from 'round these parts. But anyway, tea used to be made in a pot on the stove, and sometimes I still do. But it's just as good to make it in a coffee maker. So here goes.

2 large family tea bags
1 ½ – 2 cups sugar
1 gallon container

Place tea bags in coffee maker. Try to let them steep a little, maybe by adding a coffee filter to slow the flow of water through the tea bags. Pour a quart or so of cold water into tea container and stir in 1 ½ – 2 cups sugar. This is the trick to good tea. Stir off and on until coffee maker is done. Pour hot tea into cold sugar water and mix. Add more cold water to make a gallon. Two cups of sugar is real sweet, so you may want to try 1 ½ cups first. Keep stirring until sugar is dissolved. Place in frig. Easier than pie!

Real Lemonade

6 – 8 lemons cut into halves
1 – 2 cups sugar

A little old black lady who was a patient of mine told me the trick to real lemonade. I used to go see her once a week in her home when I worked in home care, and she always had the best lemonade I had ever had. Thank God, because she didn't have air conditioning, and I would have perished without something cold to drink, so forgive me Miss Mamie for sharing your secret. I misha a lot. She has passed now, and I think of her every time I make lemonade.

The trick is…

Wash and cut up lemons. Squeeze juice from each piece into container with lemon pieces. Do not discard lemon pieces. Pour 1 cup of sugar over lemons. Cover with plastic wrap or lid and let them "work" for at least an hour. The sugar will draw the rest of the juice out of the lemons. You will be shocked at how much liquid will be in the container when you come back. Add water to taste as you go, and add sugar as you go. Should make at least a half-gallon. It varies with lemons and personal preference. Some lemons have more juice than others. But you will taste the difference in making real lemonade. If you don't drink all of it that afternoon, remove the lemon pieces before refrigerating. The lemons rinds will overwhelm the lemonade if you leave them in overnight, but trust me, it won't last that long. Just plan ahead. Start lemons in the morning, and they'll be ready for you when you are. Just remember to wash lemons thoroughly.

www.ingramcontent.com/pod-product-compliance
Lightning Source LLC
LaVergne TN
LVHW041247080426
835510LV00009B/617